DISEASES OF CATTLE

By

Dr. Ashok Kumar

Deptt. of Zoology
Bundelkhand University
Campus Department
Jhansi (India)

DISCOVERY PUBLISHING HOUSE PVT. LTD.
NEW DELHI-110 002

Published by:
Tilak Wasan

DISCOVERY PUBLISHING HOUSE PVT. LTD.
4383/4B, Ansari Road, Darya Ganj
New Delhi-110 002 (India)
Phone : +91-11-23279245, 43596064-65
Fax : +91-11-23253475
E-mail : discoverypublishinghouse@gmail.com
sales@discoverypublishinggroup.com
parul.wasan@gmail.com
web : www.discoverypublishinggroup.com

***First Edition:* 2014**

ISBN: 978-93-5056-411-0

Diseases of Cattle

Printed at:
Dynamic Printers
Delhi

Preface

Cattle Diseases are integral to the farmer, if not for working in the fields and carrying loads, then certainly for milk production. And hence the students of agricultural sciences must have an active knowledge of various breeds their rearing and upkeep. Cattle care is not confined to the dairyman alone. The greater portions of intelligent agriculturists have perceived the necessity of paying more attention than was formerly devoted to the improvement and perfection of breeds.

Dairy cattle are susceptible to the same diseases as beef cattle. Many diseases and pests plague the cattle industries of the world, the more serious ones being prevalent in the humid and less developed countries. One of the more common diseases to be found in the developed countries is brucellosis, which has been controlled quite successfully through vaccination and testing. This disease produces undulant fever in humans through milk from infected cows. Leptospirosis, prevalent in warm blooded animals and humans, is caused by a spirochete and results in fever, loss of weight, and abortion. Bovine tuberculosis has been largely eliminated; where it has not, it can infect other warm-blooded animals, including humans.

The cause of many congenital defects is unknown, but some are inherited. The most common inheritance patternis as a simple recessive trait. The defective calfreceives a recessive gene from its sire and one from itsdam. A few congenital defects are known to be causedby genes with incomplete dominance and a few arecaused by two or more sets of genes. Genetically caused congenital defects usually run infamilies. The parents of a genetically defective calf willgenerally have at least one ancestor in common. Whenmore than one genetically caused defective calf is bornin a herd in the same calving season, their dams areusually related (for example, half sisters) and are siredby the same bull. A change in the breeding programme isrequired to correct this situation.

Cardiovascular disease present in various species, breeds, and strains, or families of animals are compared, certain differences are apparent. It is often difficult, however, to separate hereditary from environmental influences. Studies of vascular disease in zoo animals have shown that changing environmental conditions can alter the incidence of certain types of lesions in various species. Species differences, however, in resistance to diet-induced atherosclerosis appear to be genetically determined. The prevalence and types of congenital cardiac malformations appear to differ from species to species, but further systematic study is required. Arterial blood pressure is higher in the giraffe and turkey than in other species, and normal variants in cardiac rhythm are characteristic of the dog, horse, and mole.

The book is provides basic substances to proceed on practical cattle business and cattle disease.

—Author

Contents

1

Introduction

Cattle diseases cost fanners millions of rupees every year. In addition to death, they cause loss of production and frequently a loss of body condition. Unhealthy animals require more food and take longer time for growth than healthy ones. Normally, animals are born free of diseases or parasites. But, they usually acquire these maladies either through contact with diseased animals or due to improper sanitation, feeding, care and management.

One should be vigilant against cattle diseases as dairy cattle are affected by a variety of diseases. Knowledge of cattle diseases is necessary from public health point of view also as many diseases can be transmitted to man through milk. Keeping animals healthy by confining purchases to healthy herds, by proper quarantine at the time of bringing in new animals, by employing sound principles of sanitation, management and feeding and by judicious use of appropriate and dependable vaccines are the practical and economical ways to avoid losses from the disease. By proper management and feeding, the dairy farmer can, to a great extent, prevent disease out-breaks. Good housing assists in maintaining the health of the herd, whereas judicious feeding not only builds up body resistance to disease but also helps in speedy recovery in case there is a disease attack.

CATTLE DISEASES

Not considering the common ailments such as injuries, abscess etc., there are mainly five types of diseases or disorders namely infectious diseases, parasitic diseases, metabolic diseases nutritional deficiency diseases and breeding disorders. Breeding disorders may be due to hereditary infections, injury and nutritional or metabolic disorders. Since milk production is dependent on regular reproduction in cattle, breeding troubles are a serious problems in farm animals.

Infectious and parasitic diseases are caused by genus and parasites, respectively. The common cattle producing genus are bacteria and viruses. These diseases are spread from animal to animal by contact with diseased animals or their excreta or carcass. Other sources of disease are contaminated feeds, fodder, drinking water and pastures. Many disease causing germs are carried by wind also.

Further, germs and parasites can be carried by birds, dog, flies, lice, ticks, etc. These disease causing germs or microganisms enter animal body through various routes like skin, respiratory tract, alimentary canal, etc. Once they enter the body, they try to multiply in the body tissues. The body tries to destroy the disease producing agents through the defence system of the body. It consists mainly of the white corpuscles and the disease agents by engulfing them and killing. The antibodies reacts with the disease causing agents and try to destroy them. This reaction is specific in the sense that the antibody of a particular disease reacts only with the causative agent of that disease. In this process, if the defensive system of the body fails the disease appears.

SPOTTING THE DISEASE ON CATTLE

Dairymen must develop a keen eye to spot a sick animal. Common signs of ill-health of cattle are given below which should be helpful to dairy fanners in detecting diseases in their herds.

- The general posture of the animal, its movement, breathing and behaviour will change in case of sickness. Animals standing with head down or showing weariness or a tendency to separate from the herd are warning symptoms.

- Healthy cattle eat greedily and ruminate leisurely. One of the first signs of disease in cows and buffaloes is loss of appetite and stopping rumination. However, one has to make sure that the cause for animal going 'off-feed' is not due to the unsuitable feed, dirty feeding troughs or lack of water.
- The skin of animals should be soft, elastic and pliable. Skin texture can be felt by grasping a fold of skin over the side of neck between the thumb and forefinger. A coarse and dry skin is indicative of disease.
- Raised hair coat, falling or brittle and lusterless hair is undesirable. The coat should not have patches. Patches usually indicate rubbing to relieve irritation caused by parasites such as lice. The condition of the coat will vary with housing condition and grooming, but when cattle are infected with worms or wasting diseases, their coat loses glow.
- Muzzle and nostrils of healthy animals will be moist and free from any discharge. The muzzle will be dry mammals having high temperature.
- The eye in healthy animals are bright and alert. Sunken eyes with a fixed staring like often accompany the onset of fever. Lacrimation or glued eyes should be specially noted. Trouble in one eye indicates local condition, while discharges from both the eyes indicate a systemic ailment.
- The dung of healthy cattle should be semi-solid in consistency, rich green in colour and free from gas bubbles and blood clots. Constipation and scouring should be particularly noted. However, a change in the consistency of dung may occur when high green fodder is fed.
- Urine of the animal should be clear and straw coloured. It should not be dark or bloody in colour, nor should it have any abnormal odour.
- The vulva and tail should not show any evidence of discharge from the genital organs. Push containing discharges indicate septic condition of the reproduction organs.

- Change in quality and quantity of milk yield is one of the early symptoms in several diseases. Milk yield in dairy cows and buffaloes will fall even if they have only a slight chill or heat exhaustion. Blood clots in milk indicate mastitis disease.
- Variation in body temperature can be measured by inserting a clinical thermometer into the rectum of an animal for half a minute. High temperature is usually associated with the increased activity of the body in fighting off the disease. Young animals, frequently show higher temperatures than normal. On chilly days, week and debilitated animals may have sub-normal body temperature. The normal body temperatures of cattle and buffaloes are 101.5°F and 98.3°F, respectively.
- Variation in pulse rate reflects the rate at which the heart pumps blood through the body. This can be measured by placing the index or second finger on arteries where they pass near the surface of the body. In cattle and buffaloes the pulse can be felt under the tail (coccygeal artery). The normal pulse rates of cattle and buffaloes should be 50-60 beats per minute and 40 to 50 beats per minute, respectively. However, the pulse rate is generally higher in young and pregnant animals.
- Variation in rate and. depth of breathing occurs in fevered conditions. The normal respiration rates of cattle and buffaloes are 20-25 and 15-20 per minute respectively. Respiration rate can be measured by counting the hot gushes of expired air blowing against back of palm kept near the nostrils of the animals.

Incidence of coughing, whistling or grunting with pain associated with respiration should be particularly noted.

PREVENTION OF CATTLE DISEASES

'Prevention is better than cure' is a true saying and worthy of being remembered by every livestock owner. It is possible to prevent the occurrence of most of animal diseases and to prevent their spread by taking prompt precautionary and preventive, measures such as advance prophylactic vaccinations and strict hygienic measures. Following steps are to be adopted to prevent the spread and occurrence of cattle diseases.

Quarantining

Quarantining refers to a procedure of keeping the animals which are imported to a new area at the point of entry itself, in an, isolated place for a prescribed period of time. This is to keep the animals under observation and to allow time for any latent infection to develop into disease condition. If after the quarantining period the animal has not shown any disease, it is given entry into the area. In India, we do not have definite rules of quarantining for imported animals. Many countries which have controlled many of the animal diseases have formed definite rules for quarantining, so that further introduction of the diseases is prevented.

Vaccination

This is a method of protecting the animals against certain diseases. In this practice an artificial body immunity is built up in the animals against specific infectious diseases. This is done by injecting a Particular biological agent called vaccine. Vaccines ate prepared by suitably treating the disease causing organisms. Here the vaccine acts as an antigen (an agent which causes the production of antibodies). Vaccines have been developed for many of the animal diseases such as black quarter, tetanus, rinderpest, brucellosis and foot and mouth diseases. When a vaccine for any particular disease is injected into the animal body, after an interval of a few days, antibodies against the particular disease are produced, that cause active immunity against the disease. During this interval, before the antibodies make their appearance there is often increased susceptibility to the disease in question. The duration for which the immunity varies from vaccine to vaccine. Against certain diseases, a second booster dose is required after the first vaccination for achieving stronger immunity.

Vaccination may be used prophylactically to confer protection in anticipation of a disease. A vaccine is not used as a rule in a locality, where an acute infection has already broken out, because of the period of the increased susceptibility and the delay before protection is established. Vaccination is used to develop an immune zone all around an area of actual infection. This prevents the spread of disease. Also vaccination can be used routinely on animal farms as an insurance against possible disease flare-ups.

Diagnosis

Detection of disease in animals needs particular training and care. The complete history of the animal has to be extracted from the owner. The feed taken before the onset of disease, the nature of any preliminary treatment done by the owner, behaviour of the animal, etc. have to be enquired. Some of the diseases might have been caused by the feed. After the history of the animal is collected, a preliminary examination is to be made based on the external manifestation. This will be followed by a systematic examination of the animal. This involves the examination of the different systems of the body, like respiratory, circulatory, etc.

Isolation

Isolation means segregation of animals which are known or suspected to be affected with a contagious disease from the apparently healthy ones. Preferably, such segregated animals should be housed in a separate isolation ward situated far away from the normal animal houses. If a separate accommodation is not available, the animals concerned should be placed at one end of the animals building as far away from the healthy stock as possible. Attendants working on sick animals and equipments such as buckets, showels, etc., used for them should not be used for healthy animals. If this is not practicable, the sick animals should be attended to, daily, after the healthy stock. After this the equipment should be thoroughly disinfected before they are used on healthy stock next day. The attendant too should wash his hands and feet in an antiseptic solution and discard tile cloths in which he worked. The isolated animals should be brought back into the herd only when the outbreak ends and they are fully recovered.

Destroying Carriers of the Germs

When an animal recovered from a disease the causative organism as a rule is eliminated from the body, sooner or later. But there are many occasions in which the animal, although apparently in good health, harbours the organisms in its tissues. Generally, convalescent animals are carriers for short duration. In some diseases, however, the carrier state may remain for years and the animal becomes a potential danger to susceptible animals. Sometimes the animal may not become affected, the organism not assuming a parasitic existence, and yet it remains a potential source of the disease. Such animals are referred to as healthy carriers. Common diseases for which carriers have been observed in farm animals are tuberculosis and brucellosis. Carriers of diseases in the herd should be diagnosed and eliminated so that the herd may be completely free from the diseases.

Disposal of Carcasses

Proper disposal of animals died of contagious diseases is of great importance in preventing the spread of the disease. Besides, it is also necessary to prevent human infection. Carcasses of such animals should never be disposed off by depositing them in or near a stream of flowing water, because this will carry infections to the points downstream. An animal died of contagious disease should not be allowed to remain longer in the shed as biting insects, rodents, etc. can reach it and spread the infection. Therefore, it is absolutely essential that all the carcasses of animals died of contagious diseases should be either buried deep into the earth or burnt completely. For burning or burying such carcasses, an isolated place, quite away from human activities or source of drinking water or pasture, should be selected. While taking these carcasses, they are carefully lifted from the ground and put on the carriage and taken to the site. Afterwards, the carriage used for carrying these carcasses is also disinfected.

Disinfect Ion

Disinfection means destruction of pathogenic microorganisms from a place so that the place becomes free from infection. A disinfectant or germicide or antiseptic is a substance to kill organisms and spores at appropriate concentrations. The common disinfecting agents available to the cattle owner are sunlight, heat and chemical disinfectants. Sunlight possesses strong disinfecting properties. Animal houses must be so constructed that sunlight falls in the sheds at least for some time during the day.

Application of heat by steam, by hot water; burning or by boiling is an effective method of disinfection. However, sometimes it may not be practicable to use heat for disinfection. In such a case, the only option left is to use chemical disinfectants. It should be, however, noted that not all the pathogens are susceptible to the same chemical disinfectant. Furthermore, the effectiveness of antiseptics is greatly reduced in the presence of organic matter. Therefore, it is highly desirable to clean the areas before using a disinfectant. Some of the important chemical disinfectants have been given in Table 1.1.

Disinfecting animal houses is a laborious process and can not always be restored to in a routine way. Under ordinary conditions, daily scrubbing and washing off houses and the action of sunlight falling in the house is sufficient to keep moderately germ free. But when a disease outbreak bas occurred, disinfection is a must and should be carried scrupulously. All floors and walls, interiors of mangers, water troughs and other fittings and equipments coming in contact With animals are all to be disinfected.

Table 1.1 : Programme of Vaccination against Important Infectious Diseases in Cattle.

Sl. No.	*Disease*	*Type of Vaccine*	*Time of Vaccination*	*Duration of Immunity*	*Time of Revaccination*
1	Black quarter	Alum precipitated vaccine	Before onset of rainy season	One year	Before onset of next rainy season

Contd...

2	Anthrax	Anthrax spore vaccine	do	do	Do
3	Haemorrhagic septicaemia	Oil adjuvant	do	do	do
4	Brucellosis	Calf hood vaccine with otton strain 19	6 months of age	Life long	—
5	Tuberculosis	B.C.G. Vaccine	do	Life long	— —
6	Rinderpest	Carinised vaccine	do	do	— —
7	Foot and mouth disease	Polyvalent vaccine	In October-November	For one season	Next October-November

The first step in disinfection of animal houses is removal of all filth, as the power of disinfectants is greatly reduced in the presence of organic matter. In case of an outbreak of an anthrax, the dung, litter, etc. should first be disinfected in situ by thorough sprinkling of suitable disinfectant. If the floor is of earth which is generally the case in Indian villages, the top 10 cm earth should be removed and disposed of along With litter and dung. After removal of filth the place should be scrubbed and washed with 4 per cent hot washing soda solution (*i.e.* 4 kg washing soda in 100 litres of boiling water). The approved disinfectant solution can be coated liberally over the place by spraying and left so to act for 24 hours. After this period, the animal house should again be washed with clean water and left to dry by wind and sunlight.

Pastures may also be a source of such infections, but using chemical disinfectants on pasture is rather impracticable and sometimes even harmful too. What can be done is the removal of any obvious infective material, like carcass, aborted faetus, dung, etc. from the pasture and prevention of the animals from grazing in the pasture under question. During this period, the pathogens will be destroyed by the action of sunlight.

DISEASES OF COWS AND BUFFALOES

The sake of convenience, important diseases of cows, buffaloes and their calves are divided into three categories as follows:

Contagious Diseases

With the introduction of exotic animals in the country, the crossbred cows have increased in number. These crossbred animals are highly susceptible to tropical diseases and climatic variations. Contagious diseases usually take a heavier toll of purebred and crossbred cattle than indigenous. Buffaloes are more resistant to contagious diseases than cows. For example, the disease 'black quarter' is seldom found in buffaloes but takes a heavy toll of milch cows every year. On the other hand, there are a few diseases like haemouhagic secpticaemia which attack both cows and buffaloes but the infection is much heavier on buffaloes. The common contagious diseases that are likely to attack dairy cattle are:

- Bacterial diseases such as anthrax, black quarter, brucelosis, haemorrhagic septicaemia, mastitis and tuberculosis; and
- Viral diseases such as cow pox, foot and mouth disease, rinderpest, etc.

Anthrax

Anthrax is an acute disease having rapidly fatal course. It is the oldest disease known in the cattle. The disease is characterized by septicaemia and sudden death with the exudation of tarry blood from natural orifices of dead animals. This disease has a world-wide distribution. Sporadic cases occur almost throughout India. However, it is more prevalent in certain hot and humid regions of the country. The causative agent of this disease is *Bacillus antkracis*. The organism is relatively large, rod shaped and non-motile. Sporulation occurs outside the body in the presence of oxygen. The spores are highly resistant and are not killed by heat, light and disinfectants. The spores remain viable and infective for several years. The animals get infection by ingestion of food and directly from animal to animal.

Symptoms

- Shivering fits with rise of temperature. Temperature of animal body may go up to 106° F.
- Rumination stops, eyes become red, extremities get cold.
- Breathing is difficult.
- Abdominal pain and tympanities.
- Dung is stained with blood and rectum protrudes.
- Bloody discharge from mouth, nostrils and rectum. The discharge is tarry in colour.
- Staggering gaits, convulsions and animal dies within 24 hours, if the disease is in acute form.

Treatment and Control

The treatment is usually not possible in acute cases. Subacute cases are treated With antibiotics and antianthrax serum. Penicillin and streptomycin in large doses are recommended. Annual vaccination of the animals is recommended in the endemic areas. Alive spore vaccine prepared from a virulent strain of *B. anthracis* is safe for all species. Hygiene is the most important single factor in the prevention of spread of anthrax. As the sporulation of disease causing organisms takes place in the presence of oxygen, the vegetative forms present in the tissues and body fluids will die if the carcass is not opened, but is burnt or buried deep with lime. Destruction of contaminated material and disinfection of equipments and animal shed is also necessary.

Black Quarter

Black quarter is an infectious disease of cattle which may affect even healthy young animals, 6 months to 2 years of age. It is also called black leg disease (since the thigh region of the cattle is called quarter). It is rapidly falal disease caused by a bacterium *Clostridium chauvoei*. It is an anaerobic bacterium which grows only in the absence of oxygen. So bacteria entering the animal body through minute punctured wounds which exclude air get favourable environment to grow. The infection usually takes place through food, water and soil contaminated with black quarter organisms.

Symptoms

- Swelling of the muscular portions usually the quarters, thighs, shoulder, etc.
- Rise in the temperature of animal body and animal becomes dull and goes off-feed.
- Disinclination to move due to swelling. The affected muscle is black in colour.
- Pulse and respiration are accelerated.
- The animal is not able to stand or walk *i.e.* deadly lame.
- It is a Rapidly spreading disease and fatal. The symptoms escape notice because tile animal is found dead all of a sudden.

Treatment and Control

Animals can be protected by suitable vaccination. The vaccine produces immunity in 10-12 days that lasts for about one year. Animals which are showing symptoms should be isolated and treatment done for those showing early symptoms. Penicillin and tetracyclines if given promptly and inoculated into the site of lesions are of value and should be given in normal therapeutic dose. Sulphathiozole and antitoxic sera are also effective. Hygiene and prophylaxis are the methods of control Proper hygiene requires the destruction of carcasses by burning and cleaning and treatment of all wounds.

Haemorrhagic Septicaemia

This disease is widely prevalent in India among cattle and buffaloes. It occurs mostly in acute septicaemic form. Buffaloes are more susceptible to this disease than cattle owing to their greater liking for water and swamps. The disease occurs generally in low lying humid areas and is often seasonal.

Outbreak occurs during the periods of highest humidity such as during monsoon. The disease is mainly caused by *Pasteurella multocida*. However, stress due to exhaustion because of excessive work, starvation, chilling or change from rail or road journey may also pre-dispose animals to infection. This accounts for the name 'shipping fever', by which the disease is known in certain countries.

Haemorrhagic septicaemica is carried on through the carriers season after season. The organisms are maintained by carriers during the inter-epidemic period. The infection may occur due to ingestion of polluted grass or water while feeding, grazing and drinking in such places. The organisms get. into the blood through wounds inside the mouth gullet, stomach or intestine and sometimes through wounds in an animal's feet or legs. They may also be conveyed from a diseased animal to a healthy one by bitting insects. The disease may attack throat, lungs or intestines and, as such, three forms of the disease are recognizable namely throat form, lung form and intestinal form.

Symptoms

- Off-feed, high temperature (105 to 108° F) disinclination to move with the herd, shivering, starring coat, and dry hot muzzle.
- Hurried breathing and no milk.
- Dripping of saliva, pain in throat and swelling in the space between jaws, neck, fore limb and brisket.
- The swelling is hot, tense and painful
- One may notice a suffocating cough, difficult breathing and swollen and reddened eyes.
- Colicky(stomach) pain, animal groans and strains when passing faeces which first may be hard and glazed and later on watery, containing blood and mucus shreds. Mortality is very high even 90 per cent.

Treatment and Control

Treatment can be effective if it is carried out in the early stages of the disease but the rapidity of the disease often prevents it. Sulphadimidine and brond spectrum antibiotics are effective. In an endemic area prophylactic vaccination should be carried out annually about a month before the onset of rains. Healthy animals should be isolated from the sick ones and dead animals must be buried six feet deep with lime. Every thing connected with the suffering animals such as ropes, brush, baskets, etc. must be scrubbed, washed With phenyl or even burnt.

Brucellosis

Brucellosis among cattle and buffaloes produces heavy economic losses due to abortions in behind pregnancy, infertility and reduction in milk production. The disease occurs in most parts of the world. In India, the disease is fairly widely prevelent. The organism responsible for brucellosis or contagious bovine abortion is *Brncella abortus*. In a herd the disease is introduced by the induction of infected cow or, less commonly, by an infected bull. Under natural condition, the cattle get infection by ingestion of food and water contaminated with uterine discharge of aborted animals. Aborted foetuses, foetal membranes, vaginal discharges, milk and faeces of infected animals contain the organisms, which contaminate the environment, feed and water.

Symptoms

- The cow throws out a dead foetus prematurely but the placenta does not fallout.
- The cow gets sick and there is blood tinged discharge from the vagina.
- Milk yield drops in a lactating cow and the cow goes down in condition.
- There are signs of pregnancy and signs of calving will be noticeable much earlier than the due date and the calf will be thrown out prematurely. In subsequent pregnancies, the foetus is usually carried to full term but second or third abortion may take place in the same cow.

- In the bull, orchitis and epididymitis occur. One or both the scrotal sacs may be affected with acute, painful swelling.

Treatment and Control

The antibiotics are effectual in making the organisms disappear, but they may reappear when the treatment is stopped. Therefore, the treatment is not very successful. Vaccination with *Brucella abortus* strain 19 is helpful in tile control of brucellosis in a herd. The vaccine is inoculated in the calves aged 91-100 days. It stimulates the development of high level of immunity which lasts till fifth pregnancy. The general practices for the control of brucellosis in cattle are hygienic measures, identification and elimination of infected animals from herds. Hygienic measures include isolation of infected animals, disposal of aborted foetuses, placental and uterine discharges and disinfection of contaminated area.

Tuberculosis

Tuberculosis is an antique disease of man, animal and birds. Only a few countries are free of this disease. It is an infectious disease, characterized by slow development of tubercles in almost any organ of the body except the skeletal muscles. The incidence of tuberculosis depends upon a variety of factors related to husbandry, hygiene and environment. The incidence is high where intensive cattle breeding programmes are carried out in countries where animals are housed indoors during the winter months. Tuberculosis in cattle and buffaloes is caused by the bacterium Tuberculous bacilli. The bacteria enter the body usually through food, sometimes they are directly breathed into the lungs. The diseased animal may contaminate the drinking water and vessels. The excretions like faeces, urine, sputum, etc. of the diseased animal may contain the bacteria and be a source of infection.

Symptoms

The symptoms of tuberculosis depend on the limb affected as any of the organ may be involved. Moreover, an affected animal may show no clinical signs even though it may be severely affected. However, following symptoms may be observed in an affected animal.

- The infected animal gets weaker day by day and becomes inactive and dull.
- Hard, dry cough occasionally but not very pronounced in cows.
- If intestine is affected there will be tympany and diarrhoea.
- If udder is affected, there will be swelling of one or more teats with no pain. The symmetry of the udder may be lost. The milk becomes watery, the quantity reduced and gets curdled on boiling.
- When there is tuberculosis of reproductive system, the abortions occur late in pregnancy. The conception rate is very low. There is thick yellow discharge from the vagina of infected animal.

Treatment and Control

The treatment of tuberculosis is not recommended, as it is very prolonged and the results are unreliable. The animals under treatment are liable to disseminate organisms in milk for human consumption. The tuberculin is widely used throughout the world for the control of tuberculosis in animals. In India where control by test and slaughter is not possible, Bang's method of control has been found to be useful. This method is based on disposing of all the clinical cases. The calves born of tuberculosis-infected cows are free of infection. The animals not showing tile clinical sign are subjected to tuberculin testing. The reactors and non-reactors are kept separately.

The healthy group is tested every 3-6 months. Calves born of healthy animals are allowed to remain with mothers while those from reacting mothers are weaned immediately after birth. This method leads to a progressive increase in the number of healthy animals and decrease of reactors. For preventing the spread of the disease. Hygienic cattle sheds with adequate space ventilation, fresh air, etc. must be provided. The carcasses of affected animals should be burnt or burned, six feet deep with lime.

S. Mastitis

Mastitis is a disease of udder which usually occurs in heavily milking cows and buffaloes usually after third calving when the milk secretion is at its peak. There is inflamation in the udder due to the infection with micro-organisms. The infection usually occurs due to insanitary conditions of the cattle shed or due to spreading of infection from other infected cows through the hands of the milker. This may occur in anyone quarter of the udder in more than one quarters.

Symptoms

The first symptom is the tendency to kick while being milked in an otherwise quiet animal. Other symptoms are as follows.

- Very severe if the udder gets affected immediately after calving and the teats become swollen.
- Udder is hard and painful with a yellow serum-like fluid to start with, then flocculent material With blood and later on pus.
- There may be slight rise of body temperature. The animal rests her head on her chest or stretches out on the ground.
- Milk is very watery and blood tinged, often curdled, and comes out in clots or shreds, later on as pus.
- The udder loses its normal shape due to swelling of the quarters and displacement of the swollen teats out of position. Milk from the affected udder should not be used for human consumption. But if milk looks clean, healthy and without clots and shreds, it can be boiled and used for calf feeding.

Treatment and Control

The treatment of mastitis is done by antibiotics. Special preparations of antibiotics for infusion into the teats are available. The effectiveness, however, depends on the stage of development of disease. Before infusion of the medicine, the udder is completely milked out. The medicine after introduction into udder is allowed to spread properly by massaging the udder. The control of mastitis depends on sanitary precautions and early detection of affected cases. Small white clots of milk which may appear before the swelling is evidenced can be detected by a 'strip cup'. This is a wide mouthed cup with a black platform. A black cloth tied over the cup should also be used. Milk from the suspected quarters may be milked directly over the black surface to find out the presence of clots. Another method of testing for mastitis is by using special test papers, which are filter paper strips impregnated with indicators like bromthymol blue. As mastitis milk is slightly aikaline in reaction when a drop of milk is poured over the paper, the colour changes to dark green.

In order to prevent the spread of the disease, the affected cow should be isolated. She should be milked separately by a separate milkman. If a separate milkman is not available, let the available milkman milk healthy cows first and then milk the affected cow last in a separate vessel. Also, keep cattle shed and surrounding clean.

Foot and Mouth Disease

The foot and mouth disease (FMD) is highly communicable disease affecting cloven footed animals. It is characterized by fever, formation of blisters in tile mouth, udder, tests and on the skin between toes and above the hoofs. Animals recovered from the disease present a characteristically rough coat and deformation of the hoof. In India the disease is widespread and assumes a position of importance in livestock industry. The disease is caused by a virus called foot and mouth disease virus. It spreads by direct contact or indirectly through infected water, manure, hay and pastures. It is also conveyed by cattle attendants. Foot and mouth disease occurs in relatively mild form in India and is seldom fatal. It occurs practically all the year round. The disease has been existing for years and, in view of the frequent opportunities for exposure to natural infection, most of the indigenous animals have a great degree of resistance to the disease. Of late, significance is being attached to the airborne transmission of the virus.

Symptoms

The virus gains entry into the blood stream of animals through injury to the lining membranes of, tongue, intestines, clefts of hooves and other similar parts. The incubation period in natural infection is 2.5 days, whereas in artificial infection it is 24 to 48 hours only. After incubation period is complete, following symptoms may be observed.

- Rise of body temperature, dry muzzle, dullness, depression, shivering, staring coat, loss of appetite and stoppage of rumination.
- Slight constipation.
- Dribbling of saliva from tile mouth.
- Formation of blisters on the tongue, gums and cheeks.
- Shaking and kicking of legs and lameness.
- Vesicles at the cleft of the hoof become ulcer like and may get fly blown..
- Vesicles may be seen on the udder and teats also.
- The milk yield comes down in quantity and quality, and the milk coagulates on boiling.
- Tendency of the hooves to get deformed and sometimes the horns of the hooves may be shed. Consequently the animal becomes permanently lame.
- The infected animal cannot be put to hard work, especially in the sun, and it gasps from breath, a condition known as 'panting'. Panting is more severe in the cross-bred animals than in the indigenous ones.

Treatment and Control

No therapeutic agents have been establish till now to cure foot and mouth disease. The use of drugs by field worker is resorted to only as a measure of acidity in the material process of recovery. Thus, the external application of antiseptics contributes to the healing of ulcers and wards off attack by flies. A common and inexpensive dressing for lesions of feet is a mixture of coal tar and copper sulphate in the proportion of 5 : 1. Some other measures to treat the disease are given below.

- Clean the wounds and ulcers in the mouth, udder, teats and feet with 2 per cent potassium permanganate lotion or alum water.
- Decoction of *babool* bark for gargling the mouth and washing the ulcers may also be effective.
- Apply boric acid mixed with glycerin to ulcers in the mouth.
- Foot bath with a disinfectant solution such as cresol or phenol (1 : 100) may be used.
- When maggots are found, custard apple leaves ground into a paste may be applied or a few drops of turpentine are let in.
- Sores on the udder and teats of milch cows should be kept clean and dressed with boric ointment.

Johne's Disease

Johne's disease is a serious disease of cattle and buffaloes. It constitutes a potent source of threat to the dairy industry and livestock trade in many countries. It is also known as paratuberculosis as it is produced by Mycobacterium paratuberculosis.. Its insidious nature, protracted and irregular period of incubation, rather vague and indefinite symptoms in the early stage and lack of accurate methods of diagnosis defy the steps to check the indiscriminate movement of the affected animals. The infection bas thus rapidly spread all over the globe. The causative organism is excreted with faeces and will remain alive for a long period. This will cause the spread of disease to other animals.

Symptoms

The disease is very insidious at the onset, and the animal may show clinical symptoms after months or year of infection. In the early stages there is hardly any symptoms which may lead to a positive diagnosis. However, the principal symptoms are given below.

- The affected animal becomes emaciated and bas persistent diarrhoea with bad smell.

- The faeces may often be mixed with flakes of mucous and gas bubbles and are usually passed without straining.
- The appetite is not impaired and there is no fever or pain, the animal has normal body temperature.
- The coat becomes starring and the skin leathery with the progress of the disease.
- Anaemia becomes more marked and on edematous swelling (containing fluid) may develop in the sub-maxillary region.
- The animal goes on loosing condition and at last death occurs due to exhaustion and dehydration.
- In some cases, however, diarrhoea may be absent and dealt may occur due to debility only.

Control and Treatment

At present there appears to be no practical and reliable method of treatment of this disease. The organism is very resistant to chemotherapeutic agents. Because of this the practical utility of treatment in clinical cases is poor. A live vaccine bas been developed. It reduces the incidence of clinical disease. It consists of a non-athogenic strain of Johne's bacillus with an adjutant. The calves soon after birth are inoculated with the vaccine subcutaneously. The vaccinated animals become reactor of John. The vaccination is generally done in heavily infected herd.

General hygiene, test and segregation, slaughter of clinical cases, provision of clean water supply, proper disposal of infected animals improving the general nutritional level, supplementing the rations with minerals, etc. are some of the steps to prevent the spread of the disease. The carcasses of affected animals should always be burnt or buried deep into the ground with lime.

Rinderpest

Rinderpest is also known as 'cattle plague'. It is the most serious contagious disease of cattle in the country. It is a rapidly fatal disease affecting larger number of annuals and causing enormous losses in infected herds. It affects mainly cattle and other cloven footed animals including buffaloes. Unless special precautions are taken a very large percentage of the affected annuals may die. Rinderpest is caused by an ultra-visible virus.

The virus is present in the blood corpuscles of affected animals. It is excreted through the saliva or discharges from the nose, eyes and the urine and faeces of the affected animals. Outside the body the virus is rapidly destroyed by the sunlight and disinfectants.

The disease spreads through air, contaminated utensils, attendants, etc. It may be introduced in a herd by the inclusion of infected animals.

Symptoms

The incubation period of the disease is 3-7 days. After the incubation period is complete following symptoms are observed.

- High fever, dullness, staring coat, shivering, dry muzzle, and drooping of head and ears.
- Loss of appetite and no rumination.
- Milk secretion in cows stops.
- Salivation, eruptions like bran particles on the inside of lips, gums, dental pad and roof of the mouth.
- Eyelids are swollen, mucus membranes light red and there is lachrymation and nasal discharge.
- Urine becomes dark coloured and scanty.
- First there is constipation which lasts for 2-3 days followed by profuse diarrhoea mixed with mucus and blood with very offensive odour.
- The animal gets exhausted by this time and usually dies after a long period of agony.

Treatment and Control

In earlier days anti-rinderpest serum was used on a large scale for the treatment of the clinical cases of the rinderpest. This practice is now of little value. Anti-rinderpest serum has little or no curative properties once the virus has produced the clinical symptoms in the animal. Hence, the use of this serum is not recommended. Symptomatic treatment with penicillin, streptomycine, sulphadimidine and intestinal antiseptics have no action on tile virus, but may help in tile recovery of tile less severe cases of the rinderpest. It is beneficial to keep the animal on light diet, such as rice gruel with kaolin which act as intestinal astiguents to reduce the intestinal effusions and control diarrhoea. Advanced preventive vaccination if done with freezed dried rinderpest vaccine gives immunity for five years. As there are chances of spreading the disease through common grazing grounds and at cattle sheds, sufficient precautions should be taken. The affected animals are to be segregated and the newly added animals are to be quarantined for at least 10-15 days.

Cow-pox

Cow-pox attacks both cows as well as buffaloes and causes great loss by a rapid fall in the milk yield and by spreading the infection to other animals and human beings. Basically this is a viral disease but secondary infection may be caused by bacteria. The occurrence of cowpox has frequently been associated with the incidence of small-pox in human beings. Instances are on record in which cow-pox in all stages has been transmitted through the milkers. However, conclusive evidence is still lacking as to the existence of any relationship between small pox with outbreaks of cow pox.

Under natural conditions the infection takes place through inoculation by the cutaneaus route and readily spreads from one animal to another through the agency of milkers. The occurrence of this disease is not often reported since it is localised only to the teats and udder, and occasionally to the hairless parts of the body. It does not assume a serious form unless the lesions are infected with pyogenic (pus producing) organisms.

Symptoms

- The first symptom is the tendency to kick while being milked, by an otherwise quiet cow.
- Teats get swollen, hard and painful.

- There is rise of body temperature, loss of appetite and stopping of rumination.
- Eruptions appear on the skin of the udder and teats developing into vesicles, pustules and scabs by stages, sometimes on the thighs and abdomen,
- Reduction in milk yield.

Treatment and Control

The lesions heal by themselves in the normal course and the adoption of special measures is not generally required, only the usual rules of hygien need to be observed. The lesions should be cleaned with a 1 : 1000 solution of potassium permanganate followed by the application of an antiseptic ointment such as 1 : 10 boric acid. The affected animals should be isolated and milked by separate milkers. Milk from affected animals should be boiled before use. If the disease assumes serious proportions, vaccination may be undertaken.

NON-CONTAGIOUS DISEASES

These diseases occur among the animals mostly due to management irregularities, dietetic errors or deficiency in the system or sometimes due to toxic substances. Many of the common non-contagious ailments occur on all kinds of dairy cattle irrespective of breed, age or sex, mostly due to improper care and management. These non-contagious diseases will not spread from animal to animal nor will they ordinarily prove fatal because most of them are amenable to treatment if promptly detected and treated. The common non-contagious diseases or ailments met with cows and Buffaloes are milk fever, metritis, mammits, tympanities, diarrhoea, constipation, etc.

Ketosis

Ketosis in cattle is a condition occurring due to metabolic disorder. There will be an imbalance between the nutritive intake and nutrition requirement for the body. The condition usually occurs in high producing dairy cattle. There will be low blood glucose level and depletion of glycogen reserves, of the liver. As a result protein is mobilized from the body to be converted into a glucose in the liver. Stored fat of the body is also mobilized. Production of ketone bodies is increased and they accumulate in the blood and urine.

Symptoms

- The affected animal shows decreased appetite.
- Milk yield is suddenly decreased.
- Breath of animal has peculiar sweetish smell.
- The urine also gets a peculiar smell, similar to that of ammonia.
- Body weight of tile animal rapidly reduces.

Treatment and Control

The treatment consists of tile intravenous injection of glucose or fructose. Propionic acid can also be given as sodium propionate. Glycerol or propylene glycol is satisfactory when given orally. To prevent the condition in cows proper care should be taken in the feeding. Feeding balanced ration to high producers and pregnant cows and giving them molasses or jaggery will prevent this condition.

Milk Fever

Milk fever also known as parturient hypocalcaemia and parturient paresis is a disease which has assumed considerable importance with the development of heavy milking cows. Strictly speaking, the disease is not a fever because the signs of fever such as rise in body temperature are absent. Usually it occurs in cattle which have recently calved, often in the first few days after calving. The disease usually occurs in 5-10 years old cows and is chiefly caused by a sudden decrease in blood calcium level. The volume of milk secretion, particularly when the udder is completely emptied soon after birth may lower the calcium from its normal level of about 10 mg to 3-8 rug per 100 ml of blood. Inorganic phosphorus level is usually decreased from 4 to 6 mg to 1.5-5.0 per 100 ml of blood. The production of colostrum by the animal may also bring about rapid reduction in the concentration of the blood calcium.

Symptoms

- The animal becomes excited and restless, starts shivering with an impression of great discomfort by lashing its tail and paddling its hind feet.
- The animal lies down on her brisket with the head resting on one side of shoulder; snores and moans for a while and later becomes unconscious.
- Eyes become dull with pupils dilated.
- Breathing becomes deep and slow, pulse is fast but weak, extremities get cold and the temperature falls to 3 or 4 degree below normal.
- Dung and urine are not passed and the gas collects in the stomach.
- The animal loses sense, falls down With partial or complete paralysis of hind quarters and dies within 24 hours if not attended properly.

These symptoms may appear a day prior to calving or even after a month of calving though the majority of cases arise during the first 2 or 3 days of calving.

Treatment and Control

The treatment consists of the sluggish injection during about 20 minutes, into the blood torrent, of 300 ml of 20 per cent solution of calcium borogluconate and the simultaneous injection by the subcutaneous route of 50 to 100 ml of the same solution. The treatment may be repeated in 3 to 4 hours if necessary. In areas of magnesium deficiencies about 11 gm of magnesium sulphate by mouth may be administered to the animal.

The addition of calcium in the ration is contra-indicated as this may even increase the incidence of the disease, particularly if the diet is alkaline. Adding sodium propionate to the feed for 2 or 3 weeks after calving may help to some extent but the availability of sodium propionate is doubtful. The incidence of the disease may be reduced if the cows are only particularly milked during the first three days after parturition and are injected with calcium boro-gluconate immediately after calving.

Tympanitis

This is also called bloat or aphara condition. The condition is characterized by the accumulation of gas or foam in the rumen. The abdomen becomes greatly distended especially on the left side in front of the hip bone. The condition arises due to the greedy feeding on lush green especially leguminous fodder, when the animal is in half starved condition. Weak and convalescing animals are more susceptible to this ailment as they cannot digest protein rich feed and the fermentation of undigested feed takes place.

Symptoms

Formation of gas always occurs to a certain extent in the stomach of cattle. But when it occurs in large quantities the following symptoms may be observed.

- Bloated condition of the hollow of the left flank which, if topped with fingers, produces a drum like sound.
- The animal shows the signs of uncareness and pain, frequently lying down and getting up with arched back.
- Rumination is suspended.
- Tension increases leading to breathing difficult when the animal may fall down if neglected and may even die of suffocation.

Treatment and Control

Fermentation can be checked by giving internally anti-fermentative drugs such as turpentine, camphor, asafoetida and ammonium carbonate in right quantities. At the same time, try to remove the gas already formed inside, by cleansing the rectum by a warm soap-water enema. The earliest treatment in a village will be to take 20-30 gm of asafoetida, bum it, powder it and put inside a bread and shove into the oesophagus. Follow it after one hour. In severe cases when the distension is intense, a puncture may be made in the left flank with a trocar and canula to relieve the gas quickly. To prevent this condition, care in feeding lush green fodder such as legumes should be taken. Weak stomach animals should not be given fat and protein rich fodder in large quantities.

Diarrhoea

Diarrhoea is more a symptom of a disease than a disease itself. It is a condition in which dung is passed out in liquid or semi-liquid form, unlike the normal dung which is solid or semisolid. It may be caused by unwholesome feed, spoiled food, toxic food, coarse indigestible fibrous matter or feed adulterated with sand, or stones, polluted water especially after rains which may contain harmful bacteria may also cause diarrhoea. In certain contagious diseases such as rinderpest, worm infestation etc., diarrhoea is a symptom.

Symptoms

- Frequent parrage of watery motions and the soiling of buttocks, thighs and tail.
- The animal is dull, belly tucked up with a staring coat.

Treatment

At first, to remove bacteria and other possible irritants, the animal is given one litre of castor oil emulsion or one litre of linseed oil internally. A few hours later, mix 20 gm catechu, 40 gm chalk powder and 20 gm ginger powder. Feed this mixture with one litre of rice gruel to the animal. This can be repeated twice a day till the diarrhoea stops.

Animals diet should also be corrected by giving dry feed, bran, gram husk, etc. and hay or straw instead of green grass.

Constipation

Constipation is a condition where the dung is not passed out with ease, in normal quantity of consistency and is usually a symptom seen in all conditions affecting the general health of the animal, sometimes with a rise in body temperature. The causes of constipation are numerous and some important ones are being given below.

- Accumulation of dry and hard undigested feed in the stomach.

- Over-eating of not easily digestible feed such as coarse fibrous roughages.
- Hurried eating-gulping without proper chewing or rumination:
- Inadequate intake of drinking water.
- Increase in body temperature.
- Inefficient functioning of certain internal organs as liver, intestines, etc. Symptoms

Symptoms

Following symptoms are observed in constipation.

- Dung is hard, sometimes even as pellets, passed in small quantities after straining and at times not passed out at all.
- Loss of appetite.
- Animal does not chew, stops rumination and shows signs of pain and discomfort.

Treatment

The affected animal should be given laxative diet like wet wheat bran mash, rice gruel and *canji* water. Supply easily digestible green fodder. Make the animal drink adequate quantities of fresh water, if necessary by adding a little jaggery or salt or both to the water. Evacuate the rectum and give a warm soap water enema. As a first aid relief measure, use following preparation:

0.25 kg of common salt (sodium chloride)
8.25 kg of Epsom salt (magnesium sulphate)
50 g of powdered ginger
25 g powdered pepper
10 g *Nux vomica* powder.

These ingredients are mixed and divided into two parts. One part is given immediately with feed and the other after a few hours. Six hours later, give half a litre of groundnut oil mixed with 0.25 litre, castor oil, which when given internally, will certainly get the hardened mass out.

To prevent constipation in cattle following precautionary steps may be taken.

- To cows which have a tendency to constipate, supply easily digestible feed stuff With plenty of *conjee* water and drinking water with handful of salt and jaggery.
- Stop feeding straw but give easily digestible succulent grass like paragrass and doobgrass.
- Avoid fibrous feed and add a handful of common salt in the feed or *conjee* water every day as a rule.

Ephemeral Fever

This is a three days sickness condition and is often met with dairy cows especially during winter months. It is also known as rheumatic fever or stiff sickness of cows. This disease is peculiar to cattle and no other animals. The causal organism of this disease is not yet known but it is believed to be of viral origin. Lying on insanitary chill cement floors and exposure to cold may be the predisposing factors.

Symptoms

- Sudden rise of body temperature to 104-1070 F accompanied by muscular pains and lachrymation and salivation.
- The animal goes lame on only one of her legs without any injury or swelling, more commonly the front legs.
- The cow is dull, off feed, stops rumination and breathes hard.
- Milk yield is decreased, swelling is difficult.

Treatment and Control

For treatment of this disease, 2 to 4 ounces of sodium salicylate with equal quantity of Epsom salt and one tea spoonful of ginger with a little jaggery is given by mouth and repeated after six hours. The sick cow is given laxative diet and warm gruel. She is also provided with a comfortable, warm housing. Interavenous injection of sterile sodium salicylate solution by a qualified veterinary doctor, if available, will give immediate relief.

COMMON DISEASES/AILMENTS OF SUCKLING CALVES

Like grown up cattle, suckling calves also get infected with a number of diseases or ailments of various nature. Some of them such as umbilical abscess, blindness, white scour, dysentery, etc. may prove quite disastrous. These diseases are briefly described here.

Umbilical Abscess

This condition is seen in young suckling calves as on infected abscess at or near the umbilical opening. This may be caused due to neglect by the owner in not keeping the calf under hygienic condition or providing any bedding or by leaving the cut end of the umbilicus exposed to flies and bacteria Without any antiseptic dressing. In this condition following symptoms are observed.

- The part is hard, hot and painful with a foul smelling discharge at the opening.
- Slight rise in body temperature.
- Sometimes, swelling and pain at the leg joint may also occur. For the treatment, following steps should be taken.

Clean tile part with a mild disinfectant such as a few drops of tincture of iodine or phenyl in clean water. Foment and dress it with any antiseptic powder like Mycodenn or Nebasulph. Application of Horexane and Himax ointment will also be useful.

Keep the stall floor clean with disinfecting lotion like Phenyl, Salvon or ettol and provide a layer of dry straw or leaves as bedding for the calves.

Pneumonia

Pneumonia occurs in young calves soon after birth or a few days later, especially during winter season. It is caused due to exposure to cold weather or by bacterial infection. It may also occur due to worm infestation in the lungs. Following symptoms are observed.

- Rise in body temperature.
- Thick nasal discharge.
- Laboured respiration.
- Indigestion and diarrhoea.

To treat pneumonia, following measures are suggested:

- Steron inhalation with, eucalyptus or terpentine.
- Dry, warm and well ventilated stall with dry bedding.
- Antibiotic injection such as Penicillin or Amphicilline.
- The sick calf should be given warm, nutritious and easily digestible diet.

Dysentery

Dysentery in calves is caused due to irritation in intestine or sometimes due to wonns. It may also be caused by Coccidia, a protozoan parasite.

- The calf strains, it does not eat and has abdominal pain.
- Small quantities of dung are passed with mucus and blood in it. Treatment:
    1. Give castor oil emulsion (2 to 4 ounces).
    2. Give sulphaguanidine (2-4 tablets) twice a day for three days.
    3. Feed 3-4 sour pomegranate fruits, chopped with the rind, daily for three or four days.
    4. Feed the calf with rice gruel to which 10 gm of fenugreek has been added and boiled.

White Scour (Diarrhoea)

White scour disease is fairly common in most calves, especially in buffalo calves. It occurs usually within the first few weeks of birth. The condition always indicates bad management. Following factors may be responsible for this condition.

- Over drinking of mother's milk, especially when it is rich in butter fat.
- Improper feeding *i.e.* frequent feeding, more in quantity, milk rich in fat, cold and polluted milk.

- Lying in mud floor especially when it is wet and insanitary.
- Heavy worm infestation in the intestines.
- Ark, dirty and ill-ventilated calfshed.

The main symptoms of this disease are severe-whitish diarrhoea, dullness, progressive emaciation (weakness), etc. The dung of the calf is loose and watery. Often it is whitish or clayish in colour with an offensive odour. The calf strains and moarns with pain. For the treatment of white scour in calves, following steps are taken:

- Housing on dry hygienic floors, preferably with some bedding of dry straw or dry leaves.
- Good ventilation and sunlight are essential.
- Wean the sick calf, withhold whole milk and give only skimmed milk or gruel made of ragi flour and broken rice.
- Give catechu, one and half tea spoonful with equal quantity of chalk powder or jaggerry.
- Administer orally the tablets of sulphromezathine, two tablets twice a day for three days
- Add two teaspoonfuls of Aurofac, Neften or lime water to the feed for a month.
- Use a mouth gag to the calf at non-feeding time to prevent it from slicking the walls and floors.

Blindness

Blindness is a condition commonly seen in new born calves. It is caused due to lack of vitamin A. The calf develops following symptoms.

Symptoms

- The calf appears normal in all respects but standing on its feet in about half an hour as any other normal calf, it is not able to find the udder for want of vision and so keeps knocking about.
- The eyes look normal but when an attempt is made to touch the eyes with fingers or any other object, the eyelids will not close.

Treatment

To treat blindness in calves, following measures are suggested.

- Give one or two teaspoonful of good quality shark liver oil in feed at least twice a day for a month or more.
- Vitamin A preparations which are easily available in the market can be added to the feed for a month or more.
- Feeds rich in vitamin A such as yellow maize meal, chopped carrots, etc. should be fed till weaning.
- A few injections of vitamin A preparations like Prepaline, should be administered to care the calf completely.

Worm Infestation

Worm infestation is a common problem in calves, sometimes even at birth. It occurs almost invariably in all buffalo calves. It is caused due to parasitic infestation, mostly roundworms and occasionally tapeworms, hookworms and even liverflukes. Secondary factors such as insanitary conditions of housing and ill-management may also be responsible. In villages, it may also be I caused due to polluted water and fodder from marshy areas. Following symptoms may be observed.

- The infested calves get diarrhoea.
- The calf gets rough coat and depressed appetite.
- The affected calf develops the tendency to lick mud and eat any thing.
- The abdomen of affected calf becomes pendulous. Grinding of teeth may also be observed.
- Sometimes even worms may be passed out with dung.

To get rid of this affliction, the dung of affected calves should be got examined. Dewomung the calf with known anthelmintics (worm dose) such as tablets of Decaris, Helmonil, oil of turpentine arecanut, asafoetida or tender leaves of neem with salt should be practiced.

Skin Disease (Ring Worm)

Skin disease is a common occurrence among young suckling calves. Housing calves under unhygienic conditions, improper grooming and brushing and parasites like ticks, flies, lice, etc. are the factors responsible for this condition. In affected calves, hairless patches on the head, neck, face and sometimes on the legs are formed. They also get itching and irritation, which can be noticed. The animal rubs against walls, posts and trees. Affected animals should be isolated. Clip the hairs on the affected parts, remove crusts, clean the surface and paint it with tincture iodine. The calves should be given good nourishing diet and cod liver oil. Apply antifungal ointments such as Mycozol on the affected portion.

Sometimes painting the affected portion with the juice of *Leucas aspera* or applying oil obtained by burning coconut oil, are also effective. Livestock has played a very important role in the Indian economy ever since civilisation. With the increasing human population in India, demand for animal protein is increasing, due to social and economic reasons. Milk and milk products are important constituents of human diet. Some of the population also take animal meat, especially of buffaloes, due to low cost and taste. Thus control and eradication of diseases of cattle and buffaloes are very important considerations. Now with the introduction of some of the foreign breeds of cattle and their crosses, which are highly susceptible to diseases, tile demand for efficient health cover has increased considerably in order to maintain them in good health and production. For tins, control and eradication programme for these cattle diseases has become very important considering the economies of cattle and buffalo industry.

Prevention, control and eradication are the three basic methods used in dealing with any disease in the cattle population. These three methods are applied depending upon the economic importance of disease and investment cost available for the control programme. For prevention, control and eradication of all contagious diseases (which are mainly caused by virus or bacteria), a potent vaccine is very essential. For most of these contagious diseases, vaccines are available. In susceptible areas or herds, vaccination programme should be carried out well in advance.

It is also imperative that cattle and buffalo owner should know all the signs of good health and understand the condition of his animals especially when they manifest symptoms of diseased condition, so that he can take effective steps in time to get his animal treated or to control the spread of infection. Every time it may not be possible for the owner to attend his sick animal and as such, he should take the help of a qualified veterinary doctor in proper time. However, there are certain diseases for which there is no any vaccine or scientific treatment course. In such a case, improvement in hygienic conditions, management practices and feeding standards is very important.

CATTLE HEALTH

As a cattle farmer, it's essential take the necessary steps to protect the health of animals. Maintaining good health is important to ensure acceptable standards of animal welfare, but such measures will also maximise the productivity. This conduct has information about the main diseases affecting cattle, including notifiable diseases, which must be reported, and zoonoses, which can infect humans. It covers general disease prevention and legal controls to prevent specific risks, as well as describing your legal responsibilities relating to cattle feed, medicines and hormonal treatments.

CATTLE HEALTH AND CROSS COMPLIANCE

To succeed for full payment under the Single Payment Scheme and other direct payments-*e.g.* the Environmental Stewardship schemes-you must meet all relevant cross compliance requirements. These requirements are split into two types:

- Statutory Management Requirements (SMRs)
- Requirements to keep your land in Good Agricultural and Environmental Condition (GAECs).

The aim of these requirements is to stop the illegal use of substances that have a hormonal or thyrostatic action and beta-agonists in stock farming. They also prevent residues that these substances leave in meat-and other foodstuffs-from entering the human or animal food chain. The aim of SMRs 12, 13, 14 and 15 is to minimise the risk posed to human and animal health by certain transmissible spongiform encephalopathies (TSEs), foot and mouth, bluetongue and other animal diseases. These will apply to you if you keep cattle.

CRITICAL ILLNESSES OF CATTLE

Looking after animals properly and monitoring them regularly for signs of illness are the best ways of preventing disease, and of controlling its spread if there is an outbreak. The suspect signs of a notifiable disease, you must immediately notify the duty vet at your local Animal Health Office (AHO).

Cattle are vulnerable to many endemic and exotic diseases, some of which might be notified to Animal Health if suspected:

- Endemic diseases are diseases which commonly exist within Great Britain, *e.g.* common diseases such as Bovine Viral Diarrhoea (BVD), Infectious Bovine Rhinotracheitis (IBR) and Johne's disease. They can be both notifiable-those that the law requires to be reported to the veterinary authorities-and non-notifiable.
- Notifiable diseases can be both endemic, such as tuberculosis, and exotic, meaning that they are not normally found in Great Britain, such as foot and mouth and bluetongue. Outbreaks of these diseases are subject to national control policies and international trade rules. They must be reported immediately to the duty vet at your local AHO.

Endemic Diseases

The most important endemic diseases to check for in cattle are:

- BVD and BVD2-bovine viral diarrhoea

- IBR-infectious bovine rhinotracheitis
- Johne's disease
- Certain forms of tuberculosis
- Salmonella
- Mastitis
- Other viral, bacterial and mycoplasma pneumonia.

Notifiable Diseases

The main notifiable diseases which affect cattle are:

- Anthrax
- Aujesky's disease
- Bluetongue
- BSE (bovine spongiform encephalopathy)
- Brucellosis (brucella abortus)
- Contagious bovine pleuro-pneumonia
- EBL (enzootic bovine leukosis)
- Foot and mouth disease
- Lumpy-skin disease
- Pleuropneumonia
- Rabies
- Rift-valley fever
- Rinderpest
- Bovine tuberculosis
- Vesicular stomatitis
- Warble fly.

DISEASE PREVENTION AND CONTROL FOR CATTLE

Monitoring your livestock and following good farming practices are the best ways to reduce the risk of disease among your cattle. You can find out more about measures to prevent disease on your farm in our section on controlling disease.

Buying, Registering, Identifying and moving Cattle

There are rules which you must follow for registering cattle, and when moving them. These procedures make it easier to trace and identify infected animals in the event of a disease outbreak.

When restocking your herd, you should:

- Consult your vet to help you develop a plan for evaluating prospective purchases
- Buy health scheme animals-whenever possible-that have been certified as free of specific diseases
- Recognise the risks in buying older animals.

Biosecurity and Hygiene

Good biosecurity is a vital part of keeping disease away from your animals. This will also protect the health of your workers and any members of the public who may visit your farm.

Your general biosecurity measures should include:

- Restricting and controlling movements of people, vehicles and equipment into areas where your cattle are kept
- Cleaning and disinfecting equipment, vehicles, protective clothing and footwear before and after contact with farm animals.

The presence of a disease may not always be apparent - particularly in the early stages - so the measures above need to be part of your routine.

Health and Welfare Programmes

You should seek veterinary and technical advice to create a written health and welfare programme for your cattle. This should be reviewed and updated annually. As a minimum, it should include your:

- Vaccination policy and timing
- Parasite control procedures-internal and external.

Drugs are useful for preventing disease in cattle, but you must use them responsibly and record all usage.

You can reduce the risk of disease and improve the performance of your livestock by using farm health planning techniques.

One good way to improve health planning is to benchmark your cattle's health and business practices against other local farmers.

Veterinary Surveillance

As part of its disease prevention strategy, Defra constantly collects information about incidences of disease in animals. This monitoring enables any important or unusual outbreaks to be detected quickly-so that appropriate action can be taken.

The Single Payment Scheme (SPS) and Farmed Animal Requirements

If you receive SPS or other direct payments, you must comply with Statutory Management Requirements (SMRs). SMR 7, for example, sets out the requirements for cattle identification and registration whereas SMRs 10-15 are about disease prevention through the feeding and medicinal treatment restrictions set out in this guide.

DISPOSAL OF FALLEN STOCK

'Fallen stock' is any animal that has died of natural causes or disease on a farm or that has been killed on a farm for reasons other than for human consumption. To bury or burn fallen stock on farm due to the risk of spreading disease through residues in the soil, groundwater or air pollution. This ban also covers animal by-products (ABPs), including afterbirth and stillborn animals.

The only exceptions to this ban are:

- In remote areas-parts of the Highlands and Islands of Scotland, Bardsey Island and Caldy Island in Wales, and the Scilly Isles, and Lundy Island
- During outbreaks of notifiable disease-if there is a lack of capacity at rendering plants and incinerators, or if transporting carcasses would spread disease.

All fallen farm animals-including stillborn animals-must be collected by an approved transporter and taken for disposal or treatment to an approved:

- Knacker
- Hunt kennel
- Maggot farm
- Incinerator
- Renderer.

Fallen stock must be collected, identified and transported without 'undue delay'. This means as soon as is reasonably practical under the circumstances (usually within 48hrs of death). ABPs must be transported in covered leak-proof containers/vehicles and be accompanied by a commercial document.

National Fallen Stock Scheme (NFSCo)

You can dispose of fallen stock privately at an approved destination, or you can make arrangements through the NFSCo. As a farmer, you can register with the scheme for the collection and disposal of your fallen stock. Members receive a list of the approved collectors operating in their area and the prices that they charge. Members can contact a registered collector of their choice whenever they have fallen stock. You can find information on fallen stock on the National Fallen Stock Scheme website-Opens in a new window.

ANIMAL HEALTH OFFICE (AHO)

If you want to make your own arrangements, your local AHO will provide a list of approved knackers, hunt kennels, maggot farms, incinerators or renderers. If you want to burn animal carcasses in your own on-farm incinerator, your incinerator must comply with ABP controls and environmental permitting requirements. It must also be approved by the AHO. ABPs can be incinerated on the page on Compositing and incinerating animal by-products in our guide on dealing with animal by-products.

Rules for Bovine Spongiform Encephalopathy (BSE) Testing Fallen Cattle

BSE is part of a family of diseases known as Transmissible Spongiform Encephalopathies (TSEs). These are fatal brain diseases, which include classical and atypical scrapie in sheep and goats, and BSE in cattle. TSEs in fallen cattle to assess the level of these diseases in your animals. This will enable you to assess how effective disease control measures would be and help you to ensure any controls are proportionate to the risk.

Fallen stock must be tested for BSE if they are:

- Over 48 months of age
- Over 24 months of age and born outside the European Union.

PREVENTION AND CONTROL OF BRUCELLOSIS AND TSEs IN CATTLE

Cattle farmers must take steps to minimise the risk posed to human and animal health by brucellosis and transmissible spongiform encephalopathies (TSEs), such as BSE (bovine spongiform encephalopathy) and its human variant.

PREVENTION AND CONTROL OF BRUCELLOSIS

Brucellosis of cattle, known as contagious abortion, is caused by infection with the bacterium 'Brucella abortus', which can also infect people. Cases have been recorded in this country recently-despite its eradication from the UK - through the movement of infected cattle from other countries. You should therefore work out proper biosecurity with your vet before you bring imported cattle on-farm. The disease causes abortion-or early calving-of recently infected animals, with large amounts of infectious material produced. The bacterium is also excreted in milk. People can become infected by drinking untreated milk and by contact with infected animals. The bacterium is destroyed when milk is pasteurised.

All abortions in cattle, which occur at a certain stage of pregnancy, should be reported to Animal Health. The law requires cattle keepers to report every abortion or premature calving to Animal Health. An abortion or premature calving takes place less than 271 days after service or 265 days after implantation - or transfer of an embryo-whether the calf is born dead or alive. Although blood tests for brucellosis are no longer carried out routinely on beef cattle, the following surveillance and risk management measures continue to apply:

- Import controls and certification
- Exporting country alerts of brucellosis breakdowns in exporting herds
- Post-import check testing

- Post-calving check testing
- Abortion reporting and investigations.

Any suspicion of this notifiable disease, must contact Animal Health Office (AHO) immediately. Treatment for brucellosis of cattle is not permitted-all infected cattle as well as cattle that have been exposed to infection must be slaughtered. Animal Health Officers have the right to serve a notice on the owner or person in charge of the affected bovine animals to ban their movement from their current premises or require their movement to other premises. Where a notice applies, no manure, slurry or other animal waste can be removed from those premises except under a specific licence.

PREVENTION AND CONTROL OF TSEs

To reduce the risk of TSEs, you must:

- Not feed animal protein or any feeds containing animal protein to cattle, sheep, goats, camelids, bison, buffalo, deer, antelope and wildebeest-except for milk, milk-based and colostrums, eggs and egg products, gelatine from non-ruminants, hydrolysed proteins derived from non-ruminants or from ruminant hides and skins, and liquid milk replacers for unweaned ruminants containing fishmeal, if registered by Defra.
- Not use feed products containing prohibited proteins or mix prohibited proteins with feeding stuffs such as bonemeal or poultry meal
- Not use restricted proteins to produce feed for non-ruminants such as pigs and poultry-unless you have received authorisation from Defra
- Not use feed products containing restricted proteins on a farm where there are ruminant species present-unless you have received registration from Defra
- Notify the duty vet at your local AHO immediately if you know or suspect that an animal or carcass in your possession-or under your charge-is infected with a TSE
- Fully comply with any movement restrictions
- Fully comply with any order to slaughter and destroy any animal

- Fully comply with any other notices served by an inspector.

There are specific rules to prevent the spread of BSE and other TSEs through the use of animal by-products in animal feed.

PREVENTION AND CONTROL OF TUBERCULOSIS IN CATTLE

Bovine tuberculosis (bTB) is a pressing animal health issue. The incidence rate of bTB in cattle in England and Wales has been rising for 25 years and has worsened since the 2001 Foot and Mouth Disease outbreak. The disease is a largely regional problem, concentrated in England in the South West and West Midlands. As the disease can spread to humans through contaminated milk and dairy products it is unlawful for milk-raw or pasteurised-from any animal testing positive for bTB to be used for human consumption. Milk from the rest of the herd can still be sold for human consumption-as long as it's heat-treated.

Testing

Cattle with bTB are most often identified through testing using the tuberculin skin test before they develop clinical signs. This is because the disease usually progresses slowly and it can take some time for clinical signs to appear. Clinical signs of advanced bTB include:

- Weakness
- Emaciation
- Difficulty breathing
- Enlarged lymph nodes
- Coughing.

The veterinary manager of your local Animal Health Office (AHO) immediately if you know or suspect that an animal or carcass in your possession - or under your charge-is infected with bTB.

All cattle herds - except some beef fattening units - are regularly tested for bTB, as part of four different testing programmes:

- *Compulsory regular testing using the tuberculin skin test* - carried out at the Government's expense every one to four years, with the frequency determined by how widespread bTB is in a particular region
- *Gamma interferon blood testing* – in the circumstances outlined below.
- *High health risk testing* - additional annual tests where there is a potentially higher risk to public or animal health, *e.g.* producers of raw drinking milk unpasteurised, dairy products, dealers' herds, bull hirers and regular buyers of Irish cattle
- *Pre-movement testing* - compulsory tests before cattle aged 42 days or more can be moved from a high risk area
- *Post-mortem testing* - inspection carried out by the Meat Hygiene Service on all cattle at slaughterhouses, which enables bTB cases to be traced back to the herd of origin.

Tuberculin Skin Test

The tuberculin skin test is the primary screening method for bTB in Great Britain. This test is used throughout the world to screen cattle, other animals and people for TB. Testing is carried out by government-approved testers and supervised by government-approved vets. Each test has three possible outcomes:

- *Positive* - the reactor animal is isolated from the rest of the herd and slaughtered
- *Inconclusive* - the animal is re-tested
- *Negative.*

Gamma Interferon Blood Test

The supplementary sensitive gamma interferon (g-IFN) diagnostic blood test is used in prescribed circumstances alongside the tuberculin skin test, to improve the sensitivity of the testing regime and identify more infected animals more quickly.

Using both tests in this way can help to speed up the resolution of confirmed TB breakdowns by identifying as many infected cattle as possible at the earliest opportunity.

The use of g-IFN test is mandatory in the following prescribed circumstances:

- All confirmed new incidents (CNI) in 3 or 4 yearly tested herds, including those that fail to resolve through repeated skin testing or where complete or partial de-population is contemplated
- Confirmed TB incidents that have failed to resolve through repeated skin testing, in 1 and 2 yearly tested herds, including those herds where complete or partial de-population is contemplated.

Additionally, the test is used occasionally to enhance specificity in the following limited circumstances:

- Non-specific reactor procedure for unconfirmed breakdowns in 2, 3, or 4 yearly tested herds
- Suspected fraudulent reactors

Pre-Movement Testing

In addition to the above, Pre-Movement testing is a statutory requirement: cattle 42 days old and over moving from a 1 or 2 yearly tested herd must have tested negative to a bTB test within 60 days prior to movement.

Cattle Compensation

Government compensation is paid to owners of cattle compulsorily slaughtered for bTB control purposes. Compensation in England is determined primarily using table values, which reflect the average sales price of bovine animals in 47 different categories. The categories are based on the animal's age, gender, type (dairy or beef) and status (pedigree or non-pedigree).

Vaccination

Vaccination of either cattle or wildlife is a potential long-term option for reducing the risk of bovine TB in Great Britain. However, vaccines can never represent a single answer to the problem of bovine TB. Vaccination is a risk reduction measure, most likely to be successful in controlling bovine TB when used alongside other disease control. The first injectable badger vaccine was licensed in March 2010 and is available for use on prescription. Research is continuing into producing a licensed cattle vaccine with differential test and an oral badger vaccine.

Badgers and bTB

Allow controlled culling to be carried out by groups of farmers and landowners, as part of a science-led and carefully managed policy of badger control. Licences will be issued by Natural England under the Protection of Badgers Act 1992 to enable groups of farmers and landowners in the worst affected areas, to reduce badger populations for the purpose of preventing the spread of disease at their own expense. Culling will be piloted of the policy in two areas in 2012 to monitor the effectiveness, humaneness and safety of controlled shooting. Subject to Natural England's decisions on licence applications, the two areas will be West Gloucestershire and West Somerset. An independent panel of experts has been appointed to report to ministers on the findings of the monitoring of the badger culling pilots by the end of 2012. If Ministers decide to proceed following the pilots, a maximum of ten licences will be granted to start each year. A five-year Badger Vaccine Deployment Project (BVDP) is taking place in one area of Gloucestershire, near Stroud.

Farmer Advice

A figure of new measures are being implemented, aimed at helping owners of bTB restricted herds to maintain their businesses and avoid some of the practical problems created by movement controls. Farmers wishing to find out more about bTB should contact their local AHO. Government-funded advice (based on the latest scientific evidence) is being developed, covering veterinary, biosecurity, and business issues. FCN agents will provide practical support, sign-post businesses to sources of other more specialist advice, and for those in greatest financial need a dedicated FCN Business Support Group will advise farmers on their options.

PROTECTING CATTLE FROM LEAD POISONING ON FARMS

Lead poisoning can cost you money and kill your cattle. The highest incidence usually occurs immediately after turn out when animals discover lead-containing materials abandoned on the pasture. Accumulation of lead beyond legal limits renders meat, offal and milk unsafe and illegal to enter the food chain. Lead poisoning can also result in stunted animal growth, animal deaths, increased birth defects and infertility, decreased productivity, loss of market value and disposal costs for dead animals and vet fees.

Causes of Lead, Poisoning on Farms

The most frequent causes of lead poisoning in cattle are:

- *Flaking high lead paint* - mainly calves
- *Vehicle and electric fence batteries - e.g.* battery remains accidentally mixed with animal feed, or batteries fly-tipped on farm land
- *High lead soils* - usually arising from historic mining and smelting operations, land erosion-especially by water courses but occasionally landslips
- *Ash from fires in which lead materials were burned* such as painted woodwork, leaded building materials, putty, wiring
- *Lead shot* from shooting which can be eaten with soil uptake and can also contaminate certain crops, especially maize and end up in silage

Withdrawal Periods and Offal Removal

A 16-week withdrawal period before slaughter is usually sufficient but for lead which is retained in the stomach this can extend for several years. Some animals may show no signs of poisoning but have lead residues in milk, offal and meat. Offal tends to have higher levels of lead for longer periods than meat or milk. Animals and/or their produce may need to be tested to investigate whether lead residues are present and also to monitor whether a withdrawal period has been adequate or whether offal should be removed after slaughter.

How to Avoid Lead Contamination on Farm?

Present are several steps you can take to protect your cattle and the human food chain from lead contamination. You should:

- Check your fields and barns for vehicle batteries, building materials, flaking lead paint, putty, lead flashing
- Remove or fence off fly-tipped material
- Prevent access to burnt out cars and old machinery that might contain lead
- Prevent cattle access to bonfire ash.

On farms with high lead soils, you should:

- Keep your cows' soil consumption as low as possible
- Avoid waterlogged land and poached land for grazing
- Avoid overgrazing and maintain adequate sward height
- Fence off bare areas of soil
- Calibrate cutters when making silage to minimise soil uptake
- Flatten any molehills prior to cutting grass for silage
- Provide salt licks and mineral supplements
- Use mains water or tested borehole water rather than natural run-off water from high lead soils.

Suspect Lead Poisoning in Cattle

Some of your cows are contaminated with lead, you must:

- Remove your cattle from the affected area (pasture, pen or yard) immediately
- Consult your vet
- Confirm the cause of disease and if it is lead poisoning then investigate the source.

Testing for Lead in Cattle

Advice and testing for lead in cattle, produce or soil is available via your vet and from your regional Veterinary Laboratories Agency (VLA).

CATTLE FEED

Safe, good-quality foodstuffs are essential to maintain both human and animal health. Feed contaminants such as lead or antimicrobial residues-or biological agents such as botulism-may cause disease in cattle and make their produce unsuitable for human consumption.

Animal by-products as Foodstuffs

Some former foodstuffs-food previously intended for human consumption-as livestock feed, subject to the animal by-products regulations. Former foodstuffs that can be fed to cattle include:

- Milk and milk-based products
- Biscuits
- Bakery waste
- Pasta
- Chocolate
- Sweets and similar products

Such products can contain rennet, melted fat, milk or eggs, as long as they are not the main ingredients. You must ensure that the products are not contaminated by meat or other animal products before feeding them to cattle. You must not feed meat, fish and most other products of animal origin to ruminants, pigs or poultry, or allow them access to such material. Cattle should not be fed any processed or unprocessed catering waste, even if it comes from vegetarian restaurants and kitchens.

Zoonoses

Zoonoses are defined diseases and infections that can be transmitted between vertebrate animals and man. Infection may occur through a bacterium, virus, fungus, parasite, or other communicable agent. Many of these can occur in cattle feed or milk and beef products from infected animals. Notifiable zoonoses include:

- Anthrax
- BSE
- Brucellosis
- Rift Valley Fever
- Bovine tuberculosis.

HORMONAL TREATMENTS AND ANTIBIOTICS FOR CATTLE

Due to concerns about the potential risk to humans, the use of hormonal growth promoters for livestock. Antibiotic growth-promoting feed additives have also been phased out- because of concerns about the potential spread of antibiotic resistance. If you keep farmed animals there are restrictions on the use of treatments that:

- Act as beta-agonists
- Have hormonal actions
- Reduce production of thyroid hormones.

Restricted treatments include:

- Phenylbutazone
- Tetracyclines
- Sulphonamides
- Nalidixic acid
- Fusidic acid
- Florphenicol
- Ceftriaxone.

Restricted antibiotic substances include:

- Chloramphenicol
- Ampicillin
- Amoxycillin/clavulanate
- Neomycin
- Gentamicin
- Enrofloxacin
- Tiamulin.

You must:

- Observe the relevant withdrawal period-*i.e.* the period between the end of treatment and the slaughter of the animal-if your food-producing animals have been given any of the restricted substances
- Keep veterinary medicinal records relating to restricted substances available to the competent authority on request.

You must not:

- Give food-producing animals restricted substances unless with any permitted exceptions

- Use substances containing oestradiol 17ß or its ester-like derivatives
- Use substances that contain beta-agonists to slow a labour-tocolysis-in cows when calving
- Use substances containing hormones or thyroid hormone-reducing actions unless prescribed by your veterinary surgeon
- Have food-producing animals on your farm that have been given any restricted substance, unless there are permitted exceptions
- Send animals to slaughter that have been given any restricted substances, unless there are permitted exceptions
- Sell meat or any other animal product that has been given a restricted substance.

CATTLE INSPECTIONS AND RECORD KEEPING

In captivating accountability for your herd, you must have the skills needed to safeguard the animals' health and welfare. This includes being familiar with the welfare code for that species. Regular inspection of your herd is essential to maintain good health. You should be familiar with the normal behaviour of cattle and be alert for any signs of illness or distress.

MONITORING CATTLE

Signs of ill health in cattle include:

- Listlessness
- Separation from the group
- Unusual behaviour
- Loss of body condition
- Loss of appetite
- A sudden fall in milk yield
- Constipation
- Scouring (diarrhoea)
- Not cudding
- Discharge from the nostrils or eyes
- Increased saliva production
- Persistent coughing
- Rapid or irregular breathing

- Abnormal resting behaviour
- Swollen joints
- Lameness
- Mastitis.

To recognise problems in their earliest stages-so that you can identify the cause and take immediate action to resolve the issue. If the cause isn't apparent-or if your remedy proves ineffective-you should seek urgent advice from a vet or other expert.

A record of all mortalities that occur among your herd, as well as any medicinal treatment given to your animals. These records need to be kept for at least three years. Use authorised animal medicines. Your records should include:

- The name and address of the medicine supplier
- The date you treated the animals
- Which animal or group of animals you treated
- How much medicine you used.

Although it's not a legal requirement, you may also find it useful to keep a record of specific cases of-and treatment given for-certain disorders. For example:

- Mastitis
- Lameness
- Milk fever.

CATTLE WELFARE

As a cattle farmer, you must meet all relevant farmed animal welfare requirements that apply to cattle and calves. This conduct outlines the welfare requirements for keeping cattle. It also gives guidance on satisfying cross compliance requirements. The guide refers to the Department for Environment, Food and Rural Affairs (Defra) code of recommendation for the welfare of cattle and will take you to specific guidance in each level.

Welfare codes do not lay down statutory requirements but you are legally obliged to ensure that all staff attending your cattle are familiar with-and have access to-the welfare code. The codes may also be used to back up legislative require-ments, *e.g.* where a person is accused of a welfare offence, failure to comply with the provisions of the welfare code may be relied on by the prosecution to establish guilt.

2

Diseases and Conditions of Cattle

ACETONAEMIA

The NADIS data show that the number of cases of acetonaemia (or ketosis) increase significantly during the winter, and the number of cases continue to increase until turnout. So it is particularly important to look out for acetonaemia until at least a month after turn-out. Like most metabolic diseases it is important to remember that for every cow that shows clinical signs, there will be several more which are affected sub-clinically.

INTRODUCTION TO ACETONAEMIA

Acetonaemia occurs when the cow's energy intake does not match its requirement and the cow is unable to compensate and mobilises its body reserves too quickly. In the beef cow, this is most likely to occur in late pregnancy when the cow's appetite is at its lowest and the energy requirement of the growing calf near its peak. In the dairy cow, the mismatch between input and output usually occurs in the first few weeks of lactation, because the cow is not able to eat enough to match the energy lost in the milk.

Clinical Signs

- Reduced milk yield: Initially a moderate decline, eventually a sudden drop

- Body condition and weight loss
- Reduction in appetite (initially non-forage feeds)
- Dull, stary coat
- Firm, 'waxy' dung
- Acetone (pear drop) smell of breath or milk-not always detectable
- Temperature, pulse rate and respiratory rate usually normal
- A few develop nervous signs including excess salivation, licking, incoordination, aggression.

Acetonaemia is more common in the dairy cow, probably because the energy difference of the lactating cow is more difficult to overcome than that of the pregnant cow, which means that most dairy cows in the UK are in negative energy balance during the first few weeks of lactation. Acetonaemia occurs when the cow is not able to cope with this energy deficit, either because it is too great or if it continues for too long. If it occurs in one cow, it usually indicates that although the other cows in the herd are currently compensating, many are suffering from an energy deficit that is significantly reducing their productivity. A clinical case of acetonaemia is the tip of the iceberg, and therefore it is advisable to discuss blood testing other cows in the same lactation group, for the subclinical form of the disease.

Prevention

Each treated cow is the tip of the iceberg, so prevention is very important. The aim of any prevention regime is to maximise dry matter intake during the critical period. This can be achieved by:

- *Avoiding over-fat and over-thin cows:* Aim to calve cows at condition score (CS) 3.0. Fat cows have lower appetites and mobilise more fat and so are more prone to ketosis Dry-off cows at CS 3.0. Cows should not gain or lose weight during the dry period. Thin cows should be fed to gain condition during late lactation. Fat cows should be fed to lose condition during late lactation.
- *Preventing disease around calving*: Cows with calving difficulties, retained membranes, endometritis, milk

fever, toxic mastitis, and hypomagnesaemia all have an increased risk of acetonaemia, so preventing these diseases reduces the risk of acetonaemia.

- *Feeding correctly:* Introduce the milking ration to the dry cows from two weeks before calving. This allows the rumen time to adapt to the milking diet Maximise palatability. Good quality forage and feeding as a total mixed ration both increase intake and thus reduce the energy deficit Maximise feeding time. Increasing the feeder space, particularly for self-fed silage, can increase intake and thus reduce energy deficit Keep the diet consistent. Avoid sudden changes to the diet even if only batch changes of concentrate.
- *Reduce stress:* Keep freshly-calved cows separate from the milking herd for at least two weeks after calving. Acetonaemia is a significant cause of economic loss, but these losses can be reduced by good management and attention.
- *Early treatment* leads to early recovery, so treat as soon as possible Veterinary advice should be sought to ensure that displaced abomasum is ruled out as a cause of the acetonaemia.

If acidosis occurs in one cow, it usually indicates that although the other cows in the herd are currently, compensating many are suffering from sub-clinical acidosis that is significantly reducing their productivity. A clinical case is the tip of the iceberg, and therefore solutions have to be for the whole herd not the individual animal. Many diseases have been linked to acidosis. For some, such as liver abscesses, the evidence is very strong. For others, such as sole ulcer and white-line disease, the link is not so strong.

Diagnosis

- Difficult as signs are non-specific.
- Ketosis (acetonaemia) must be ruled out.
- Reduced milk fat is strongly indicative of excess starch feeding.

- Most diagnoses are based on eliminating other causes of reduced appetite and yield.

Treatment

- Most treatment is supportive to allow the rumen to return to normal.
- Ruminal stimulants are of little value.
- Feeding of buffers such as sodium bicarbonate can help in the short term, particularly in animals in the same group.

Prevention

Every treated cow is the tip of the iceberg, so prevention is vital. The aim of any prevention regime is to give the cow time to adapt to change and not to expect the rumen to be able to adapt to whatever is thrown at it. There are two types of sub-acute acidosis. The first occurs in freshly calved cows (up to 20 days after calving). This occurs because of a failure to adapt the rumen to the lactation diet before calving. In this case, dry cow management is the key to prevention. In particular, feeding a transition diet and minimising calving stress are important.

The second type of acidosis affects cows from peak to mid-lactation. At this time rumen adaptation to the diet should have occurred, so acidosis in these cows occurs as a result of feeding diets that are low in fibre and high in starch (or which allow for feed selection). In all herds with an acidosis problem there needs to be a full assessment of the feeding, with attention paid to what the cows are being fed and to what they are eating. Each individual situation will be different and require a different range of solutions. Nevertheless there are several factors which are likely to be of importance in most situations:

- Forage to concentrate ratio. Except in very high yielding cows a ratio of 60:40 will significantly reduce the risk of acidosis
- Feeding total mixed rations with forage and concentrates mixed can significantly reduce acidosis, provided selection of the concentrate portion doesn't occur

occur

- Feeding space: If there is insufficient space average meal size will increase, increasing the risk of acidosis (even with a TMR). (This can also occur if feeding time is restricted or if feeding times are irregular).

ANAPLASMOSIS

Anaplasmosis is caused by a protaozoan parasite (Anaplasma marginale) that is spread by ticks and biting insects. Additionally, it can be transmitted by needles or surgical equipment. Once the parasite reaches the blood stream in infects red blood cells (RBCs) where they multiply, writes Dr. Grant Dewell, Iowa State University Beef Veterinarian. Anemia results from a phagocytosis of the RBCs. Anemic animals will develop icterus (jaundice) but not hemoglobinuria (red urine) because RBC destruction occurs from phagocytosis in the spleen rather than RBC lysis in the blood vessels.

CLINICAL SIGNS

Clinical signs of anaplasmosis are associated with anemia. In acute anaplasmosis cattle will be febrile and anemic with an increased heart and respiratory rates. Cattle may also have muscle weakness, inappetence and depression. Mucus membranes will be pale. Icterus develops several days after onset of symptoms. Peracute anaplasomosis can be seen in highly susceptible animals such as adult purebred animals or high-producing dairy cows. These cattle can succumb to the infection within hours. Chronic anaplasomosis may follow an acute infection for up to 3 months of poor response. Young animals will show less severe clinical signs, due to a more responsive production of RBCs. Abortions are common in pregnant cattle with acute anaplasmosis. Bulls may show a temporary infertility which could be important in a fall breeding programme.

Diagnosis

Diagnosis during the acute stage of the disease is usually based on clinical signs, presence of anemia and microscopic examination of a stained blood smear. In cattle the *A. marginale* organisms are located on the periphery of the RBC. However, in some acute infections the organism is not visible on a blood smear because all infected cells were removed from circulation and immature erythrocytes are usually not infected. Serology for *A. marginale* can be useful to aid in diagnosis in these cases. Necropsy examination of cattle that die from anaplasmosis reveals either pale and anemic or icteric depending on stage of disease. An enlarged spleen and a swollen liver with enlarged gall bladder are also present. Urine will not be discoloured with hemoglobin. Submission samples include blood smear or EDTA blood tube sample, Serum sample or clotted blood sample for serology. Tissues to submit include liver, spleen, kidney.

Treatment

Tetracycline is the drug of choice for clinical anaplasmosis. A single dose of long-acting 200 mg/ml oxytetracycline is usually sufficient. General supportive care is also important for anemic animals. Blood transfusions are of limited benefit. Large volume is needed because of the severe anemia and because the erythrophagocytosis system is activated transfused RBC are removed from circulation in 24-48 hours.

Control

Typically, cases of anaplasmosis increase in late summer and fall as insect vectors increase. Therefore, control of vectors is key to preventing anaplasmosis. If necessary herd treatment with oxytetracycline injection every 3 to 4 weeks during high risk times may be necessary will prevent clinical disease but animals can become carriers. Another option is oral administration of chlortetracycline at 1.1 mg/kg daily. To remove carrier state cattle need to treated with long acting oxytetracycline every 3 days for 4 treatments or 2 mg chlortetracycline per pound body weight orally per day for 50 days. Cattle will become serologically negative 3-4 months after the carrier state has been removed.

ANTHRAX

In the UK, all cases of unexplainable sudden death have to be reported to the Divisional Veterinary Office, so that a decision can be made whether the animal is to be tested for anthrax as sudden unexplained death is the most common presentation of anthrax in cattle. However, although the number of cases of sudden death has increased there have been no cases of anthrax in cattle for over three years. However, it is important that owners and stock people are aware of anthrax, as contact with animals or animal products is, despite the recent American outbreak, still the most important cause of human anthrax.

- Sudden death (often within 2 or 3 hours of being apparently normal) is by far the most common sign
- Very occasionally some animals may show trembling, a high temperature, difficulty breathing, collapse and convulsions before death. This usually occurs over a period of 24 hours
- After death blood may not clot, resulting in a small amount of bloody discharge from the nose, mouth and other openings

Diagnosis

- On the clinical signs
- Rod-shaped bacteria surrounded by a capsule are visible in blood smears made from surface blood vessels
- Post-mortem examinations should not be undertaken on suspected anthrax cases (including any cow that has died suddenly for no apparent reason) until a blood smear has proved negative)
- If a carcass is opened accidentally, the spleen is usually swollen and there is bloodstained fluid in all body cavities Suspected anthrax cases are covered by the
- Anthrax Order 1991 (which replaced the Order of 1938). Any suspicion of the disease must be notified to the DEFRA Divisional Veterinary Manager (DVM), who if they see fit will instigate a veterinary enquiry to determine whether anthrax is present on the farm. Usually the DVM will arrange a visit (often by the owner•fs own vet) to take a blood sample to look for

bacteria with capsules. The animal or carcass must not be moved before this has been done, fines will be levied if movement does occur. If the tests prove negative, the veterinarian will send in a certificate stating this and nothing further will happen. If anthrax is still suspected then orders banning movement and requiring disinfection will be instigated.

Treatment

- Due to the rapidity of the disease treatment is seldom possible
- High doses of penicillin have been effective in the later stages of some outbreaks

Prevention

Infection is usually acquired through the ingestion of contaminated soil, fodder or compound feed. Sterilisation of meat and bone meal used in animal feed (and more recently its complete removal from cattle feed) has been the main factor responsible for the rarity of anthrax in the UK over the last few years.

Botulism

Botulism is a lethal food poisoning in cattle caused by eating material that contains *Clostridium botulinum* toxins. The incubation period before clinical signs appear varies from a few hours to two weeks, making it difficult to identify the causative material eaten by affected animals. The most common manifestation of the disease in cattle is a subacute disease with restlessness, incoordination and difficulty to swallow developing into recumbency, paralysis and death within 1-7 days.

The bacteria and the disease occurrence are worldwide. In the UK, cases are likely to occur either due to ingestion of contaminated silage or contact with animal carcasses or skeletons of dead animals containing the toxin. The use of poultry litter as fertiliser on cattle pastures has been identified as a risk factor, due to the poultry mixed with the litter.

Bacillary Haemoglobulinuria

Bacillary haemoglobulinuria is a rapidly fatal disease caused by *C. oedematiens* type D. The disease is associated with liver damage primarily caused by liver fluke. The condition is fairly rare in the UK. Young stock or dry cows inspected less regularly are often found dead. In lactating cows, a sudded drop in milk yield associated with high fever is seen. Other clinical signs include ruminal stasis with or without apparent abdominal pain, rapid breathing, dark red urine, jaundice and death within a short time of the onset of clinical signs.

Spores of *C. oedematiens* type D can be found both in the soil and in the livers of normal cattle on farms where the disease occurs.

Blackleg

Blackleg infection is caused by *Clostridium chauvoei* and is almost allways associated with wound infection in cattle. Most cases occur in young stock between 10 months and two years of age. Feet or legs and the tongue are often the predilection site. Within 48 hours there is a high fever and if limb muscles are involved the animal becomes stiff and unwilling to move. Skin discolouration, subcutaneous oedema and gas production may be present and perineal oedema is sometimes seen. Infections of the head may produce marked oedema and even bleeding from the nose. Death usually follows a period of anorexia, profound depression and prostration. The spores of *C. chauvoei* survive well in the soil.

Malignant Oedema

Malignant oedema is caused by the infection of wounds with bacilli of the genus *Clostridium* (*C. oedematiens* type A; *C. chauvoei*; *C. perfringens*; *C. sordellii*; *C. septicum*). The condition is fairly rare and sporadic, but outbreaks involving several animals may occur after an event that has caused bruising or wounds (*e.g.* penning for a short period). Clinical signs appear rapidly after infection and at the site of infection a swelling will develop which will 'pit' on pressure. Gas may be detected, as the skin becomes darkened and tenser. A high fever is present and toxaemia develops. The animal dies within 1-2 days.

Tetanus

Tetanus is caused by the toxin tetanospasmin released from the spore-forming bacillus *Clostridium tetani.* The disease in cattle occurs most often after surgical intervention or difficult calving after spores gain entry to a wound. Germination of spores occurs only if the microenvironment is anaerobic. After germination of the spores within the wound the *C. tetani bacilli* proliferate and produce toxin.

The incubation period can be very variable from 3 days to several months but most cases occur usually after about 10 days. At first the animal appears slightly stiff, becomes unwilling to move and develops a fine muscle tremor. The temperature rise is variable (39-42°C). The general stiffness of the limbs, head, neck and tail increases after 12-24 hours. The animal shows hyperaestesia and repeated spasms. Mastication becomes difficult due to tetany of the masseter muscle (lockjaw), food is chewed with difficulty, the animal drools saliva and bloat often occurs. There is retention of the urine and constipation. The animal becomes recumbent, with the legs rigidly extended, opistotonos and the jaws become rigid. The animal usually dies due to respiratory failure 3-4 days after the onset of clinical signs. Milder cases, which develop more slowly, can recover over a period of weeks or even months.

BLOAT IN CATTLE

There was an increase in the number of reports of bloat from NADIS vets this spring. Bloat is most commonly seen in spring and autumn, when grass growth is at its peak. It is one of the most common causes of death in adult cattle at grassp>

WHAT IS BLOAT?

Bloat is simply the build up of gas in the rumen. This gas is produced as part of the normal process of digestion, and is normally lost by belching (eructation). Bloat occurs when this loss of gas is prevented. There are two sorts of bloat. The least common type is gassy bloat, which occurs when the gullet is obstructed (often by foreign objects such as potatoes) or when the animal can't burp (such as with milk fever or tetanus). The second type of bloat is frothy bloat, which happens as the result of a stable foam developing on top of the rumen liquid, which blocks the release of the gas. This is by far the most common form of bloat, and unlike gassy bloat, it is highly seasonal with peaks in the spring and autumn. This is because the foam is formed by breakdown products from rapidly growing forages (particularly legumes such as clover and alfalfa). These increase the viscosity (stickiness) of the rumen fluid and prevent the small bubbles of gas formed by rumen fermentation from coming together to form free gas that can be belched off

CLINICAL SIGNS

- Distended left abdomen is the most obvious sign
- Usually associated with pain, discomfort, and bellowing.
- Death can occur within 15 minutes after the development of bloat
- Gaseous bloat is usually seen in one or two animals. Frothy bloat can affect up to 25 per cent of cases
- In some cases sudden death may be the first sign seen by the stockman, although in such cases it is likely that there will be other cattle with bloat that are still alive

Diagnosis

- On the clinical signs described above
- History of access to lush pasture
- Passing a stomach tube will distinguish between gassy and frothy bloat. If it's gassy bloat a stomach tube passed into the rumen will allow the gas build-up to escape through the tube. No such gas is seen in frothy bloat.

Treatment

- Passing a stomach tube is the best treatment for gassy bloat. Once the gas has been released, the cause of the obstruction should be looked for.
- In a few cases a trochar and cannula punched through the side into the rumen will relieve gassy bloat when a stomach tube has not worked. But such cases are rare, and as the trochar provides a tremendous opportunity for introduction of infection, it should only be used as a last resort.
- For frothy bloat, antifoaming agents that disperse the foam should be given by stomach tube. Old-fashioned remedies such as linseed oil and turpentine are effective but newer treatments such as dimethicone or polaxolene are easier to give as the effective dose is much smaller.
- If an outbreak of frothy bloat occurs all cattle on that pasture should be removed immediately and put onto a high fibre diet (hay or straw), and any cows showing bloating signs treated with an anti-foaming agent. The pasture should not be grazed for at least ten days.

Prevention

It is much more effective to prevent bloat than treat affected animals. Management and planning can significantly reduce the number of cases. To prevent frothy bloat:

- If possible avoid using high-risk pastures at high-risk times. Pastures with a history of bloat problems or with a high clover content should not be used for cows soon after turnout.
- Stagger turnout with buffer feeding as this will allow the rumen to adapt to the new diet. In particular try and keep up fibre intakes at risk periods.
- If you have to use high-risk pastures, introduce the cattle to them slowly. In some cases restricting access to as little as ten minutes per day at the start may be necessary to prevent bloat.

- Avoid starting to graze high-risk pastures when they are wet.
- Administer anti-foaming agents daily if bloat is a severe problem. If this is the case and you can strip graze then spraying antifoaming oils (emulsified with water) onto the grass can significantly reduce labour costs.
- Remove high-risk animals. Some animals have recurrent bloat despite prevention and treatment.

BOVINE TRICHOMONIASIS

Trichomoniasis is a venereal disease of cattle, characterised primarily by early pregnancy loss and, occasionally, by abortion and pyometra. Bovine trichomoniasis (trich) is a reportable disease in many parts of the US. It appears to be mostly those states West of the Mississippi that have problems. In recent years, thanks to an increased awareness, the number of cases have dropped significantly.

Symptoms

There is no outward evidence of the disease that makes it recognisable to producers, said Dr. Roehr. It can only be confirmed by tests. Trich, does however, significantly reduce fertility, which can have a devastating economic impact for producers. The disease is spread between cows, by bulls. Any bull found with the disease must be culled. Dr. Roehr says that the majority of cows (97-99 per cent) will self clear of the disease within 120 days.

Whilst it is beneficial that cows can clear themselves of the disease, during this time period they will have missed a valuable time frame for coming into calf. There are no accepted treatments out there for trich, said Dr. Roehr, and there is a possibility that the disease may re-occur within cows. With this in mind he advices producers to sell non-pregnant cows.

Prevention

Bulls should be tested annually for trich. This, Dr. Roehr said, is an excellent strategy to ensure that trich is not present in herds. He also advised producers against buying non-pregnant cows, as they may be a source of the infection.

It is hard to put a dollar figure on trich, said Dr. Roehr. However, if a producer only has a 50 per cent pregnancy rate for one season, that could put him out of business. There is mandatory testing of all bulls when they are imported or change ownership. However frequent bull testing will control the disease, within the state, he said. Concluding, Dr. Roehr advised producers to work with their local veterinarians to subscribe a plan that works with each individual herd. It is also advisable to test bulls before breeding.

BOTULISM

Botulism is caused by *Clostridium botulinum* bacteria that produce toxins under certain environmental conditions. C. botulinum bacteria are commonly found in the environment and will grow to high levels in decaying organic matter including animal and bird carcases. It is believed that contamination of broiler litter with the carcases of chickens that have died, from various causes during production, can render the litter dangerous for ruminants. Even small fragments of carcases transferred onto pasture by scavenger animals, such as foxes, dogs or crows may pose a risk to grazing ruminants. Scavengers may gain access to this material during storage or following spreading on land. While the Animal By-Products (Enforcement) Regulations (NI) 2011 permits the spreading on land of poultry litter, the spreading of litter contaminated by carcases is an offence.

It is important to note that that manure from egg laying hens has not been associated with outbreaks of botulism in cattle. A possible reason for this is that husbandry arrangements for layers reduce the likelihood of contamination of litter with carcases.

Symptoms of Botulism

Cattle and sheep of all ages are susceptible to botulism, which is characterised by a progressive muscle weakness (paralysis). Affected animals may be weak, stagger about, or go down. Cattle characteristically display flaccid paralysis and occasionally protrusion of the tongue. Signs in sheep and goats are similar to cattle but protrusion of the tongue may not be as obvious. In most cases the disease is fatal although some animals may recover.

In many cases of botulism euthanasia is justified on welfare grounds. Cattle are extremely sensitive to the effects of the toxin meaning that ingestion of very small amounts of toxin can result in clinical disease. The progression and severity of the disease depends on the amount of ingested toxin. When a large amount of toxin has been ingested, the animal may be found dead without having shown any signs of disease. Conversely if only a small amount of toxin is ingested the progression of the disease may take a more chronic course and clinical signs may be less severe.

Diagnosis of Botulism

Diagnosis of botulism is based primarily on clinical signs and a history of known exposure to risk factors such as contaminated broiler litter or carcase material. Laboratory confirmation is frequently difficult and relies on detection of the toxin in samples harvested from suspect cases and elimination of other possible causes of disease.

Control of Botulism in Ruminants

Careful disposal of all animal or bird carcases and poultry litter is essential to minimise the risk of botulism to livestock. Poultry carcases should be promptly removed and disposed of by incineration.

Following removal of the broiler crop, all poultry house doors should be kept closed until the litter is removed. The litter should not be removed from the house until it can be loaded directly onto spreading equipment, covered vehicles or immediately stacked and covered. At no time should it be accessible to dogs, foxes, crows or other scavengers that may carry carcases onto adjacent pasture or into livestock housing. Washings from poultry houses and yards should be collected in tanks rather than be allowed to flow onto adjacent land.

Poultry litter should not be spread on agricultural land that is to be grazed, or from which silage or hay is to be harvested, in the same year. Spreading litter on a windy day may also pose a risk of contaminating adjacent fields. Any animal or bird carcases, or portions of carcasses, visible on pasture or in livestock houses, should be promptly removed. Even small fragments of such material may be dangerous to livestock and should be disposed of by incineration or rendering, as required by current legislation.

Vaccination

No vaccine is available under general licence in the UK for the protection of cattle against botulism. However, veterinary surgeons may apply to the Veterinary Medicines Directorate (VMD) to obtain and use vaccines under 'special treatment certification' (STC), to protect animals at risk of botulism. There are currently two inactivated vaccine products available by STC for use in Northern Ireland. For full protection the vaccination course must be completed. Vaccination should not be used as a substitute for the hygiene measures.

BRACKEN POISONING IN CATTLE

Many plant poisonings, including bracken poisoning, are common in the autumn. The highest risk period is when grass growth is poor, particularly if this has been combined with bracken control so that rhizomes or new young fronds are available for cattle to eat. Bracken contains a variety of toxins. For cattle the two most important are a toxin that depresses the bone marrow, and a cancer–causing toxin. These toxins are still active in hay made from pastures with bracken.

CLINICAL SIGNS

Acute Poisoning

This occurs as a consequence of eating large quantities of bracken. Disease develops because of depression of the bone marrow, which stops the production of the white cells that fight infection and the platelets that help blood to clot. Signs can up to eight weeks after cattle have stopped eating bracken;

- Depression and loss of appetite
- Bloody diarrhoea accompanied by straining
- High temperature
- Weakening, collapse and death (usually within five days of the onset of signs)
- Secondary infection is very common.

Enzootic Haematuria

This occurs as the result of eating small quantities of bracken over a long period of time. Cancerous changes occur in the bladder leading to:

- In mild cases-persistently bloody urine (haematuria)
- In severe cases – severe blood loss and difficulty passing urine with visible blood clots.

In some animals, cancer occurs in the gut as well as the bladder. The signs depend on the site of the tumour. Get veterinary advice in animals showing unusual gut signs that have had access to bracken.

Diagnosis

- On the clinical signs described above
- History of access to bracken
- Blood sample for haematology
- In many cases a post mortem will be essential to confirm the diagnosis.

Treatment

- here is no specific antidote for bracken poisoning.
- Broad-spectrum antibiotics to prevent secondary infection can help in acute cases
- For animals with haematuria no treatment is effective.

Prevention

- Limit access to pastures with bracken, particularly if grazing is poor

- Never allow cattle access to recently ploughed land where bracken has been. Exposed rhizomes are the most dangerous part of the plant as they are attractive to cattle. Particularly if they have started to reshoot
- Bracken control by burning, ploughing, reseeding, and herbicide is the best method of prevention.

BULLS AND BIOSECURITY

The acquire of a bull is one of the commonest ways in which disease enters farms. Too many farms think they are closed but buy bulls. A bull is as likely to be infected with an important disease as a cow and, because of the close contact during mating, far more likely to spread it.

So what should you be doing when buying a bull to prevent disease getting on your farm?

Bull Health Declaration

The first thing to do is determine his disease status. The best bulls will have a Bull Health Declaration covering the major diseases: BVD, Leptospirosis, IBR, TB and Johne's. This declaration will show whether the bull's herd is free of the specific disease in addition to showing that the bull is free of that disease. In addition it will show whether the bull has been vaccinated.

Testing

If such a declaration is not available then you should get the bull tested. This is best done before moving the bull onto the farm. If this is not possible then the testing should be done as part of the quarantine system. Bulls should be tested for BVD, Leptospirosis, IBR, TB and (if older than two) Johne's. The test results need to be interpreted by your vet as the bull's history (particularly vaccination) can have a major impact on the test results. However, it is important to remember that a negative Johne's result does not mean a bull is free of disease as many infected bulls can test negative. The only way of ensuring that an animal is free of Johne's is to buy it from a herd that has been tested and shown to be free of disease.

Never buy a Johne's vaccinated bull as this is likely to have come from a farm with a significant disease problem and vaccination does not prevent infection.

Quarantine

If the bull passes these initial tests it should then go into quarantine on your farm. For BVD, Leptospirosis and IBR, it pays to retest negative animals that you have bought at a sale as they could have been infected at the sale and so be capable of spreading disease for another eight to ten weeks. Also ask your vet about treating the bull with antibiotics to prevent the excretion of Leptospirosis, which can happen even if the bull has no antibodies.

Other Disease Checks

The quarantine period is also useful for checking for digital dermatitis, Salmonella and Campylobacter. The latter is one of the commonest causes of infectious infertility, but only occurs in herds using natural service. Get your vet to test for Campylobacter and if necessary wash the prepuce with antibiotics to clear potential infection. Bulls bought from TB areas should also have an additional TB test while in quarantine, so that the only bulls from such areas which are allowed to enter the herd have had two recent clear TB tests

This testing will significantly reduce the risk of bulls bringing disease onto your farm, preventing such disasters as the 80-cow suckler farm that lost 30 calves in one year due to BVD and the farm on which less than half of the cows got pregnant during the service period as a result of a bull infected with Campylobacter.

Vaccinate

Although the biggest risk is the bull bringing disease onto your farm, don't forget that infection can spread the other way. So if you have IBR, BVD or Leptospirosis and the bull you are buying tests negative, vaccinate to prevent it getting infected as these diseases can have significant effects on bulls as well as cows.

CALF PNEUMONIA

Respiratory Diseases

Enzootic pneumonia in young calves is a multifactorial disease that occurs mainly in two different systems: in housed dairy calves reared for replacement or in housed calves reared for beef in a herd other than the herd of origin. Dairy calves are likely to suffer from the disease at any age, with it manifesting itself as a chronic, coughing pneumonia, or as a more acute, enzootic calf pneumonia. Older dairy calves are also vulnerable after housing in the autumn. Suckler calves are more likely to suffer from respiratory disease between two and five months of age, following weaning or transport from one herd to another. Outdoor reared beef suckler calves can also be severely affected by pneumonia.

In older calves, mainly in weaned suckler calves aged six months to two years, respiratory disease is likely to occur after transport or other environmental stress and is often called shipping or transit fever. This condition is discussed elsewhere in this compendium. Similarly, a respiratory disease caused by lung parasites, husk, occurs in older calves and is discussed elsewhere. A viral respiratory disease caused by the infectious bovine rhinotracheitis virus is also more significant in older animals and discussed under its own heading.

Respiratory diseases in young animals were ranked very low in importance in a survey of British organic beef and dairy farmers. Late weaning, a whole milk diet, the requirement for good housing standards and a closed herd policy reduce the risk factors for respiratory disease in calves in organic dairy herds. The Soil Association standards further prevent the sale of calves via the cattle markets when calves are sold for fattening. This should reduce the stress of moving from one farm to another and the risk of acquiring new infections.

Enzootic Pneumonia in Calves

Enzootic pneumonia in young calves may be a chronic disease with very few clinical signs apart from a dry cough and slightly increased respiratory rate. The acute form of the disease usually manifests itself in an outbreak involving several calves going down with the disease within a 48-hour period. Fever, dullness, inappetence and coughing, often combined with nasal discharge, are the most common symptoms. There is very little data available on the prevalence of enzootic pneumonia in UK cattle herds, as recording of calf diseases is seldom carried out. Respiratory diseases are, however, considered the second most important cause of death and ill drift in calves. The condition is farm related, with some farms suffering serious losses due to calf pneumonia, while on others the disease is either very mild or non-existent. Sporadic outbreaks can, however, be experienced by farms that normally see very little respiratory disease in calves.

Causes of Enzootic Pneumonia

Enzootic pneumonia in calves is a multifactorial disease. Infectious agents, environment, management and the immune status of the calves are all-important factors in determining the outcome of an infection.

A multitude of infectious agents, including viruses, bacteria and *Mycoplasma*, are involved in different combinations on different farms. It is often suggested that the viral and mycoplasmal agents are the primary infections and the bacterial agents cause a secondary infection in an animal whose defences have been weakened by the first infection. The most common viral agents isolated from enzootic pneumonia cases are respiratory syncytial virus (RSV), parainfluenza III virus (PI3), infectious bovine rhinotracheitis virus (IBR) and bovine viral diarrhoea virus (BVD), some of which are discussed separately as herd problems elsewhere in the compendium.

Mycoplasmal agents are usually considered to be the most common agents causing the chronic form of enzootic pneumonia, even though *Mycoplasma bovis* has been identified as the causative agent in many acute outbreaks as well. The most commonly isolated bacterial organisms are *Pasterurella* and *Hemophilus* subspecies. The major environmental factor predisposing calves to respiratory disease is poor ventilation in calf housing. Cold, humid conditions, sudden changes in air temperature, stress due to different causes and change in the environment have also been associated with outbreaks of pneumonia in young calves.

Insufficient intake of colostrum or poor quality colostrum will affect the calves' defence against respiratory agents and make them more susceptible to infection. Weaning of calves before five weeks of age has been associated with increased respiratory disease. Rearing systems where calves of different origin are mixed together at a young age suffer from high levels of respiratory diseases. Large, shared air spaces, calves from different age groups and poor sanitation between calf batches often make these systems even more vulnerable. Calves that have suffered from diarrhoea are also more likely to suffer from respiratory disease. The stress associated with management procedures such as disbudding and castration may also be associated with a high respiratory disease incidence.

COPPER POISONING IN CATTLE

Cattle are commonly supplemented with copper to prevent copper deficiency (often due to molybdenum toxicity). Unlike sheep, which are very prone to copper poisoning, it has been thought that cattle are relatively resistant. In the past most cases of copper poisoning have been associated with cattle inadvertently eating pig food or grazing pastures fertilised with pig manure (pigs are fed high levels of copper to increase growth rates). However, cases of copper toxicity are now being seen in cattle with no connection to pigs or pig by-products. Copper toxicity in cattle is usually chronic in development (occurring as the result of a build–up over a long period of time), but is usually seen as an acute disease. The signs occur as the result of liver failure when the lèvel of copper stored in the liver gets too high and damages the liver cells it is stored in)

Clinical Signs

- Depression
- Colic (abdominal pain)

- Paleness and jaundice (yellowing)
- Reduced appetite and milk yield.
- Dark red urine (haemoglobinuria)
- Death.

Diagnosis

On clinical signs noted above you can be suspicious of copper poisoning. However your veterinary surgeon would carry out further tests to confirm copper poisoning:

- *Blood copper*: will be elevated in ill animals, and in many apparently normal animals (unless there is a single small point source of copper. Blood copper measurement will show the extent of the problem
- *Tissue copper*: Measurement of liver and kidney copper is confirmatory. This can be done by biopsy, but is best done post-mortem.

Treatment

Identify dietary sources of copper, and if possible remove them. Remove copper from all minerals. Individual treatment with ammonium molybdate and sodium thiosulphate can be effective but may not be economic. Other supportive therapy such as fluid therapy and antibiotics is of limited value

Prevention

It has not yet been clearly established what the cause of the increased rate of copper poisoning in cattle is. However, the risk of copper poisoning can be reduced by

- Ensuring you know what the copper intake of your cows. Pay particular attention to the copper content of your mineral and your forage
- Using chelates with care. So-called 'organic copper' may be better absorbed than inorganic copper, but this increase the risk of copper toxicity, particularly if the same amount of copper is fed.
- Do not supplement with copper unless you have clear evidence of copper deficiency (or molybdenum toxicity).

COCCIDIOSIS IN CATTLE

The NADIS data show that the number of cases of coccidiosis is at its lowest in late winter, and then rises during the spring to peak in June and July. This peak is followed by a slight, short-lived fall in late summer, and then another rise to a peak in November.

Coccidiosis is caused by single-celled parasites (not bacteria) known as coccidia. There are several species in cattle, not all of which cause disease. The species that cause disease are primarily found in the large intestine, and the diarrhoea results from damage to the cells lining it.

Coccidiosis is seen in animals up to two years old, and is particularly common in calves between three weeks and six months of age. Cattle become infected when placed in environments contaminated by older cattle or other infected calves. This can happen either indoors on bedding, or outdoors around drinking or feeding troughs. In order for the coccidial oocysts (the egg stage of the parasite) to become infective they require warmth and moisture. It is probably the lack of moisture in late summer and the low temperatures in late winter that result in the low level of coccidiosis during these times, however coccidiosis can be a significant problem at any time of year.

Clinical Signs

The most common sign is a watery diarrhoea, which because the coccidia damage the large intestine is often accompanied by straining (which can become very severe), mucous and blood. Other signs can include depression, loss of appetite, weight loss, and, much more rarely than with diarrhoea in milk-fed calves, dehydration. Death is rare. Infections that fail to produce diarrhoea can, nevertheless, result in reduced growth and weight gain. This sub-clinical infection is very common, with up to 95 per cent of cases being of this type.

Diagnosis

- On the clinical signs described above
- Examination of diarrhoea for the presence of large

numbers of oocysts. However, care must be taken when interpreting these results and it is best to consult a veterinarian in suspect cases.

Treatment

- Most cases will recover without treatment. Discuss the necessity of treatment in particular cases with your veterinary surgeon.
- If calves become dehydrated then electrolytes should be given.
- Once high numbers of oocysts are found, then treatment is unlikely to be of any benefit
- Treatment is better given to in-contact animals that have not yet started showing signs, or to combat secondary infection. A large number of products are available for treatment, but only two are licensed. Specific recommendations should be obtained from your veterinarian.
- All calves with diarrhoea should be separated from clinically normal calves, to reduce contamination of environment with oocysts.
- If possible, during an outbreak stressful procedures, such as dehorning, castration and weaning should be avoided.

Prevention

To achieve effective control of coccidia, good management and hygiene is vital. This should include:

- Reducing stocking density
- Regularly moving feed and water troughs
- Preventing faecal contamination of feed and water troughs, by raising or covering
- Increasing the bedding to reduce contamination
- Clean and disinfect all buildings with products that kill oocysts
- Mass medication can be used as a preventative, but it is no substitute for improving management.

DIGITAL DERMITITIS

Lameness is a common problem in all classes of cattle and can greatly affect the welfare and productivity of the animals. Researchers reported 24 per cent lameness in a DAISY survey of 90 herds in 1992-1993, while a more recent survey on 50 farms during 1995-1996 found 38 per cent lameness. There are a large number of factors contributing to lameness in cattle. These can be broken down into external, farm, animal and foot factors.

External Factors

Most important external factors is the time of year, the number of cases being greater in winter than in summer. Wet weather conditions are also conducive to maintaining high bacterial levels. Lameness in grazing cattle tends to increase about three weeks after heavy rainfall.

Farm Factors

Farm factors associated with lameness include herd size: veterinary practitioners saw proportionally fewer cases of foul-in-the-foot but more cases of sole ulcer in larger than in smaller herds. Overcrowding, especially of first calved heifers, leads to reduced lying times and increased lameness.

Stockmanship is important, as farmers who know more about lameness or who have been trained tend to have lower overall prevalence of lameness in their herds than untrained herdsmen. Housing is a very important factor. The overall incidence of lesions is lower in strawyards (0.71 cases/100 cows/month) than in cubicles with yards (0.93 cases/100 cows/month). The difference is thought to be due largely to longer lying times in strawyards. Cattle at pasture tend to lie down for longer periods than those in cubicles. This is thought to be beneficial. Straw yards also reduce the exposure to bacteria causing digital dermatitis.

The floor surface is another important factor. A two-year survey of 37 farms showed that only 25 per cent of floor surfaces were satisfactory in the first winter and 34 per cent in the second winter. 55 per cent and 33 per cent were considered smooth or very smooth and 20 per cent and 33 per cent were rough or very rough in the two periods. There is no doubt that feed input has an important role to play in lameness associated with lesions of hoof horn and laminitis.

Animal Factors

The differences between breeds in claw score traits for certain foot conditions. Ayrshires and Jerseys had better scores than other breeds. The Brown Swiss had the worst scores for corkscrew claws, laminitis and sole ulcers. White line score was worst in Guernseys and heel erosion and digital dermatitis were worst in Friesians. There is evidence that Jerseys tend have harder feet and less lameness. It has also been suggested that heavier cows are more prone to clinical lameness. Claw colour has also been implicated in lameness, with cattle with less pigmented feet being more prone to lameness. The heritability of clinical lameness in dairy cows from 24 herds was estimated as 0.10 and 0.22 using linear and threshold model analysis respectively.

An initial peak in lameness occurs in young first calving heifers. There appears to be a marked reduction in horn growth in late-pregnant heifers, making them more prone to bruising and haemorrhages when housed on concrete floors. The reduced growth leads to softer horn formation, causing a weakening and possible separation at the white line and predisposing to mechanical bruising of the underlying sensitive corium. Older cows are mainly affected between five and eight years old. There is evidence that low dominance-ranked cows spend less time lying down than high-ranking animals, leading to higher lameness risks. Many foot lesions are also related to the early post-calving period.

Lameness Lesions

Over 90 per cent of lameness involves the foot, with leg injuries being far less common. Lameness lesions can be classified into four main categories: horn, skin, joint and leg problems:

HORN DISEASES

Laminitis

Laminitis is an acute or chronic inflammation of the laminae, which lie immediately below the outer horny wall of the foot. The disease may cause lameness in its own right, often in all four feet, but usually it is a predisposing cause or risk factor for other types of lameness lesions, such as sole ulcer and white line abscesses. Factors causing laminitis include housing systems and management factors that decrease lying times and increase stress on the feet, such as:

- Cubicle design and overall cow comfort;
- Competition for cubicle space;
- Cubicle bedding material;
- Sudden changes in calving, especially at calving.

Nutritional factors have also been implicated in predisposing laminitis. These factors include:

- Diets high in starch and low in fibre, leading to ruminal acidosis;
- Possibly, diets high in crude protein content;
- Sudden, major changes of diet at calving, especially from low to high concentrate diets;
- Excessive cow condition at calving, where overfat cows have a lower appetite for forage and hence are more prone to ruminal acidosis;
- The way food is offered-large amounts of concentrates at one time can produce acidosis.

Sole Ulcer

Sole ulcers are the most common disease of the foot and most typically occur in the outer claw of the hind foot. Events such as laminitis may cause the pedal bone to drop and damage the underlying horn of the sole. As a result, an ulcer appears in the typical position-the centre of the sole towards the heel. The ulcer sometimes appears as a haemorrhage, with a softening and yellowing of the horn, progressing to necrotic tissue and often infection. Lumps of proud flesh-granulation tissue-may protrude from the ulcer area.

Sole ulcers can cause severe losses and reduced fertility, especially when occurring 70-120 days after calving. Many sole ulcers never fully heal and cows may suffer from chronic lameness for the rest of their productive lives. Solar ulcers may also predispose other conditions, such as septic arthritis.

White Line Abscess

The white line is the site at which the horn of the wall of the hoof joins that of the sole. It is a naturally weak area in the horn and cracks can allow dirt and bacteria to enter, causing abscess formation, pain and lameness. The initial weakness in the white line may be a result of laminitis, abnormal conformation and possibly dietary effects. The abscess most commonly occurs on the outside of the outer claw of the hind foot. This type of lameness is the most common form of lameness in yarded cattle, especially on slats. Excessive activity on poor underfoot surfaces can lead to a high incidence of the condition. Restrictions of trough space in yarded cattle may also predispose the condition.

Slurry Heel

Slurry heel is also known as heel erosion and is very common. Almost all older cattle which are housed show some degree of irregular loss of the bulbar horn. The problem may occur in all four feet, but often it may only affect the hind feet. The lateral digit is most commonly involved. It is thought the bacterium *Dichelobacter (Bacteroides) nodosus*, an obligate anaerobic bacterium producing keratolytic enzymes that are able to erode the horn, is involved. As a result, the hoof might rotate backwards and the toe may no longer be weight-bearing, the pedal bone rotates and leads to an increased risk of lameness. The predisposing factors include moist conditions, which soften the horn, unhygienic conditions allowing bacterial proliferation, and overgrown feet and chronic laminitis, which produce poor quality horn.

SKIN DISEASES

Digital Dermatitis

The Digital dermatitis is the most common skin disease

of the foot, often associated with housing. It is a contagious inflammation of the epidermis. Classically, it occurs between the bulbs of the heels, but more recently it has also affected the interdigital space. There is a severe form that attacks the horn/skin junction at the coronary band.

Digital dermatitis is likely to be caused by an infection. *Spirochaetes* (a type of bacteria) are most probably involved. They have a predilection for keratinised cells and produce a toxin which is keratolytic. It can produce two types of lesion: erosive (strawberry-like) or proliferative (wart-like). The erosive form is most commonly found in the United Kingdom. It is very painful and has a pungent smell. The wart-like lesion occurs when the infection is not treated and is due to a chronic irritation reaction of the skin.

Foul-in-the-foot

The Foul-in-the-foot is caused by an infection with *Fusobacterium necrophorum,* usually following damage to the interdigital skin by a foreign body. The infection results in sudden lameness, often in one limb. Body temperature is raised. There is swelling of the coronary band area, forcing the claws apart, and a split in the interdigital skin often associated with pus and dead tissue. The degenerated skin causes a 'foul' odour. At certain times of the year (wet, muddy and often warm at grazing) there can be herd outbreaks. 'Super foul' is an aggressive form of the disease that has become more common in recent years. It produces severe interdigital necrosis with rapid extension deep into the surrounding structures.

JOINT DISEASES

Septic Arthritis

Septic arthritis usually involves the pedal joint between the pedal bone and the second phalangeal bone. It results from the direct extension of infection from a foot lesion (*e.g.* sole ulcer or white line infection) into the surrounding tissues and eventually involving the structures such as the joint itself. It is associated with swelling of the joints, acute pain, reduced appetite, weight loss and longer periods of recumbency.

Joint-Ill

Joint-ill is a disease of newborn calves and results from any form of septicemia that spreads to the joints of the limbs. The most common causative bacteria involved are *E. coli* and *Streptococcus*, which are found in great numbers in damp, dirty bedding. It causes severe lameness, usually in one or two joints.

LEG INJURIES

Hock Damage and Carpal Hygromas

Hock damage, such as hygroma and traumatic arthritis, primarily results from chronic mechanical irritation due to rough floors with little or no bedding, poor cubicle or building design, and poor hygienic conditions. A hygroma is a swelling on the outside face of the hock joint and is produced by changes in the skin and underlying structures. The skin is often hairless, thickened and flaky. The underlying tissues are thickened and swollen, mainly with fibrous tissue. A cavity may develop, containing blood clots and serum, but infection often produces an abscess, which will eventually burst and drain. A fibrous lump will remain.

E. COLI DIARRHOEA

According to NADIS data most common cause of diarrhoea in calves continues to be *E. coli.*

E. coli is a bacterium that is present in the guts of normal animals. Most types of E.coli do not cause disease, however three types of E.coli are associated with diarrhoea in calves. One type (known as ETEC) attach to and damage the small intestine and produce a special type of toxin (known as an enterotoxin), the second (EPEC) attaches to and damages the small intestine but do not produce enterotoxins, and the third (EHEC) attaches to and damages the large intestine

Clinical Signs

ETEC: Young calves (usually <3 days old)

Calves become depressed, don't drink, dehydrate and die rapidly Diarrhoea is very watery.

EPEC: Older calves (usually <21days)

Usually not so rapid or as severe as ETEC

Diarrhoea yellow and watery.

EHEC: Older calves (around 14 days)

Often bloody diarrhea.

Diagnosis

ETEC

- Age of calf
- Severity and nature of diarrhoea
- Laboratory tests can identify the protein used by bacteria to attach to the gut.

EPEC/EHEC

- Difficult to diagnose as signs are very similar to diarrhoea caused by other organisms, and non-disease causing E.coli are present in most faecal samples
- Examination of material from post-mortems can confirm E.coli –related disease.

Treatment

- Replacing lost fluids is the most important part of treatment. This can range from oral electrolytes for moderately affected calves to intravenous fluids for severely affected calves.
- Commercial electrolytes are more expensive than the home-made version but in moderate to severe cases they are much more effective
- Antibiotics can help in some cases, but they should be used with caution and if possible sensitivity testing should be undertaken.

Prevention

- Keep the environment as clean as possible, this refers to the calving yards as well as the calf pens.

- Single penning of young calves will significantly reduce the spread of diarrhoea
- Sick calves will pass a vast number of disease-causing bacteria. Disinfection is vital
- If possible use an all-in-all-out system. This allows pens to be disinfected between batches and prevents disease being passed on to every new calf that enters the building.
- Ensure good colostrum intake. In herds with problems, feeding bulked colostrum for at least 7 days can significantly reduce the number of cases of scour
- For ETEC diarrhoea only, vaccination is available. This is given to the mother in late pregnancy. The colostrum then contains antibodies that help prevent ETEC infection. For the best effect colostrum feeding should continue for at least a week.

FATTY LIVER SYNDROME

The Fatty liver syndrome is the accumulation of fat within the cow's liver. The dairy cow does not normally store fat in the liver, so fatty liver does not occur when a cow increases its body condition and puts fat on its back. Fatty liver occurs as a result of the cow breaking down too much fat for the liver to process properly, the broken down fat products are then converted back to fat in the liver to prevent them becoming toxic.

Thus the liver becomes fat when the cow is losing condition, the more loss in condition the more fat in the liver. Fatty liver syndrome (> 20 per cent fat) reduces liver function, depresses appetite and milk yield, increases the risk of diseases such as RFM, metritis and mastitis, reduces fertility, and when severe (when it is usually called fat cow syndrome) can lead to death.

Once it is deposited in the liver, the concentration of fat in the liver does not fall until the cow gets into positive energy balance, which can be over ten weeks after calving, particularly if the fatty liver is severe. Fat cows (>BCS 3.5) are much more prone to fatty liver.

CAUSES OF FATTY LIVER

Fatty liver, ketosis and displaced abomasum are closely

interconnected. Cows which have one of these conditions are much more likely to get another. The most important cause of fatty liver is negative energy balance.

Clinical Signs

- High incidence of diseases such as milk fever, ketosis, mastitis after calving
- Reduced fertility
- Rapid weight loss after calving particularly in cows that were fat at calving
- Reduced milk yield (often on a herd basis).

Diagnosis

- Clinical signs
- Blood samples: increased NEFA (free fatty acids), increased ketones (such as beta-hydroxy butyrate), increased liver enzymes Liver biopsy: this the best diagnostic test.

Treatment

- Use the same treatment as for ketosis: Glucose, propylene glycol, corticosteroids.
- However treatment is often ineffective.
- Prevention is far more important.

Prevention and control

Fatty liver occurs because of too much fat breakdown after calving. This occurs primarily in cows that are too fat at calving. Therefore ensuring that cows calve at a body condition score between 2.5 to 3.0 will significantly reduce the risk of fatty liver. Cows should be dried off at a body condition score of 2.5 to 3.0 and maintain their body condition during the dry period. Any alteration of body condition score is best done during mid to late lactation.

FOOT ROT IN CATTLE

The Foot rot is a term loosely used to describe lameness associated with the bovine foot. However, true foot rot is characterized by acute inflammation of the skin and adjacent soft tissues of the interdigital cleft or space. It is accompanied by diffuse swelling, varying degrees of lameness and in most cases, by a foul-smelling necrotic lesion of the interdigital skin. Foot rot is the term commonly used in the United States for this lameness disorder, but internationally the disease is better known as foul, foul-in-the-foot, interdigital phlegmon, interdigital necrobacillosis, or infectious pododermatitis. It is a frequent problem of beef and dairy cattle, especially in poorly drained, muddy pens or lots and pastures. Normally, occurrence is sporadic, affecting only 1 or 2 animals at a time, but it may affect larger numbers of cattle in outbreak situations or problem herds.

Causes and Contributing Factors

For many years *Fusobacterium necrophorum or Bacteroides melaninogenicus* were considered the primary causes of foot rot with *F necrophorum* most commonly isolated. Recently with improved technology and taxonomic changes there is evidence that the companion organism *Porphyromonas levii* (formerly considered in the *Bacteroides genus*) may play an important role with *F necrophorum* in foot rot infections. Healthy epithelium (skin) is resistant to bacterial organisms, whereas diseased or injured epithelial tissues are susceptible to infection. High rainfall with wet feces and mud can soften the interdigital skin, making it susceptible to injury. Infectious agents gain entry through the skin as a consequence of injury caused by sharp pieces of stone, metal, wood, stubble, thorns, and frozen manure. Other factors that may encourage damage to the interdigital skin may include irritation and erosion of the interdigital skin caused by interdigital dermatitis, believed to be in part a consequence of the constant exposure of feet to mud and manure.

Clinical Signs and Diagnosis

The earliest and most obvious clinical sign of foot rot is lameness, which increases in severity as the disease progresses. Once the infectious organisms become established, they cause inflammation and necrosis of tissue, resulting in slight to severe swelling and pain. The swelling is usually more evident in the interdigital space and around the coronet (or skin horn junction). The swelling is usually sufficient to cause separation of the digits. A break or fissure in the interdigital space develops which may extend from the front of the foot to the bulbs of the heel. These lesions are sometimes difficult to see unless the foot is elevated and properly restrained for examination. The interdigital lesion is often necrotic along its edges and has a characteristic fetid or foul odour, hence the name foul-in-the-foot.

The signs of foot rot in cattle include lameness with holding or raising a foot, reluctance to move, impaired locomotion, loss of appetite, weight loss, low-grade fever and reduction in milk yield for lactating cows. Hind feet are affected most often and cattle tend to stand and walk on their toes. If left untreated, lameness becomes increasingly severe with infection extending to the distal and proximal interphalangeal joints and other deeper structures of the foot. Diagnosis of foot rot is made by observation of the animal and physical examination of the foot for the characteristic gross lesions. Cattle producers often diagnose any lameness associated with foot swelling as foot rot, but a more careful examination may reveal other causes of the swelling and lameness.

Treatment

The affected foot should be cleaned and inspected for characteristic clinical signs and to rule out other causes for the swelling and lameness such as foreign bodies, infectious arthritis, or wounds caused by trauma. Historically, an antiseptic and bandage were applied after cleaning and trimming the foot, but topical treatment and bandaging are considered less important than systemic therapy. Prompt diagnosis and initiation of antimicrobial therapy are essential to achieve a satisfactory response. The treatment of choice is parenteral antibiotics administered for three to five days. In commercial beef cattle that are difficult to handle, feed additives such as chlortetracycline and oxytetracycline have been used for control and treatment of large numbers of cattle with the disease. Although this is convenient, there are no feed-grade antimicrobials labelled for control or treatment of foot rot. According to the Animal Medicinal Drug Use Clarification (AMDUCA) extralabel use of feed additives is prohibited in the United States. Readers are advised to seek advice from a veterinarian for specific recommendations. In some severe cases where the infection has extended into deeper tissues of the foot, surgical correction including amputation of the affected claw may be indicated. Recovered cattle can usually function well with one claw.

Prevention

Preventive measures include removing sources of injury and keeping feet dry and clean. Mudholes should be filled and stagnant pools drained or fenced off. Lots should be well drained and manure removed frequently to reduce the amount of muddy filth. In areas where cattle walk frequently, such as in lanes or gateways, grading or filling in low areas to provide a well-drained pathway for walking may help to prevent foot rot cases. Pouring a concrete pad around feed bunks and water troughs will help keep feet dry. In dairy cows, beef cows and bulls, regular foot care including claw trimming as needed helps prevent foot diseases and injuries. Animals may also be walked through a foot bath containing copper sulfate, zinc sulfate or formalin (where permitted). Footbaths are more commonly utilized in dairies and may be impractical for most beef herds.

Historically organic iodide (EDDI) was added to salt mixtures to reduce the incidence of foot rot. Although organic iodide can be effective, the current US Food and Drug Compliance policy guide states that all therapeutic and prevention claims for EDDI are considered as unapproved new animal drugs, thus restricting their use. Foot rot can be a cause of economic losses in beef and dairy herds. Early treatment, control and prevention under the direction of a veterinarian will help to keep losses to a minimum.

LICE IN CATTLE

The NADIS data show that last winter there was an increase in the number of cases of lice seen by NADIS vets. Lice populations are highest in winter and lowest in summer. There are two main reasons for this. Firstly, housing significantly increases the rate of transfer of lice between cattle. Secondly, low light levels and cooler skin temperatures are associated with increased louse activity. The denser winter coat and cooler weather thus favours lice survival.

THE EFFECT OF LICE

Lice cause irritation of the skin. This leads to biting, scratching and rubbing by affected cattle. These cows may also damage fences, trees and buildings while rubbing. The effect of lice on the production and growth rate of cattle has been the subject of much research but is still is a matter for continued debate. Their effect on the skin of cattle is probably best understood. Lice are probably the primary cause of 'light spot and fleck', a blemish visible on the hide of cattle which down grades the value of leather and is estimated to cost the leather industry £20 million per year.

Other effects such as weight loss, poor milk production and anaemia are less proven, even when there are large numbers of lice involved. This is probably because large numbers of lice are usually seen in animals that are under stress or under-fed or that have other current disease, which can all result in poor productivity without lice involvement

Types of Lice

There are four common species of lice in the UK, which can be divided into two different categories:

- *Sucking lice:* There are 3 species commonly found in the UK. These have relatively small narrow heads designed piercing the skin and sucking blood. In large numbers they can cause anaemia. They are usually found around the head and neck of cattle
- *Biting lice:* Biting lice have larger rounder heads. They feed

on skin debris, blood and scabs. Despite being apparently less invasive than sucking lice, it is biting lice that produce the most severe irritation. There is one species of biting louse found throughout the world. It is a reddish-brown louse about 2 mm long with a brown head. It is mostly found on the neck, shoulders, back and rump.

The life cycles of all species are similar. The female lays a few hundred eggs over the period of one month. These eggs are glued to the hair shafts, and hatch within a few days as nymphs (which resemble small soft adults). These develop, grow and moult three times before they become adult, with each stage lasting approximately one week. The entire life cycle takes between three and six weeks.

Diagnosis

On clinical signs and finding one of the three stages of the life cycle. Eggs are usually the easiest stage to spot, being found on hairs adjacent to bald, rubbed areas. Careful examination of nearby skin, with a magnifying glass, will usually detect nymphs and adults.

Treatment

Lice are spread only by direct contact between cattle. Adults, nymphs and eggs cannot survive more than a few days if removed from cattle. If properly applied treatment can eradicate lice from a farm. Most insecticides are effective against adult lice and nymphs. However most are not very active against louse eggs. This means that after treatment, eggs can still hatch and continue the infestation, unless there is some residual action. Ask your vet for advice as to which product has the best persistence.

It can be important to know whether you have sucking or biting lice, because the different method of feeding means that they have different susceptibilities to treatments. This is particularly important if you are going to use an avermectin injection (such as ivermectin) as these are much more effective against sucking than biting lice. If you want to use such a product ensure you have the lice on your cattle identified.

The timing and frequency of treatments depend very much on individual circumstances. In many cases treatment in late autumn or early winter will give adequate control of cattle lice for the whole housing period. Whichever product you use, dose accurately, ensuring that you do not under-dose as under-dosing is the best way of ensuring the development of lice that are resistant to treatment. Treat all cattle on the property at the same time if possible, choosing a time when they are not stressed or in poor condition. If groups have to be treated separately, such groups should be kept apart to ensure there is no contact between treated and untreated groups.

Is Lice Treatment Necessary?

For cattle that have light to moderate numbers of lice, treatment cannot be justified in terms of improving growth rate, body condition or productivity. Treatment can improve hide quality, but as yet this is not of economic importance in the UK. However some quality assurance programmes in other countries (*e.g.* Australia) have made hide quality of economic importance and it is possible that this will come in the UK. Treatment may also become necessary on welfare grounds because of the easily appreciated discomfort that even moderate lice infestations cause.

MANGE IN CATTLE

Mange is the term used to describe infection by mites, microscopic relatives of spiders. They inhabit and damage the skin of domestic animals and man. Problems are most frequently seen in the autumn and winter but can occur all year round. There are three main species of mite that affect cattle in the UK, the surface mite (*Chorioptes bovis*), the burrowing mite (*Sarcoptes scabiei*) and the sheep scab mite (*Psoroptes ovis*) The surface mite is the most commonly seen in the UK.

The Effect of Mites

The surface mite is usually found on the neck, legs, and tail head. It produces limited hair loss, which only increases slowly in size. However, the lesions are obviously itchy which results in hide damage elsewhere as the cattle try to rub the affected areas. The sheep scab mite is found on the flanks and around the tail head and anus. Although this mite feeds on the surface of the skin, its mouthparts pierce the skin, producing blisters, which are very irritant.

The burrowing mite prefers the neck and the loin area next to the tail (leading to the description of 'neck and tail' mange). As they burrow into and out of the skin they produce a much more intense irritant reaction so that the skin damage rapidly develops with much larger areas being affected and the skin becoming very thickened and crusty. Infection of the damaged areas often develops and affected animals have much reduced production.

Life Cycle

The surface mite and the sheep scab mite both spend their entire life cycle on the surface of the skin. Females lay around 90 eggs which once hatched take around ten days to develop into mature adults. The burrowing mites lifecycle is more complex. The female mite tunnels into the skin, and lays around 50 eggs. These hatch in four or five days, each releasing a larva. Some of these tunnel to the surface to become adult others develop in the tunnels; this process takes around two weeks. More tunnels are often formed during the mating process.

For all three species, infection is spread mainly by direct contact between cattle. However, the burrowing mite can survive for some time off the host, so, for this species, bedding and objects that come into contact with infected animals may become contaminated and help spread the infection. For the sheep scab mite, although mites found on cattle are very similar to those found on sheep, it is very unlikely that natural spread from cow to sheep (and *vice-versa*) occurs.

Diagnosis

Areas of thickened skin in obviously itchy animals are very suggestive of mites, particularly if there is no evidence of lice. To confirm a diagnosis get your vet to take a skin scraping for examination under a microscope.

Treatment

A range of products is available to treat mange in cattle. The choice is between pour-on products and injections. The first are easier and quicker to use and are often cheaper. However, in severely infected animals (as is often seen in burrowing mite problems), the skin reaction can mean that contact between the product and the mite is limited. In such cases, scabs may have to be removed before treatment. If very severe then injectable products are probably a better bet. For very severe surface mite problems, an injection should be followed up by a pour-on treatment when the skin has recovered, as in this species (unlike the burrowing mite) injections only control but do not eliminate. Sheep scab mite can be effectively controlled with injections.

The timing and frequency of treatments depend very much on individual circumstances. In most clinical cases, two treatments will give adequate control of cattle mites for the housing period. Whichever product you use, dose accurately, ensuring that you do not under-dose as under-dosing is the best way of ensuring the development of mites that are resistant to treatment. Treat all cattle on the property at the same time if possible, choosing a time when they are not stressed or in poor condition. If groups have to be treated separately, such groups should be kept apart to ensure there is no contact between treated and untreated groups.

PHOTOSENSITISATION IN CATTLE

Photosensitisation occurs when the presence of a chemical makes skin become sensitive to sunlight (particularly UV wavelengths). This leads to skin damage and loss. It is not very common in the UK, but it causes significant economic loss, particularly when it occurs in groups of animals.

There are three sorts of photosensitisation. Direct photosensitisation occurs when the chemical comes from a defect in the animals metabolism of its red blood cells, or, more commonly, from plants such as St. John's wort. Secondary photosensitisation occurs in animals with liver damage. This damage interferes with the complete breakdown of chlorophyll, resulting in the accumulation of a photosensitive chemical. Local photosensitivity can also result as a reaction to the sap of some plants. Most commonly affected sites are those exposed to direct sunlight, including the udder (which is exposed when the animal lies down).

Clinical Signs

- Non-pigmented skin affected
- Hair loss, reddening, peeling
- Ulceration of skin
- Crusting, bleeding.

Diagnosis

- On the clinical signs described above
- A veterinary diagnosis is important in order to rule out liver failure.

Treatment

- Removal to cool shaded housing
- Fly control
- Supportive therapy
- Treatment of liver failure (if present).

Prevention

Do not breed from animals with photosensitisation due to a genetic defect Identify and remove possible plant sources of photosensitising chemicals.

RINGWORM IN CATTLE

The NADIS data show that as winter progresses, particularly if wet, there is a significant increase in the numbers of cattle, especially growing cattle and calves, with skin disease,. Ringworm is one of the commonest skin diseases in such cattle

Ringworm is caused by infection with a fungus that lives in hairy skin.

Clinical Signs

- Grey-white areas of skin with an ash like surface
- Usually circular in outline and slightly raised
- Size of lesions very variable, can become very extensive
- In calves most commonly found around eyes, on ears and on back, in adult cattle chest and legs more common.

Diagnosis

- On the clinical signs described above
- Culture of skin sample can be used in unusual cases to confirm ringworm and identify type of fungus.

Treatment

- Ringworm is usually self-limiting, this means that the skin will usually heal without treatment. However this can take up to nine months
- The most commonly used treatment was griseofulvin in the feed, however, this is no longer available for use in food producing animals.
- The only remaining treatments are sprays. These are expensive, but can be very effective
- Many unlicensed treatments have been used from snail slime to copper sprays. They are cheap but have no proven efficacy.

Control

- The environment is the major source of infective fungi. Effective control of ringworm will only occur if the environment is properly cleaned and disinfected. This must be done between each batch of calves
- Vaccination will significantly reduce the number of animals affected with ringworm, and affected calves will have fewer, smaller crusts. On most farms, this may be of little benefit, but vaccination can be extremely useful on farms with a severe problem, particularly if this is in adult cattle.

- Ringworm can spread from cattle to humans. Thus if there is a lot of human: cow contact, such as on open farms, vaccination is essential if ringworm has been previously identified.

SCHMALLENBERG VIRUS

Schmallenberg virus gets its name from the German, Winterberg, where the virus was first identified in cattle in November 2011. After testing ruled out various other illnesses, the orthobunyavirus (Schmallenberg virus) was identified by metagenomic analysis and virus isolation of infected cattle in Germany. The Schmallenberg virus is related to the Simbu serogroup viruses, in particular Shamonda, Akabane, and Aino virus. So far, research confirms that the virus is vector-borne, spread by insects, mainly flies/midges.

The virus affects cattle, bison, sheep and goats. The disease has mostly been recognised in small ruminants around the time of partuition, with offspring showing signs of brain damage or malformations. There is no risk to human health, says the OIE.

Clinical Symptoms

Manifestation of clinical signs varies by species: bovine adults have shown a mild form of acute disease during the vector season, congenital malformations have affected more species of ruminants (to date: cattle, sheep, goat and bison). Some dairy sheep farms have also reported diarrhoea.

Adults (cattle)

- Probably often inapparent, but some acute disease during the vector-active season
- Fever
- Impaired general condition
- Anorexia
- Reduced milk yield (by up to 50 per cent)
- Diarrhoea
- Recovery within a few days for the individuals, 2-3 weeks at the herd scale.

Malformed animals and stillbirths (calves, lambs, kids)

- Arthrogryposis (abnormal joints)
- Hydrocephaly (build up of fluid in skull)
- Brachygnathia inferior (overshot jaw)
- Ankylosis (stiff joints)
- Torticollis (twisted neck)
- Scoliosis (deformed spine).

As of yet there is no vaccine for the virus, which will take some times, perhaps up to two years, to develop. Farmers are urged to stay vigilant and report any suspected cases.

TETANUS IN CATTLE

Tetanus is a fairly common disease occurring in all types of livestock. It is relatively rare in cattle, but cattle can get tetanus and outbreaks of disease can cause very severe losses.

Tetanus is a highly fatal disease caused by toxins produced by the bacterium Clostridium tetani. This bacterium is found in the soil and the guts of animals and humans. The disease starts when the organism gets into wounded or damaged tissue as a result of contamination. In the absence of oxygen the bacteria multiply and produce a local infection. As they grow, the bacteria produce poisons (toxins), which spread along the nerves to the brain and cause the clinical signs of tetanus. We don't know how the toxins are transported or how they produce their effect on the nervous system. The time between infection and disease can be very short (two or three days) or quite long (four weeks or more), depending on how long it takes for the contaminated area to develop a low level of oxygen (such as by a wound healing over sealing off the tissue from the outside). The disease is seen in all ages of stock. Calving and castration seem to be the most common procedures linked to the development of tetanus

Clinical Signs

- Stiffness and reluctance to move are normally the first signs
- Twitching and tremors of the muscles
- Lockjaw

- Prominent protruding third eyelid.
- Unsteady gait with stiff held out tail
- Affected cattle are usually anxious and easily excited by sudden movements or handling.
- Bloat is common because the rumen stops working
- Later signs include collapse, lying on side with legs held stiffly out, spasm and death.

Diagnosis

The clinical signs are characteristic and in many cases the only information available for making a diagnosis Post mortem investigation is very useful for ruling out other causes of similar disease, such as CCN, staggers or lead poisoning Growing the bacterium from the suspected site of infection is a useful finding. However, it is often very difficult to culture *Cl. tetani*, because the numbers of bacteria are usually small and the site of infection is often hidden

Treatment

- Cattle with early tetanus probably respond to treatment better than most other livestock
- In very early cases very high doses of penicillin may be helpful, particularly if combined with local treatment of the infected site.
- Antitoxin is probably of little value unless given in the very early stages.
- In some cases sedatives and relaxants can aid recovery
- Good nursing is important. Treated animals need dark quiet surroundings with lots of space and plentiful bedding
- It is not worth treating cattle with fully developed tetanus.

Prevention

Undertaking surgical procedures (such as castration) properly, in a clean environment, with disinfected instruments and surgical area, will significantly reduce the risk of tetanus. The same rules apply to calving, be as clean as possible and minimise contamination. Antitoxin can be useful as a short-acting (up to 21 days) preventative if used at high risk times, however on such farms vaccination may be better as a three dose course of vaccination can result in protection for over three years.

TRAUMATIC RETICULITIS

Though far less common than it used to be 30 years ago, NADIS data shows that Traumatic Reticulitis has increased in recent years and is a significant cause of ill-thrift and culling on many farms What is traumatic reticulitis Traumatic reticulitis is primarily a disease of adult cattle. It occurs when pieces of wire, or other sharp metal objects, which have been eaten by the cow along with its food penetrate the reticulum wall (as a result of the contractions during the cudding process). Infection spreads along the wire to the surrounding abdomen, producing an abscess and adhesions. In some cases the wire will penetrate into the chest of the animal causing abscess in the chest, and in severe cases infection of the outside of the heart (pericarditis). In the UK the most common cause of traumatic reticulitis is tyre wire, coming from old tyres used on silage clamps.

Clinical Signs

- Traumatic reticulitis is a progressive disease with the signs changing as the infected abscessed area spreads
- Reduction in feed intake
- Reduced milk yield
- Abdominal pain, reluctant to move, often grunts when made to move
- Stands with arched back and tense abdominal wall
- Initially temperature will be raised, but as progresses this can fall to normal
- Rumen movements reduced and weak.

Diagnosis

- On clinical signs, but these are often very vague
- Blood tests may show increased white blood cells, a secondary ketosis

- Exploratory rumenotomy can be used to locate wire
- Animals will grunt when withers firmly pressed down
- Pericarditis identified by muffled heart sounds accompanied by splashing
- For many cows in chronic phase the only diagnosis possible is a non-specific indigestion, because the signs of traumatic reticulitis are limited.

Treatment

- Surgical treatment (rumenotomy and removal of wire) can be useful in early cases if spread is not too great
- Conservative treatment (antibiotics, anti-inflammatories and a rumen magnet) can also be effective in mild cases.
- Severely affected cases, particularly those with pericarditis, should be humanely slaughtered as soon as possible as treatment will almost certainly be ineffective
- Injections of anti-inflammatories significantly improve cow wellbeing and help to restore the cow to normal production more quickly.

Prevention

- Removing the source of wire is the best method of prevention. Old tyres with wires that show any evidence of wear must be thrown away and not used on silage clamps
- Magnets can significantly reduce the incidence of clinical disease.

ULCERATIVE MAMMILLITIS

Ulcerative mammillitis is a relatively uncommon condition but it can spread rapidly in herds which are affected for the first time and cause significant pain and discomfort. It tends to occur most commonly in early winter.

Ulcerative Mammillitis

Ulcerative mammillitis is an infection of the skin of the teats and udder of dairy cattle. It is caused by a herpes virus (known as BHV-2)

Clinical Signs

The clinical signs vary from small irregular fluid-filled blisters to larger areas of ulcers and scabs.

Diagnosis

- A veterinary examination can confirm that ulcerative mammillitis is very likely
- Scrapings of blistered skin will contain virus which can be seen with electron microscope.

Treatment

- No specific treatment is available. Treatment should be aimed at speeding the healing of the skin and preventing spread to other cattle.
- Separate and milk affected cows last
- Disinfect clusters between cows and after milking
- Dip teats with iodine-based dip
- Emollient udder cream can speed healing of skin
- Check regularly to ensure tha skin damage hasn't resulted in mastitis. (In some cases cannulation may be necessary to milk cow properly.

Prevention

Once on a farm ulcerative mammillitis is difficult to eliminate. If you are buying in cattle, try and ensure you don't buy ulcerative mammillitis as well. Check the teats and udder of all cows before you purchase them. This will significantly reduce, but not eliminate, the risk of buying in ulcerative mammillitis. Once you have ulcerative mammillitis is established on your farm, it will be most commonly seen in first lactation heifers during winter housing. Pay particular attention to this group and separate and treat affected heifers as soon as you see signs of diseases. Good parlour hygiene and controlling biting flies can significantly reduce the impact of this disease.

WORMS

Parasitic gastroenteritis is associated with large numbers of nematodes in the abomasum and intestines. The nematodes in the abomasum are generally considered to be the primary pathogens, with those in the intestines playing a lesser but synergistic role. In the United Kingdom, the predominant worms in the abomasum belong to the genus *Ostertagia,* with *Ostertagia ostertagi* the most abundant. In the small intestine, *Cooperia oncophora* and *Nematodirus helvetianus* are commonest. There are two common forms of ostertagiasis, type I and type II.

Type I *Ostertagia* infection

This disease is most common in late summer and autumn and causes profuse watery diarrhoea in calves at grass. The faeces are usually green because of the grass diet. Developing larvae within the gastric glands of the abomasum cause the lumen of these glands to distend and stretch the cellular lining. As a result, the mature functional parietal and peptic cells are superseded by undifferential cells. As the infection progresses adjacent non-parasitized glands also become affected and their parietal cells replaced by non-functional undifferentiated cells. The pH of the abomasum increases and leakage of macromolecules and protein occurs across the damaged mucosa, resulting in hypoproteinaemia and increased concentrations of pepsinogen in the plasma. There is a rapid loss of weight, largely due to changes in grazing behaviour. In chronic cases, submandibular oedema may result.

The straight cause is the ingestion of large numbers of *O. ostertagi* infected larvae over a relatively short period of time. The number of infected larvae on pasture is lowest in May and June, but rises to a peak in late August and September. This pattern arises from a sequence of events which starts with calves turned out in April or May onto pasture grazed by cattle (and especially calves) during the preceding year. These calves ingest some of the infective larvae which have overwintered. It takes three weeks for these larvae to develop into adults and start laying eggs. The rate of hatching of these eggs depends on climatic conditions, reaching a peak in midsummer. The hatched larvae migrate or are washed out of faecal pats onto surrounding herbage to await ingestion by the eventual host. Wet summers produce an early peak, but numbers decrease more rapidly due to rapid depletion of numbers in faecal pats and dilution due to the more abundant grass growth. Conversely, dry summers delay the build-up, as the release of the larvae from the faecal pats is delayed until the autumn rains.

In dairy herds typical cases of type I *Ostertagia* infection occur in spring-born calves turned out in midsummer onto pastures grazed and contaminated in the spring and early summer by autumn-born calves. In a recent survey, it was found that 65 per cent of farmers used the same pasture each year for calves. The disease is not usually a problem in spring-calving beef herds, as the calves are too young to consume much grass in the early part of the season. As a result, the peak of infective larvae does not develop until September or October, when most calves are weaned and housed. However, autumn-born beef calves may suffer from type I *Ostertagia* infection in the absence of preventative measures. In areas where climatic conditions allow autumn-born calves to be turned out in March or early April, type I *Ostertagia* infection may occur 4 to 6 weeks after going to grass.

Type II *Ostertagia* infection

Infective larvae ingested from September onwards undergo a change in their normal parasitic development, resulting in a period of delayed development at the early fourth larval stage while within the abomasal wall. The change is thought to be brought about by either cold or desiccation in their preparasitic exposure. In the late autumn, calves may harbour many thousands of such larvae. Type II ostertagiasis results when these inhibited larvae resume their development, usually from February to May, the emerging larvae causing the same lesions as those causing type I disease.

Although adult cattle acquire immunity by the age of 18 months, occasionally bulls grazing calf paddocks or cows suffering from immunosuppression due to other diseases, such as fascioliasis, may suffer from type II ostertagiasis.

NEMATODIRIASIS IN CALVES

Nematodirus battus, mainly a parasite of sheep, has recently been found to be transmittable by cattle, both on farms where annual alternation of sheep and cattle has taken place, and even where cattle only are kept. It has caused severe outbreaks of diarrhoea in calves.

3

Diseases of Cattle
Their Causes, Symptoms and Treatment

The sluggish nature of cattle some drugs do not have the same effect upon them that they do upon horses. Aloes, even in large doses, have little or no effect while Epsom salts are an effective purge. Oil is also excellent as a mild purge or laxative; in the absence of oil, lard may be used instead. None of the preparations of mercury should be used by the novice as their action is sometimes violent and injurious. All medicines are best given in liquid form and should be of considerable bulk, owing to the great capacity of the digestive apparatus. The dose also is, as a rule, double the size of that given to the horse and, in some medicines, even larger.

SIGNS OF DISEASE IN CATTLE

In cattle, as well as in horses, it is necessary that the at tendant should know the signs of health before he can learn to distinguish the symptoms of disease. A staring coat and dry, harsh skin; a dull, sunken eye; a cough; a poor or a capricious appetite; a dry muzzle and suspended rumination are all indications of interference with the functions of some part of the animal organism, while the opposite of these conditions affords good grounds for considering the animal in good health.

PULSE, TEMPERATURE AND RESPIRATION

The heart as it pumps the blood throughout the system causes a beat or pulsation which can be perceptably felt wherever an artery passes near the surface an idea of the circulation can be obtained by 'taking the pulse.' The places where the pulse may be taken are at the angle of the lower jaw as in the horse, about the middle of the first rib, or on the under side of the root of the tail; or in fact it may be taken at any point where an artery nears the surface, especially if it passes over a bone. The number of pulse beats per minute in cattle is from 45 to 55 and should be regular, full, round and soft.

The temperature in cattle is also somewhat higher than in horses, being from about 100 degrees to 101 degrees Fah., and anything above this may be looked upon as indicative of some functional derangement. The respirations, in health, are from 10 to 15 per minute which may easily be seen from the heaving of the sides of the chest. But in examining for disease it should be remembered that surrounding circumstances exert a powerful influence upon the condition of an animal. Thus anything which tends to worry or excite, and especially being chased by dogs, will increase the frequency of both the pulse and respirations and will sometimes even cause an elevation of temperature.

DISEASES OF RESPIRATORY ORGANS OF CATTLE

CATARRH OR COMMON COLD

Catarrh or cold is the result of exposure to cold or wet weather. Standing in damp, filthy stables or in a current of cold air are prolific sources of the disease.

Symptoms

There will be poor appetite, staring coat, dry muzzle and a watery discharge from eyes and nostrils. The mucous membrane lining the nostrils will be red and inflamed, and sometimes this condition will extend to the throat and larynx and then there will be swelling of the throat and difficult breathing and sometimes a cough.

Treatment

Place the animal in a warm, but well-ventilated stable, and if the weather is cold put on a blanket. Give a pint of lard or raw oil at once. Give the following drench every four hours until the muzzle becomes moist and there are signs of improvement. Sweet spirits of nitre, two ounces; nitrate of potash, four drachms; sulphate of cinchonida, one drachm; water, one pint. When there is well-marked improvement this may be reduced to three times a day. Steam the nostrils occasionally with boiling water to which an ounce of turpentine has been added. If the throat is sore or there is a cough apply the ammoniacal liniment, rubbing it in well three or four times a day, until the skin becomes sore. Give plenty of cold water to drink and feed on soft food as bran mash, boiled oats, vegetables and good, clean, sweet hay.

PNEUMONIA OR INFLAMMATION OF THE LUNGS

Pneumonia is inflammation of the lung substance and may be in one or both lungs. It is often caused by exposure to cold or wet, or by sudden changes of the weather; it may follow a severe case of catarrh.

Symptoms

One of the first symptoms is a chill or shivering, but this often passes unnoticed. The appetite fails, rumination ceases, the muzzle becomes dry, and the nostrils are dilated. The breathing becomes more rapid and difficult and if the ear is held against the side of the chest there will be an absence of the natural respiratory murmur, and instead will sometimes be heard a dry wheezing sound or, if the pleura is involved, there will be a rasping sound as of two pieces of dry leather being rubbed together. The pulse will be strong and full at first but as the disease progresses it will grow small, weak and wiry an d gradually increase in frequency. The temperature may be from 103 degrees to 105 degrees Fah., which can only be determined by the use of the thermometer. The animal stands with its fore legs wider apart than usual. Unlike horses, cattle sometimes lie down in pneumonia always resting upon the sternum; they evince signs of pain and do not remain in a recumbent position long at a time.

Treatment

In this disease prompt action and good nursing are of the greatest importance; the patient must be shielded from cold and wet. Give four drachms of nitrate of potash and one drachm of the sulphate of cinchonida every four hours until the fever begins to abate then give the same dose three times a day. If the patient is thin in flesh or appears weak, give with each dose two ounces of sweet spirits of nitre or three ounces of Mindererus' spirit. If the bowels are not already loose give from one to three drachms of calomel in the beginning of the disease. These medicines are best given in gruel. Rub the sides of the chest thoroughly with ammoniacal liniment three or four times a day, or until the skin becomes tender. Give the animal all the cool water it can drink and feed on laxative, nourishing diet. If treatment is begun in the early stages the chances for recovery are good.

PLEURISY-DISEASES OF RESPIRATORY ORGANS

Pleurisy is the term used to designate inflammation of the pleura or membrane lining the chest and covering the lungs. It is often complicated with pneumonia and then becomes more serious.

Symptoms

The symptoms are somewhat similar to those of pneumonia, except that the breathing is more painful; the elbows will stand out more than usual; the ribs will appear fixed and the breathing will be done by the abdominal muscles. There is generally a short, painful cough which sounds as if the animal was trying to suppress it. There will be a crease, called the 'pleuritic ridge,' running from the flank downward and forward along the lower ends of the ribs towards the elbows; the animal will walk with difficulty, as though stiff in the shoulders, giving a short, quick grunt at each step. In the beginning, if the ear is held to the side of the chest, a rasping sound will be heard; but, after a few days, this will be absent owing to the effusion of fluid into the thoracic cavity.

Treatment

The treatment prescribed in pneumonia will be equally effective in pleurisy if begun in time. If there is no improvement after several days, effusion takes place, the chest begins to fill with water, producing the condition known as hydrothorax, when there is little hope for the patient except in the hands of the most skilful practitioner.

DISEASES OF DIGESTIVE ORGANS

CHOKING

Cattle are very liable to choke, especially when fed on roots, nubbins of corn, chopped pumpkins, or any other hard food.

Symptoms

The animal will stop eating, stand apart from the others, drool freely and sometimes gulp as if trying to swallow. The obstruction may also be seen and felt from the outside of the throat and neck. Sometimes when an animal has remained choked for some time there will be severe bloating which may have to be relieved by puncturing, as described under Bloating.

Treatment

If the obstruction is up near the throat, place a gag in the animal's mouth and endeavour to reach the offending object and draw it out through the mouth. But, if the choke is low down or cannot be reached with the hand, a probang must be inserted and the object pushed down into the stomach. If the choke should be of bran or other ground food, or of oats, do not pass the probang, as it will only pack and make the matter worse. In this case a little oil may be poured down; or better, a half pint of water in which has been dissolved a heaping teaspoonful of saltpetre, and then try to start the choke by working on the outside with the hands. If a choke cannot be removed by any other means it may be done by laying the walls of the esophagus or gullet open with a sharp knife, but this will require the skill of a surgeon.

BLOATING

Bloating is of very common occurrence in cattle, especially in districts where red clover is raised for pasture. Allowing animals to graze upon clover in the morning while the dew is on, or even when it is wet from rain, will often cause severe bloating. Frozen roots or vegetables of any kind, grass when covered with frost, half-wilted tops of garden vegetables are all likely to cause trouble.

Symptoms

The symptoms cannot be mistaken. The left flank will be most prominent, being often raised above the level of the backbone, and having a drum-like sound when struck with the hand When the stomach becomes greatly distended it presses forward upon the diaphragm and lungs so much as to interfere with the breathing; and if not relieved the animal reels, falls and dies of suffocation.

Treatment

In moderate cases, where death from suffocation is not imminent, a heaping tablespoonful of pulverized charcoal mixed with water and given as a drench, and repeated in half an hour, is sometimes very effectual. Four drachms of carbonate of ammonia, given in a quart of water every half hour will often stop the formation of gas. But in urgent cases puncturing in the flank is the only resort. This is best done with trocar and canula, which every stock raiser should have and know how to use. In the absence of a trocar, a long, slender-bladed knife may be used. The point at which to puncture is high up on the left flank at an equal distance from the last rib, the point of the hip, and the transverse process of the vertebrae. An incision half an inch long should be made in the skin, the point of the trocar inserted and pushed downward and slightly inward and forward. The trocar should then be withdrawn, leaving the canula in the opening until all the gas has escaped and its formation ceased. The trocar should then be inserted and the canula removed and a little carbolized oil rubbed on the wound. The animal should then have a pound of Epsom salt dissolved in half a gallon of water and given as a drench.

INDIGESTION

Indigestion in the chronic form is of frequent occurrence among milk cows, especially in towns and cities where large quantities of corn chop and other heating food-stuffs are fed. Mouldy or course innutritious hay, or wintering around straw stacks will also cause it.

Symptoms

Staring coat, sunken eyes, loss of appetite, hollow flanks, dry, flaky, mucous-covered droppings, and sometimes they will be blood-stained and are always small in quantity. The muzzle will be dry at times and at others moist. The breathing is generally increased and the animal grunts and frequently moans, especially when moved.

Treatment

The first step is to cleanse the bowels. If there is diarrhoea give a quart of raw oil If there is no diarrhoea give one pound or more of Epsom salt dissolved in half a gallon of warm water, repeating the dose if the first does not operate in twenty-four hours. When the bowels have been opened give the following dose twice a day until the bowels become regular: Bicarbonate of soda, powdered charcoal and powdered gentian root, of each half an ounce. Feed on oil cake, bran mash, roots or any other easily-digested, laxative food. If in summer give green grass; if in winter give good, sweet hay for roughness and allow plenty of good water at all times.

CONSTIPATION

Constipation in cattle is always more or less associated with indigestion, and the same treatment will apply to both.

If the case is an obstinate one, a half a pint to a pint of raw oil every day or two will assist in keeping the bowels open.

DIARRHOEA

Diarrhoea sometimes becomes a very serious affection in cattle. It may come from chronic indigestion or it may be due to an overfeed of grain; it also frequently happens from eating some irritating or poisonous substance.

Symptoms

The symptoms are very apparent. The discharge from the bowels is very profuse; it is often very dark in colour and has a fetid odour. In the beginning there is generally great thirst, but no appetite for food. If the disease continues for some time the animal becomes so prostrated that it cannot rise to its feet, and the discharge becomes thin and watery.

Treatment

It will do no good to give astringents to check the discharge until the bowels have been cleansed of all irritating substance; hence, one and a half pints of raw oil and two ounces of laudanum should be given at once, and if there is much pain, an ounce of laudanum and four ounces of raw oil may be given every two hours until the pain ceases. An ounce of hyposulphite of soda should be given every three or four hours, either in a quart of water or slippery elm tea. After the oil has operated, take four heaping tablespoonfulls of wheat flour and make into thin gruel by boiling over a slow fire; give this at one dose and repeat every six hours until the bowels begin to check. Feed on light, nourishing diet for a few days until the stomach has had time to recover from the shock.

AFFECTION OF GASTRIC DELIRIUM

Treatment

Give a dose of Epsom salt sufficient to open the bowels (a pound or more to an ordinary cow) dissolved in half a gallon of warm water. Half an ounce of bromide of potassium should be given with the salt and the same dose repeated every four or six hours until the delirium subsides. In severe cases, cloths wet in cold water should be kept on the head. If the first dose of Epsom salt does not open the bowels in twenty-four hours a second dose should be given. For after-treatment an ounce of hyposulphite of soda may be given in drinking water two or three times a day.

Sometimes cattle are seen chewing old bones, licking a stone wall, eating earthy matter, etc. This generally indicates some gastric derangement and will nearly always yield to the treatment prescribed for indigestion. Some cows get into the habit of eating horse dung, probably due to starvation at first, unless it originates from the filthy habit which some dairymen have of feeding their cows upon the cleanings from livery stables, simply because they can get it for the trouble of hauling.

DISEASES OF EYE

INJURIES OF EYES

Cattle are liable to receive injuries to the eyes from brush and weeds while grazing; also from chaff and other substances getting into the eye, causing it to become inflamed and throw off a watery discharge.

Treatment

Examine the eye carefully to remove any foreign body that may be there. If there is much pain, bathe the eye for ten or fifteen minutes night and morning with water as hot as can be borne with the hand. If the irritation is only slight, cold-water bathing will be all that is necessary. In very severe cases the animal should be kept in a dark stable in the brightest part of the day.

BLEEDING FUNGUS OF EYES

This is a cancerous growth which sometimes affects the eyes of cattle. A fungus growth grows in the eye and tissues around it, protruding from the orbital fossa and sometimes crowding the eye out with it. There is a constant discharge and a fetid odour from it.

Treatment

The only remedy is to remove the entire growth, eye and all tissues involved; scrape the bone clean and then apply powdered sulphate of copper to all raw surface and fill the cavity with cotton. In twenty-four hours the cotton should be taken out and the wound washed and dressed once a day thereafter with the following ointment: Pine tar and lard, of each, four ounces; acetate of copper, half an ounce; mix.

CONTAGIOUS OPHTHALMIA IN CATTLE

Contagious ophthalmia in cattle is comparatively a new disease in Kansas, only having made its appearance about five or six years ago. It does not sweep the entire country, but is rather enzootic in its habits, although when it enters a herd it continues until all have had it. It is an inflammatory condition involving some of the inner structures of the eye and the eyelids.

Symptoms

There will be a watery discharge from the eye; the lids will be kept closed. As the disease progresses, the eyelids will become swollen; the cornea will have a whitish colour, and the animal will grow dumpish and lose its appetite. In very severe cases the swelling continues until the eye-ball is ruptured and its contents discharged, precluding all possibility of restoring sight.

Treatment

Place the patient in a dark, cool stable; four ounces of Epsom salt should be dissolved in a quart of water and given as a drench twice a day; if the bowels become too loose, give only once a day. In mild cases, bathing twice a day with cold water may reduce the inflammation; but, if there is much swelling, bathe twice a day with hot water, and each time wipe the skin dry and apply a little of the following, all around and in the eye: Nitrate of potash, forty grains; sulphate of zinc, forty grains; fluid extract of belladonna, four drachms; water, one pint. If the eye-ball ruptures, syringe it out with the same lotion.

PARASITIC DISEASES OF CATTLE

ACTINOMYCOSIS-LUMPY-JAW

Actinomycosis, or lumpy-jaw, is characterized by swellings on the jaws. The swelling may be on either upper or lower jaw and may be somewhat soft at first, but soon grows hard, as the disease affects the bone. It is due to the parasite actinomysis, a vegetable fungus supposed to be on the fodder or other food and enters the animal organism through some abrasion of the skin. It sometimes affects the tongue, causing it to thicken up and become hard, in which condition it is the so-called 'woody-tongue.' The general health of the animal does not appear to be much affected by the disease as long as the animal can masticate its food, but after a time the jaw becomes affected to such an extent that the animal can scarcely eat, then it soon becomes emaciated. Theorists differ as to whether the flesh of such an animal is fit for food. The safest plan is to let it alone.

Treatment

There have been many methods of treatment prescribed and some 'sure cures'(?) advertised. But the only thing most of them affect, with any certainty, is the owner's pocket book. The best treatment known for this disease at the present time is that recommended by the Bureau of Animal Industry, which is as follows: Give a daily dose of iodide of potassium, allowing fifteen grains for each one hundred pounds of the animal's weight. This may be dissolved in water and given as a drench, and should be continued until symptoms of iodism are produced, which will be in from ten to fourteen days.

The animal will become languid and disinclined to move about; the appetite will fail and there will be a discharge from the eyes and nostrils. In some subjects, not all, there will be a vesicular eruption of the skin; there will be abstinence from water, and elevation of temperature. When these symptoms occur, the iodide should be withheld for a few days until the appetite returns and the other symptoms subside, when the treatment should be repeated as before. The treatment should be continued in this manner until the enlargement begins to decrease in size, which may be two or three months.

TUBERCULOSIS CONSUMPTION

Tuberculosis, or pulmonary consumption, is an infectious disease due to the bacillus tuberculosis which, through various channels, invades the animal's body. The most important consideration, with regard to animal tuberculosis, is the bearing that it has upon the health of the human family. That animal and human tuberculosis, or consumption, are identically the same has become an established fact; and it is also the belief of the most scientific investigators that animal, and especially bovine, tuberculosis is, to an enormous extent, responsible for the same disease in the human race.

The disease may be communicated from the animal to the human being in various ways. The milk of diseased animals is known to be one of the most prolific sources of communication. The flesh, though not always, has been known to contain the bacilli, and, as many people eat their meat 'rare done,' it thus becomes a source of danger. The discharge from the nostrils and from abscesses of diseased animals falling upon the ground or upon stable floors, becoming dry and being taken up as fine dust by the moving air, may be inhaled by other cattle and also by human beings. Milk, containing the bacilli, spilled upon floors of dwellings and dairy rooms, in this manner becomes a source of communication by inhalation, even to those who do not drink it.

A most serious aspect of this subject is the fact that this disease is not easily detected in its first stages; its progress is often slow at first, the animal being apparently in fair health for a year or two after the disease has begun its work. There was affected breathing, and a slight wheezing sound in the lungs. Tuberculosis was mentioned at the time, but as we had no microscope and did not then know the use of tuberculin, no test was made; and, as after a few doses of stimulants and tonics, the cow seemed to recover, nothing more was thought of the case until two years after, when your humble servant was again called to deliver a calf from the same cow. The cow was very thin in flesh, and she had not been doing well for a month or two. The calf was dead, but was soon delivered, and when the placenta was taken away its uterine surface was found thickly studded with nodules and small ulcers. Having access this time to a microscope, the writer prepared several specimens, in each of which were countless numbers of the bacilli of tuberculosis.

Symptoms

The symptoms are often so slight at first as to be almost unnoticed, or may be mistaken for a common cold. The animal may be slightly off its feed for a few days; the muzzle may be dry, and, if a cow, there may be a decrease in the quantity of milk. Good nursing, with a few doses of medicine, soon checks the disease, and the animal is all right for a while. These attacks become more frequent and each one leaves the system in a worse condition until finally the symptoms never abate entirely. The hair will begin to look rough; the appetite will be capricious; the breathing will be affected; the animal cannot stand exertion; the ear placed against the side of the chest will detect a wheezing or whistling sound; there may be a cough and, as the disease progresses, there may be a discharge from the nostrils with a fetid odour; as the symptoms become more aggravated, there will be great emaciation; there will be complication with bowel troubles, and some times tubercular tumors or abscesses form about the head and neck and other parts of the body.

But, though these symptoms are sufficient to excite suspicion, the only true test is with the microscope, or by the hypodermic injection of tuberculin, both of which methods require experience. The disease is incurable, and as soon as its existence is proven, the affected animal should be destroyed and the carcass burned. The milk of tuberculous cows should not even be fed to pigs. The writer has seen several well-marked cases of the disease in swine.

ERUPTIVE APTHA, OR PSEUDO-FOOT-AND-MOUTH DISEASE

This disease first made its appearance in the State of Missouri a few years ago and was thoroughly investigated by Dr. Paul Faquin, State Veterinarian of Missouri at that time, and found to be due to some vegetable parasite. Through a misconstruction of some statement made by the doctor, a report became widely circulated that the cases were of the true foot-and-mouth disease, and considerable excitement prevailed for some time and the excitement, as well as the disease, soon became quiet.

Nearly every season since, there have been a few cases in Missouri and Kansas (and probably other Western States), but it has never become, serious, and if any animal ever died with the disease it must have been because the owner neglected to furnish proper food for it while its mouth was sore, and it starved to death. The disease is simply an eruption of the mucous membrane of the mouth and of the skin of the body; and although the two diseases have many symptoms in common, yet it lacks the virulence of the foot-and-mouth disease of European countries.

Symptoms

Small blisters form on the tongue and inside of the lips; these burst open, forming small sores, and sometimes the lips become dry and cracked. The animal eats readily if food is placed well back on the tongue, but cannot take it up because of the soreness of the mouth. The jaws are kept moving and the saliva flows freely. Small eruptions appear over the body; and about the udder and other parts where the hair is thin, the skin becomes of a reddish colour. The soreness on the skin extends down to the feet and sometimes cracks form around the hoofs, and, in severe cases, the hoofs come off. The animal often gets very lame and is inclined to lie down a great deal.

Treatment

If there is diarrhoea, give a dose of raw oil; if no diarrhoea exists, give a dose of Epsom salt sufficient to open the bowels moderately; give hyposulphite of soda in the drinking water to the amount of three ounces in twenty-four hours. Swab the mouth three times a day with the following: Alum, one ounce; water, one quart; mix. Sponge all sores on the body and feet with a solution of sulphate of copper, one ounce, to water, one quart. Keep the patient in a cool, shady place, and feed on gruel, bran mash, boiled oats and other soft food.

PARTURITION AND ITS SUBSEQUENT DISEASES

PARTURITION

Although cattle in their wild and untrammeled state, guided by natural instincts, scarcely ever have any trouble during the process of parturition, the changes in their mode of life, consequent upon domestication, have rendered timely assistance frequently necessary to a safe delivery. Hence, every one who has the care of cattle should be somewhat familiar with the proceedings in a case of natural presentation and delivery. The period of gestation in the cow is, approximately, about nine months. Some cows, and especially heifers with first calf, go a week or two over, or a week or two under the regular time without causing any material difference in the offspring. A record of the date of service should always be kept as a guide to the time about when parturition can be expected to take place. As the time for calving comes near, the udder fills out with milk; the hips will begin to spread apart, and the muscles on each side of the backbone between the hips and the root of the tail become sunken.

When the time for delivery arrives the cow generally goes away from the others, if allowed to do so. There will be uneasiness, lying down and getting up again, as the labour pains come and go. In a short time the water bag makes its appearance, breaks, and the two front feet present themselves with the nose lying between them. As long as the labour pains continue to come on and the calf is being forced through the passage, even though slowly, it is better, as a rule, not to interfere; but, if it seems to be on a 'stand still' and the pains are diminishing, or the cow becoming weak from prolonged labour, aid may be given by pulling gently on the calf's feet just when the pain comes on, but at no other time.

If, after the water bag has been presented and broken, the pains subside, or continue for some time without the appearance of the calf's feet, the hand and arm should be well oiled and introduced carefully into the vagina to ascertain the cause of the delay. If there is a wrong presentation, endeavour to bring the calf into proper position. No special instructions can be of any service on this point; but only a few general hints will be given, leaving the operator to use his own good sense and judgement, according to the circumstances.

The proper presentation is of the front feet and head, and if only a part of these are presented and the others lagging, bring them carefully into position. If the two hind feet are engaged in the passage, bring the calf away backwards. If both fore and hind feet be presented at the same time, retain the hind feet, return the front ones, and deliver the calf backwards. When delivery has been effected the cow will generally give the calf all the care that is necessary.

PARTURIENT PARALYSIS

It frequently happens after a difficult case of parturition, and sometimes where delivery was easy, that there is partial paralysis of the hind quarters. Sometimes a few days of good nursing will bring about recovery; but, if the cow does not show improvement by the second day, a moderate dose of Epsom salts should be given to open the bowels, and one drachm of nux vomica combined with two drachms of nitrate of potash should be given twice a day. If there is still no improvement after five days, increase the dose of nux vomica to two drachms. The spine should also be rubbed three times a day, till sore, with ammoniacal liniment. Feed nourishing, laxative food and give plenty of fresh water to drink.

PARTURIENT APOPLEXY

This is an affection of the brain and spinal cord and, although many different theories have been written in explanation of its origin, pathology and treatment, nothing very satisfactory has ever been reached It generally attacks only the best milkers, and the best in flesh. It comes on within four or five days after calving, the earlier, the more likely it is to be fatal.

Symptoms

First there will be a slight unsteadiness in walking; the patient will lie down, then get up again, showing uneasiness; there will be constipation and scanty urine. The symptoms may come on very rapidly and in a short time there will be paralysis of the hind quarters and inability to rise when down; the head will be thrown around to the side and there will be a snoring sound in the breathing, and in time the animal will become unconscious.

Treatment

As soon as possible after the attack begins to come on give six drachms each of chloral hydrate and bromide of potassium dissolved in one pint of water, and, each two hours thereafter, give a dose of four drachms each of the chloral and potassium until three more doses are given, then gradually diminish the dose each time and also lengthen out the time between the doses. Great care must be exercised to prevent choking while drenching, and just as soon as swallowing is done readily a dose of Epsom salt, sufficient to open the bowels, should be given. Plenty of drinking water should be given at all times, and a little nourishing food as soon as the animal will eat. The animal should be rolled over occasionally and be kept well bedded. Cloths wet in cold water should also be kept on the head for the first day or two.

GARGET FREQUENT

Garget is of frequent occurrence among good milkers, especially in cities where cows are highly fed. It is often the result of careless milking, but may come from exposure to cold or wet.

Symptoms

Part or all of the udder becomes swollen and hard, and is sometimes very painful, The milk becomes thick and curdled and sometimes the secretion of milk is stopped, and only a watery fluid comes from the teat.

Treatment

Open the bowels with a dose of Epsom salt, then give half an ounce of nitrate of potash twice a day for a week. Bathe the udder twice a day with hot water, wipe dry and apply the following: Gum camphor rubbed fine, two ounces; fluid extract lobelia, two ounces; olive oil, six ounces; mix. Milk thoroughly clean several times a day.

INVERSION OF THE UTERUS

Sometimes inversion of the uterus or 'calf bed' takes place after the calf has been delivered. It can be known by the large bloody-looking, pear shaped mass protruding or hanging from the vagina.

Treatment

Remove all straw and dirt from the mass with warm water, and place a clean sheet under it to keep it from the ground. Oil the hand, insert the closed fist into one of the horns (two openings at the large end of the uterus), and push it as far in as possible; have an assistant to place his hands against this and hold it while you do the same with the other side. When the entire mass has been returned take a large needle and a strong twine and put four or five stitches across the vulva or mouth of the vagina to prevent the uterus from being expelled again. If the cow continues to strain, a couple of ounces of laudanum may be given in a pint of water as a drench. After trying all other remedies to prevent the uterus from being thrown out again, I have found nothing else so effectual as blistering the cow along the spine with ammoniacal lininent. The stitches should be left in for six or seven days.

RETENTION OF PLACENTA

Sometimes the placenta or afterbirth does not come away. A pint of scalded flax seed fed to the cow will often have the desired result. If it does not come away it should not be taken sooner than twenty-four, nor later than forty-eight hours, as to take it sooner might cause bleeding and later than forty-eight hours, decay would begin.

SPECIFIC CEREBRO MENINGITIS IN CATTLE

The so-called 'mad itch' in cattle has long been a mystery to cattlemen, as it seemingly attacked cattle in all conditions, fat cattle in the feed yards frequently falling victims. Many causes have been assigned for the disease. Frozen pasturage, poisonous vegetation, corn cobs and husks which hogs had chewed and covered with saliva, and then dropped upon the ground, were supposed to be eaten by the cattle and cause the peculiar symptoms. But all these theories faded one after another as experimental tests only brought contradictory results. The disease has been described under different names, some even calling it hydrophobia. The name Specific Cerebro Meningitis was suggested by Dr. Paul Paquin; and by reading a report of some investigations made by Dr. Paquin regarding the disease.

It is well known that in many pastures cattle get their water supply from ponds; or if there is a stream of water running through the field it goes dry except a few deep holes. Now as the dry, hot weather comes on the water in these ponds or holes grows less in quantity and more filthy from the manure and from the tramping of the cattle until, finally, there is only a filthy, mucky mass left and the cattle go elsewhere for water. After a few weeks the rains begin to fall; the old watering places are filled with fresh, clear water, and the cattle are turned into the old pasture again and in a few days begin to die.

There is some mystery the owner cannot comprehend. He does not look to the water for the cause, for he knows that it looks better than when the cattle were in the field before. He does not know that during this undisturbed period the old pond was a regular hot-bed for the development of fungi and micro-organic ferments; that in that clear, fresh water, so inviting to thirsty throats on a hot summer's day, lies the death dealing germ that is causing such terrible havoc among his cattle. There have been outbreaks of this disease where no pool of stagnant water existed; but examination proved the soil to be of that moist, mucky character favourable to the development of disease germs, and, as it dried out, it was left full of deep indentations from the hoofs of the cattle. When the rain fell, these indentations were tilled with water, and the cattle drank from them, thus taking in the germ as from the water in the pond. Sharp frosts and cold weather tend to check the ravages of the disease; but it starts again with warm weather, and, if the cattle are not removed, continues until the summer heat dries up the water. There is no cure for the disease when an animal once takes it. The only hope lies in preventing it.

Symtoms

There will be a dull, and sometimes anxious, look about the eyes; loss of appetite; suspension of rumination; dribbling of frothy saliva from the mouth; shivering of the muscles; sudden jerking of the feet; lying down and immediately getting up; walking with an unsteady gait; shaking of the head, with frequent attempts to scratch the shoulders and sides with the horns; rubbing the head and neck against other objects; sometimes holding the head near the ground, and at other times holding it high in air. As time goes on the symptoms become more aggravated; the eyes assume a wild, staring, frenzied appearance; the animal will sometimes give a sudden start, snort, bellow, and run as if attacking some imaginary foe; it will often attack anything that may come in its way, man or beast, in a most threatening and aggressive manner. Thus the animal goes on for several days, when it generally sinks to the ground, either from exhaustion or paralysis, and often becomes comatose before it dies. These symptoms will not all be exhibited in every case; some cases will be mild and, to some extent, controllable; while others will be so frenzied and vicious as to lead the attendant and, sometimes, even inexperienced veterinarians to pronounce it hydrophobia.

Prevention

When possible, water only from deep wells or running streams. If ponds must be used, clean them often, and, if the disease breaks out, move to higher ground, and change feed and water.

INFECTIOUS ABORTION IN CATTLE

It is a well known fact that outbreaks of abortion among cows frequently occur in certain localities which cannot be traced to any visible or ordinary cause. No condition of flesh or health seems to be exempt, but fat and lean alike fall victims to the infection. These abortions generally occur at some time from the fourth to the seventh month of pregnancy and generally without any premonitory symptoms. In some instances the abortions of different cows have seemingly occurred at regular intervals of a certain number of days, which might point to a necessary period of incubation. Experiments of smearing the vagina of a cow with the mucus from a cow that had just aborted, have produced abortion, thus proving that it can be communicated from one cow to another; but the fact that the succeeding cases in a stable have often stood far apart from the preceding ones, goes far to prove that actual contact is not necessary to its communication. As no curative treatment has ever yet given satisfaction, the preventive treatment is the only one to be recommended.

First, when an abortion occurs, get rid of the foetus and all its membranes by burning; gather up all straw and other litter that may have become infected, and burn this also. If in a stable, close all doors and burn sulphur until the fumes penetrate every crevice, then whitewash all walls with a strong lime wash to which has been added a pound of salt to each two gallons of the wash, and sprinkle all floors with the same.

SNAKE BITES WITH CATTLE

Sometimes it happens that animals are bitten by poisonous reptiles. If the Wound is discovered immediately after it has been inflicted, the best plan is to cut it out and touch all raw surface with lunar caustic-but it is not always seen in time for this.

Antidotes: Dissolve half a pint of common salt in a quart or two of water and give as a drench, and bind salt moistened with hot water on the wound. Whiskey may be given in half pint doses every hour. An ounce of aqua ammonia well diluted with water and given every hour is good. The wound may also be bathed with ammonia. If great swelling takes place, little can be done.

CORNSTALK DISEASE IN CATTLE

The disease known by this name is characterized by symptoms of indigestion followed by delirium. Various opinions have been advanced in regard to its cause, but no satisfactory treatment has yet been found. It is believed by some to be due to a minute parasitic fungus which grows upon stocks and blades of fodder left standing in the field, while others adherc to the theory of impaction in the stomach.

'This affection has been known for ages past, under the different names of 'dry murrain', 'fardle-bound', 'grass staggers', 'impaction of the many plies', 'wood evil' and 'indigestion'. The different names simply indicate the ideas of the different individuals in regard to the nature of the disease, its causes, etc., according to the construction they each placed upon the peculiar symptoms exhibited by the animals affected. But, by whatever name the disease may be called, the pathology is just the same, namely, a disordered condition of the stomach, an imperfect performance of its functions, and either a partial or a total suspension of the process of digestion. The peculiar construction of the stomach of the ruminant or cud-chewing animal, makes its mode of feeding so entirely different from that of the non-ruminant, that, in order to make the subject more closely understood, a description is necessary.

The stomach of the ox is very large as compared with that of the horse, and capable of containing a great amount of food. It is divided into four distinct compartments as follows: The rumen or paunch, reticulum or second stomach, the omasum or third stomach, sometimes also called the manyplies, and the abomasum or fourth stomach. The rumen is the largest of the four divisions, and is equal in capacity to all the others combined The esophagus or gullet through which all food and drink passes from the mouth to the stomach, enters the rumen near its junction with the reticulum or second stomach, and continuing along the roof of the second stomach, not as a complete tube, but in the shape of two movable lips attached by one border to the walls of the second stomach, the other border being free, it enters the third stomach by a circular orifice. These lips, when open and passive, allow all food as it is swallowed to pass into the rumen, but, when they are drawn together, they form a channel known as esophageal groove and through which food can pass directly into the third stomach, and thence into the fourth, without stopping in the first or second. At the entrance of the esophagus into the rumen are also numerous small, fleshy points or papillse, which help to work the food to the place where it should go.

Now, when any ruminating animal feeds upon grass, hay or other coarse material, the food passes very rapidly and with very little mastication into the first stomach, where it becomes saturated and softened by the fluids supplied by that division, and also by the saliva which is secreted by the salivary glands and poured down the animal's throat, and by a sort of churning process, caused by the contracting and relaxing of the muscular walls of the stomach, it is prepared for the next step in the process of digestion. From the first stomach the food is gradually worked into the second, where it is worked into pellets or cuds and, by a peculiar spasmodic action, is thrown up by the reticulum, and grasped by the esophagus and returned to the mouth to be remasticated, when it is again swallowed, this time passing along the esophageal groove into the third stomach. This division is made up of numerous folds or leaves, between which the semi-ground food passes, and again undergoes a triturating or grinding process, and is then passed on to the fourth or true digestive stomach, where the process of digestion is easily completed.

But should the food be more of the nature of chaff, or finely broken fodder, a great amount of it passes by the first and second stomachs into the third, where, if the food be of an especially dry and non-nutritive character, it becomes lodged between the manyplies, and not being saturated as it should be with the liquids from the first and second divisions, the fluid secreted by the third division alone is insufficient, and the result is an impaired condition of the stomach and the beginning of a case of impaction. Now, if this is allowed to go on day after day without change of food, the impaction increases, until finally the spaces between the manyplies become entirely filled up, leaving only a small channel through the lesser curvature of the stomach, along the edge of the manyplies, through which only food in a semi-fluid state can pass. The other divisions soon become affected, through sympathy with this one, and there is complete suspension of the functions of the entire digestive tract. Then the sensory nerves soon begin to transmit the disordered sensations to the brain, hence the train of nervous symptoms, so often seen in such cases.

If the case can be taken when the animal only appears stupid, with impaired appetite, it will pay to treat it. Give Epsom salts, from one to two pounds, according to size of animal, dissolved in half a gallon of warm water, with one pint of molasses added, and follow with two quarts of warm linseed tea, or thin gruel, every two hours, and injections of warm water per rectum, and moderate exercise occasionally. If the medicine does not operate in twenty-four hours, repeat the dose, and continue the other treatment as before. But as our object in the beginning was to throw some light on the trouble in cornstalk feeding, we will proceed to that. It is a mystery to some why cattle will sometimes feed in one stalk field for weeks without any loss, and then be changed to another, and soon begin to die rapidly. Also that they will be turned into a field and seem to do well for a week, and then suddenly the mortality will begin. And then again, we often hear, that of two neighbours living side by side, one turns his cattle in the field and lets them remain there, with no loss whatever; while the other turns his in only a few hours at a time and tries to take every precaution against loss, as instructed by writers on the subject, yet his cattle will die as if a curse had been set upon them. This, we think will all be clear enough if we will note the difference in the condition of the fields. If the corn is of good, large growth and well matured, the danger is not very great. But if the stalks are small and not matured, the cob soft and spongy, the grains undeveloped, and the ears half covered with smut; blades, stalks and all, bitten by the frost and then dried by the sun and wind until they are capable of being ground up fine enough by a few strokes of the jaw, so that when swallowed, the whole mass will pass at once into the third stomach, and, being very dry and of almost no nutritive value, finds lodgment there from day to day, until the stomach becomes filled to such an extent that no medicine will relieve it.

A few good ears of corn may have been left in the field to be gathered by the cattle, and this will ward off the catastrophe for a few days, and thus account for their not dying when first turned in. In view of these facts, then, we should be able to form some idea of a preventive treatment.

In the first place, the cattle should have free access to both salt and water, and should be driven to the latter every day, if they do not go of their own accord. They should never go into the stalks except with full stomachs; they should not be left in over an hour at a time, and after the first two days leave them out a day, and continue in this way two days in and the third day out for at least two weeks, and when they are out of the stalks do not turn them into an old dry field to go hungry till the time comes to go into the stalks again, but feed liberally on good hay or well cured, green-cut fodder, accompanied by corn, bran, oil-cake, sliced roots or anything else that will form a nutritious and laxative diet, and see that they eat it before they are again allowed to enter the stalk field, and they should still be fed a little grain of some kind, even after they have become accustomed to the stalks. If this method of feeding does not prove a complete remedy it will at least lower the death rate, and those that live will be all the better for having had the extra care.'

BLACKLEG IN CATTLE

This is a disease which affects only young cattle, and is due to a micro-organism taken into the system from the soil in some localities. As many theories have been advanced regarding the origin of the disease, its treatment and prophylactic measures, we will not discuss the merits or demerits of these different theories here, but enter at once upon a description of the plans most feasible to the farmer for saving his cattle. It has often been said that 'only fat cattle take the disease.' While this is not true, yet it is a fact that only those which are thriving rapidly take it no matter whether fat or lean. And it is also a fact that depletion or a sudden check in the thriving of an animal will check the ravages of the disease, for the time being at least.

Symptoms

At first there will be loss of appetite and rumination will cease; a slight lameness may be noticed, gradually growing worse until the animal is unable to rise to its feet when down. There will be swelling in the lame limb, and, if the hand is rubbed over this gently, a crackling sound will be heard from underneath the skin. If the skin is split open, the blood will be of a black tarry appearance and too thick to flow.

Treatment

After an animal is down and unable to stand upon its feet when helped up, no medicine will save it. But, if found while yet able to walk about, give a dose of Epsom salt, raw oil or melted lard, sufficient to open the bowels, then get upon a horse and keep the patient on a trot for an hour or two unless the bowels open freely sooner. If you succeed in getting a full, free evacuation of the bowels, the chances are you will save the calf. Also as soon as a case of blackleg is found among a lot of young cattle, the entire lot should be taken from the pasture and put in a high, dry yard where they can get neither water nor feed for twenty-four hours. It may also be well enough to give each animal a dose of Epsom salt to open the bowels. The animals should not be returned to the same pasture, but should be kept on higher and drier ground. Many preparations have been recommended as preventatives, but experience has proven them all to be of doubtful value A mixture composed of common salt, wood ashes, sulphur and saltpetre, will be found as good as any. It should be kept in troughs in the pasture where the cattle can get it at Will.

We do not wish it understood that we ignore the theories that have been advanced by learned men in regard to this disease. On the contrary, we appreciate every effort of science to fathom the true cause of, and to discover a preventative against the disease, and, as preventive inoculation in the hands of some of our most noted scientists has produced comparative immunity from the disease, we recommend every farmer to give it a trial when opportunity affords; but until such opportunity is afforded, we recommend the afore-described treatment, which we have given many trials and have never yet failed to check the ravages of the disease for the time being.

GONORRHOEA IN CATTLE

Occassionally a bull, from serving a cow suffering with leucorrhoea, will be attacked with an inflammation of the penis and mucous membrane lining the sheath which, if allowed to continue, often causes ulcers on the penis and swelling of the sheath. There is a muco-purulent discharge through which the disease will be communicated to cows if served by the bull while suffering with the disease.

Treatment

The affected parts should be thoroughly cleaned with warm water and, if ulcers exist, they should be touched with nitrate of silver. After the first cleansing, wash the inflamed part once or twice a day with cold water, and each time make an application of the white lotion as described in Medicines and How to Prepare Them. When cows become affected, syringe out the vagina with warm water and inject the lotion.

ACETONAEMIA IN COWS

Acetonaemia also called ketosis, sweet breath, and hypoglycaemia, is a disease commonly seen either in high producing dairy cows, or in any cows on a poor diet. The disease is caused by a deficiency of glucose in the blood and in body tissues. It is important to remember that cows cannot be fed glucose in their diet, because of their complex digestive processes. Glucose is made in the rumen from suitable carbohydrates in the diet. Cows need considerably more energy during the latter part of pregnancy and in early lactation. A high producing cow may be not able to consume enough carbohydrate (particularly if the ration is pasture based only) to produce enough glucose. Cows need considerably more energy during the latter part of pregnancy and in early lactation. If glucose demand cannot be met by additional feed of the right sort, fat is broken down in the body. If this is excessive, there is a build-up of by-products called ketones in the blood. The clinical condition-acetonaemia is caused by these toxic substances.

Clinical Signs

Acetonaemia has two major forms - the wasting form and the nervous form. They usually occur during the first 60 days of lactation. Cows of any age may be affected but the disease increases in prevalence to peak at the fourth calving. In the wasting form, the disease shows up as the gradual but moderate decrease in appetite and milk yield over 2-5 days. Body weight is lost rapidly, resulting in the coat having what is described as a 'woody' appearance. The dung is firm and dry but the animal is not constipated. Reluctance to move and a hangdog appearance is also seen as the syndrome progresses. A sweet smell of ketones can be smelt on the breath and sometimes in the milk. Without treatment, the milk yield falls by as much as 25 per cent but spontaneous recovery usually occurs over about a month.

Sometimes, the disease is very mild-the only signs being a small reduction in milk production and a sweet, acetone smelling breath. Acetonaemia is sometimes seen as a secondary sign to some other more major disease disorder in the animal. For example displacement of the fourth stomach, mastitis, metritis, peritonitis, milk fever and other conditions that result in reduction of the cows appetite for a length of time.

The nervous form is less common but more dramatic. There is a sudden onset of signs that may last 1-2 hours. These signs include walking in circles, straddling or crossing of the legs, head-pushing, apparent blindness, aimless wandering, staggering, vagourous licking of the skin, depraved appetite, nervousness and slobbering. Affected cows may injure themselves during one of these episodes, which may occur 2 or 3 times a day. The animal is very sensitive when touched and bellows when the skin is pinched. Movement of the limbs often seems to be stiff and uncoordinated.

Treatment

The aim of treatment is to restore body glucose levels as fast as possible. This can be achieved by drenching with glycerine at a rate of half a litre twice daily for two days. Ceton® and Ketol® are suitable alternative commercial preparations. It is important not to give glucose by mouth to cattle since their complex digestive system will make the acetonaemia worse.

Dextrose can be administered intravenously to give a quick initial response, and long-acting corticosteroids may be given by intra muscular injection but both these treatments are only available through a veterinarian. Where there is a lack of response to treatment, an underlying cause must be diagnosed and treated.

Prevention

Prevention is always preferable to treatment and depends on adequate feeding and management. Cows in late pregnancy must be well fed so that they calve in Body Condition Score

4.5 to 5.5 on a condition score scale of 1-8 where 1 is very thin and 8 is very fat. A condition score outside the range of 4.5 to 5.5 increases the cow's susceptibility to acetonaemia.

After calving, suitable high energy feed must be available. Acetonaemia is often seen in Tasmania where freshly calved cows are fed only on lush, fresh pasture. This pasture has a high moisture content and may not supply sufficient energy to satisfy the needs of high producing cows. Supplementary feeding with grain early in lactation may be necessary to overcome any shortfall in energy.

PERENNIAL RYEGRASS STAGGERS

Ryegrass staggers is a disease of grazing animals that causes muscle spasms, loss of muscle control and paralysis.

What Causes Ryegrass Staggers?

It is caused by a group of toxins that accumulates in the leaf sheaths of perennial ryegrass. The toxins are produced by a native fungus called ryegrass endophyte, *Neotyphodium lolii*, that grows within the leaves, stems and seeds of perennial ryegrass. The toxins accumulate in the plant – peaking in summer/autumn and may remain high in the pasture for five to six months. Silage made during this time may also retain similar concentrations of toxin as the source grass for more than 200 days. In hay the toxins appear to decline significantly over a similar period. Neither the fungus nor the toxins adversely affect the plant. In fact, the presence of the fungus increases seedling vigour and the productivity of mature plants. Also, the toxins deter a wide range of insect pests from attacking infected plants and interfere with the lifecycle of the ryegrass stem weevil.

The fungus can only spread to ryegrass plants from infected seeds as it lives entirely within the plant and does not produce spores. It cannot spread from plant to plant in the field. The fungus has only a short life (18-24 months) in the seed under normal grain storage conditions. Seed with a high fungus content that is sown in the first autumn after harvest, three months old, will produce pastures with a high proportion of infected plants. The same seed sown one year later will give a lower and more variable level of infection, while two-year-old seed will produce pasture that is virtually free of fungus.

Stock Affected

Sheep and cattle are most commonly affected but horses, aplaca and deer are also susceptible. Ryegrass staggers has not been recorded in goats, however, there is no evidence to suggest that goats are not susceptible to this disease. Their clean record may simply be due to their grazing/browsing habits. As the fungus and the toxin occur mainly in the leaf sheaths, very close to the ground, hard grazing of infected pasture is likely to induce ryegrass staggers.

The acute problems created by this disease occur when trying to move affected animals. They have a stiff gait or are unable to walk, and may injure or kill themselves in transit. The toxins can induce high body temperatures thus animals will try to cool themselves in mud wallows, dams and troughs, drowning or otherwise injuring themselves in the process. Younger animals tend to be worst affected. There is growing evidence of chronic production losses due to the toxins themselves as well as the indirect effects such as missed drenchings because the animals could not be moved to the yards. For example, young sheep grazing highly infected pasture grow at a slower rate than normal and milk production is reduced in dairy cows.

The symptoms of ryegrass staggers usually develop 7-14 days after stock start grazing the toxic parts of the plant. Animals that are not severely affected recover two to three days (sometimes up to 14 days) after they are transferred to 'non-toxic' pasture. The rate of recovery will, amongst other things, depend on how free of toxin is the 'non-toxic' pasture. Prolonged exposure to toxic pasture can lead to permanent neurological damage. The typical symptoms of ryegrass staggers are listed below:

Sheep

- Behavioural changes-more flighty
- Slight tremor of the head and twitching of muscles in the neck, shoulder and flank.

- Nodding of head and jerky limb movements.
- Swaying and staggering.
- Stiff stilted gait, short prancing steps to stiff legged bounding gait.
- Collapse, extension of head, arching of back, rigid tetanic extension of legs.

Cattle

- Behavioural change-more flighty
- Leg and trunk stiffness causing hesitancy in movement.
- Tendency to fall, stand with legs splayed out.
- May kneel on forelegs or 'dogsit' on hind legs.
- Collapse, flexion rather than extension of legs.

Horses

- Turn with difficulty, stand with legs splayed out, tendency to fall.
- Reeling drunken gait, move slowly.
- Paralysis of hind quarters.
- Trembling, muscle spasms, hypersensitivity to sudden stimuli.

It is of utmost importance that affected animals are managed appropriately – those that can no longer fend for themselves must be nursed or humanely destroyed. Preventative measures include the fencing of dams and waterways and ensuring an alternative feed supply is available. Monitoring the animals is vital so that the early signs of staggers can be detected and the animals moved to safe pastures.

Controlling the Disease

Avoid stock management practices that encourage animals to graze close to the ground. Maintain a close watch on stock whenever feed is in short supply because most problems occur at these times. Consider feedlotting weaners during the peak toxin period. If feed regularly becomes very short throughout a property, sow pastures of other species (*e.g.*

cocksfoot, phalaris) or forage crops for grazing in the summer-autumn period. Perennial ryegrass with low endophyte or non-toxic endophyte is becoming increasingly available.

Set-stocking often leads to uneven grazing, with small areas of the pastures grazed closely and the rest untouched. However, a rotational grazing system that leaves very short stubbles (such as block grazing with a two to three day grazing period) may also lead to staggers. Moving stock daily, so that longer stubble remains, can avoid this problem. The choice of pastures and their management can also reduce the incidence of staggers. Appropriate practices include:

- Block grazing and balanced fertiliser use, to promote pastures with a high clover content.
- Using mixed pasture swards containing cocksfoot, tall fescue, prairie grass and phalaris, to reduce the ryegrass content of the pasture.
- Sowing pasture with perennial ryegrass seed that is at least 15 months (and preferably two years), old, as the fungus dies in the seed under normal storage conditions. However, these pastures may be less productive and persistent than those with a high level of fungus infection.

There is no evidence to support claims that the use of different fertiliser regimes, or the application of salt or other additives to the sward or drinking water, will prevent or cure staggers while stock continue to graze infected pastures.

Annual Ryegrass Toxicity

This is a distinctly different disease to perennial ryegrass staggers although the similarity of the names often causes confusion. Annual ryegrass staggers occurs when stock graze Wimmera ryegrass Lolium rigidum at or after heading and the seed heads are infected with a particular type of nematode and species of bacterium. The bacteria produce a toxin that is fatal to stock.

The disease is confined to areas of Western Australia, South Australia and Victoria. It has not been detected in Tasmania to date, neither have pastures or grass seed infected with the nematode and bacteria. The Seeds Regulation prohibits seed containing the nematode from being imported to, or sold in, Tasmania.

CUTE BOVINE LIVER DISEASE

ACUTE BOVINE LIVER DISEASE

Acute bovine liver disease (ABLD), previously known as phytotoxic hepatitis, is a disease of beef and dairy cattle. Although it occurs sporadically throughout Tasmania, most recorded cases have been in the Northern Midlands and South, particularly the Derwent Valley and Copping area. Cases have also been recorded interstate. Facial Eczema is a disease that may appear similar to ABLD, and has been recorded in dairy herds in north eastern Tasmania. It also occurs sporadically in sheep, beef and dairy cattle in mainland south eastern Australia.

Signs of the Disease

The signs of ABLD are variable. As the name of the disease suggests, signs are related to liver disease of sudden onset. In the worst cases, sudden deaths of cattle over six months of age occur and these may be sporadic or they may involve large numbers within a herd. In cattle that don't die suddenly, signs observed are mostly related to photosensitisation, which occurs when plant breakdown products react with sunlight in the skin. Affected cattle may be distressed, agitated, seek shade and develop sunburn on the muzzle and areas of pale skin, such as white faces, white patches, udder and vulva. Other signs may include fever, a drop in milk production and depression. Other species such as sheep and horses are not affected.

Cause

Although ABLD may be a very severe liver condition, the cause is unknown. Cases of ABLD are often associated with the introduction of cattle into certain paddocks, particularly those that have been under-utilised and contain considerable standing and/or fallen dry feed. Signs of ABLD may be observed within hours of introducing cattle to the 'toxic' paddock. An annual grass known as Rough Dog's Tail (*Cynosurus echinatus*) is often associated with cases of ABLD, however it is unknown whether the plant is directly involved or whether it is merely an 'indicator' of some other factor.

Because many cases of ABLD are associated with warm, moist weather in autumn or spring, a fungal toxin associated with Rough Dog's Tail has been suggested as being a possible cause. There is no current evidence that the plant itself is toxic. State departments of agriculture and primary industry are currently studying cases in an attempt to identify the cause(s).

Complications

Surviving cattle generally have a prolonged recovery. Areas of affected skin eventually slough off and may become infected. A drop in milk production can be significant and if teats are involved, mastitis may occur.

Treatment

There is no known cure for the condition. Although recovery is normally prolonged, early intervention by a veterinarian may assist with recovery by the use of medications such as anti-inflammatories, anti-histamines and zinc. Affected animals should be provided with shade and easy access to drinking water, and may require hand feeding. Skin treatments, particularly those containing zinc and lanolin (*e.g.* nappy rash cream), may help if applied to affected areas of skin. Severely photosensitised cattle may have to be humanely destroyed.

Prevention

Paddocks may remain 'toxic' for variable lengths of time (hours to months) following an ABLD event. It is unknown whether 'toxic' paddocks will be 'toxic' in future years. Management options include: (1) eating out the paddock with sheep to reduce the amount of dry standing material, (2) cultivation of high risk paddocks, (3) avoiding grazing cattle on paddocks with an abundance of dry material which have been spelled for extended periods of time, and (4) trying cattle again but with only a few animals at first to test for 'toxicity'.

Cattle should be frequently observed if grazed on 'at-risk' paddocks during 'danger' periods, particularly during autumn and spring. Cattle should be moved off the paddock immediately if any unusual signs are observed.

BOTULISM ON THE FARM

Botulism affecting humans are rare, it is a common disease of animals and birds. Botulism occurs in animals or birds in some areas of Tasmania. Botulism is not an infectious disease even though it is caused by bacteria. The bacterium *Clostridium botulinum* abounds in nature and, under certain conditions, multiplies rapidly producing a deadly toxin in the process-it is said to be the most poisonous known biological substance.

A feature of the toxin is its ability to survive naturally for long periods, sometimes for years. Likewise, spores of the bacterium can survive in the environment for over 30 years. When the toxin is ingested with food, it produces the symptoms of botulism. However, unless the same food has been shared by another person, or another animal, with the same effect, a diagnosis may be difficult.

The disease cannot be transmitted by contact. The botulinum organisms belong to the same family of bacteria as those responsible for tetanus, gangrene, enterotoxaemia, black disease and blackleg. Like all clostridial organisms, *Cl. botulinum* needs anaerobic (airless) conditions in which to reproduce. It also requires the right environment. In the case of *Cl. botulinum* types C and D, the ones responsible for botulism in Tasmania, this includes decaying animal or vegetable matter.

Before the use of superphosphate on farms was widespread, and even occasionally today, carcase-initiated botulism resulted from stock chewing old bones while attempting to satisfy their craving for phosphorus. A common source of vegetable-initiated botulism in livestock is turnips.

Calves seem particularly susceptible and sometimes seem to possess an ability to locate the odd dangerous turnip in a whole paddock full of safe ones.

Outbreaks of botulism are difficult to predict but, if a property has a history of botulism, it could pay to discuss the merits of vaccination with your veterinarian. The onset of the disease is rapid and symptoms may pass unnoticed, a dead animal being the first indication of an attack. The initial symptoms in ruminants are slobbering and the inability to swallow. This is followed soon after by ataxia and death.

Treatment of botulism in cattle and sheep, once the disease strikes, is practically impossible. Occasionally, slightly affected animals recover but they usually die from asphyxia after an ascending muscle paralysis, the rate of which is proportional to the quantity of toxin absorbed. Horses are more resistant to the toxin.

Botulism in domestic poultry, especially ducks, is fairly common. There are also many places in yards and duck ponds for the bacteria to multiply. Usually ducks and fowls affected by botulism die quickly. Occasionally there are signs of paralysis beforehand to give a clue. This is very characteristic and has given rise to the name 'Limberneck' for the disease in poultry, because paralysed neck muscles make it impossible for the bird to raise or control its head. Diarrhoea is also a symptom. Despite the rapid advances of modern science, it is practically certain that botulism will persist. Care is important at all times.

GRASS TETANY/GRASS STAGGERS

Grass tetany (cattle), grass staggers (sheep) and hypomagnesaemia are names given to a condition that can affect stock in late autumn, winter and spring. It can cause significant losses in production, even when there are no signs of illness. Grass tetany or grass staggers occurs when blood magnesium levels fall below a critical level-hence the term hypomagnesaemia. This occurs when animals are running on pasture which has low available levels of magnesium, or as a result of increased body demands for magnesium during lactation or late pregnancy.

Symptoms of the disease include restlessness, staggers, an over-alert appearance, being excitable and in some cases, aggressiveness. In severe cases, animals may fall down and go into convulsions or just die without warning. There are some common factors that are always present with grass tetany.

- Animals are usually grazing grass dominant pasture or lush cereal crops, often without any hay supplementation.
- Cold and wet windy weather with little or no shelter, resulting in short periods of fasting. The danger period in Tasmania extends from May to October.
- Animals are either fat and losing condition or very thin.
- Animals recently moved to a different paddock.
- Heavy use of nitrogen and/or potash fertiliser on pasture.
- Dairy cows in peak lactation are most commonly affected, but dry cows and, under certain conditions, beef steers, may also suffer.

Clinical Signs

Signs of the disease include restlessness, staggers, an over-alert appearance, being excitable and in some cases, aggressiveness. In severe cases, animals may fall down and go into convulsions or just die without warning. There are some common factors that are always present with grass tetany.

- Animals are usually grazing grass dominant pasture or lush cereal crops, often without any hay supplementation.
- Cold and wet windy weather with little or no shelter, resulting in short periods of fasting. The danger period in Tasmania extends from May to October.
- Animals are either fat and losing condition or very thin.
- Animals recently moved to a different paddock.
- Heavy use of nitrogen and/or potash fertiliser on pasture.
- Dairy cows in peak lactation are most commonly

affected, but dry cows and, under certain conditions, beef steers, may also suffer.

Treatment

Treatment must be prompt to be effective. It is best to inject a combined calcium and magnesium solution (350ml for cattle, 100ml for sheep) under the skin in the area behind the shoulder and over the ribs. Massage the area well after injecting the solution to spread the fluid and aid its rapid absorption into the blood stream. Treated animals should be given adequate shelter and identified so that a response to treatment can be judged. In some cases, repeat treatment may be needed. A frustrating aspect of grass tetany is that animals often relapse and die or become 'downers' which eventually have to be destroyed. The success rate depends on getting to the animals soon enough and reducing stress from the weather. Often affected animals do not eat-this can be a very serious complication, especially in pregnant ewes which then succumb to pregnancy toxaemia and die.

Prevention

Prevention is preferable to treatment as grass tetany often occurs without warning. Basically, prevention involves supplementing the animals with magnesium during the period of greatest risk. However, the provision of hay during periods when there is lush, rapid pasture growth can reduce the incidence of the disease. For dairy cows the risk period is one month before calving to two months after calving. Magnesium stored in the body is not rapidly available so it must be supplied at least every second day during the 'danger period'.

There are several magnesium supplements available from rural suppliers or veterinarians that can be used-magnesium oxide, magnesium chloride, magnesium sulphate (epsom salts) and grass tetany blocks. They may be given in several ways:

- Dust pasture with magnesium oxide at the rate of 60 g per cow per day or 10 g per sheep per day. Apply powder early in the morning and strip graze through the week. Redusting may be required if heavy falls of rain (25 mm or more) occur.

- Magnesium oxide may be sprayed on hay. This is one of the cheapest and most reliable methods of providing magnesium. A mixture of 600 grams of magnesium oxide and molasses mixed in two litres of water is poured evenly onto the cut edge of the bale about 12 hours before feeding. Feed this treated hay at the rate of 10 cows or 100 sheep per bale. Don't feed untreated hay until this hay has been eaten. Hay may be treated with this magnesium oxide solution before baling-allowing 600 grams of magnesium oxide, to a 'bale length' of windrow. Magnesium oxide may also be added as a dry powder (600 g/bale) during baling, by means of a salting applicator attached to the baler. The treated bales should be put in a separate stack to allow them to be used during the danger period.
- Grass tetany blocks provide magnesium as a palatable 'lick'. A major disadvantage of this method is that all the animals may not consume sufficient magnesium. Follow the manufacturer's instructions concerning the number of cows per block. When buying blocks, be sure that they are recommended for the prevention of grass tetany.
- Epsom salts or magnesium chloride may be added to the water supply. This is best done through a Dosatron® at a rate of 500g per 100 litres of drinking water for Epsom salts and 420g per 100 litres of water for magnesium chloride. The salts can also be added at the rate of 60g per cow per day (60 g is about two level tablespoons). The dose must be split and added to the water on two occasions during the day. The normal water flow should be maintained. The capacity of the trough should be at least nine litres per cow so that the salts are sufficiently diluted. Cattle will scour if they get more than 140 g of Epsom salts per day. Also, because cattle don't like the taste, the Epsom salts need to be added

gradually over 2-3 weeks. There are several disadvantages in using this method. Epsom salts are unpalatable and not readily accepted by stock. In winter, water consumption is variable due to the high moisture content of the feed and as a result insufficient salts may be ingested.

- Drenching stock with magnesium oxide or Epsom salts mixed in water is an effective but time consuming, method. The daily rate is 60g/cow mixed in 100 ml water. Epsom salts may be mixed with pluronic-type bloat treatments but the volume of water will need to be increased if such a mixture is used. The magnesium oxide drench mixture must be constantly shaken to prevent it settling out.
- Magnesium oxide may be added to feed fed in the bail at the rate of 45-50 g per cow per day but there are indications that levels greater than 30g per cow per day may predispose the cows to Salmonella.
- Fertilizers rich in potassium and nitrogen reduce the availability of magnesium from the pasture, and increase the risk of grass tetany. So avoid grazing these pastures soon after fertilizer application.

If magnesium is fed over a long period it is important to add phosphorus (dicalcium phosphate powder or bone flour) as a precautionary measure because magnesium can reduce phosphorus absorption. Grass tetany is difficult to treat but, with magnesium supplementation, it is easy to prevent. Saving one cow will pay for the cost of supplementation for at least a year. If there is any doubt about the prevention or treatment of grass tetany contact your local veterinarian.

BOVINE PESTIVIRUS

As its name indicates, bovine pestivirus affects cattle – both dairy and beef. Pestivirus is a group (genus) of viruses. It includes not only bovine pestivirus, but also other viruses that cause border disease in sheep and classical swine fever in pigs. Bovine pestivirus infection of or by other species is very rare.

Present in Tasmania

Yes. Recent test results from the Department of Primary Industries and Water's Animal Health Laboratory indicate that pestivirus in cattle may be as widespread in Tasmania as it is on the mainland, where an estimated 70 per cent of herds are actively infected. While the production losses of pestivirus can be substantial, this will not always be the case. In most cases, the aim should simply be to manage the risk effectively and this can prevent the infection becoming a costly problem.

Pestivirus Risk be Actively Managed

Pestivirus can cause several problems. By far the most common in Australia are reproductive losses. These can show up as aborted or stillborn calves, deformed calves or simply a failure to conceive. The productivity losses arising from pestivirus can range from minor to substantial. The key factor is whether the infection causes a 'PI' that can then cause a wider spread of disease across the herd. Where a herd of non-immune and pregnant animals comes into contact with 'PIs', the reproductive problems can become major.

Transient and Persistent Infections

A healthy animal becomes infected after birth, the infection is usually short-lived and is cleared by the immune system. With such transient infections, the short period of virus shedding (typically around 10 days) and, with Type 1 viruses, the low concentration of virus means that the risk of spreading to other cattle is not high. With Type 2 viruses, the virus shedding period is the same but concentration of virus excreted is much higher so the risk of spread to other cattle is also higher. Outbreaks of clinically severe disease have been seen overseas.

Where a cow becomes infected during the early stages of pregnancy, the foetus does not recognize the virus as being a foreign invader and the foetus does not produce antibodies to the virus. This is because during the early stages of pregnancy, the foetal immune system is still being developed. At this early stage of pregnancy, a foetus that becomes infected with pestivirus does not develop immunity to the virus and therefore if the calf survives (as it does in about 70 per cent of cases), that calf is likely to be a 'PI' – that is, it is likely to be persistently infected and thereby a carrier of the virus for the rest of its life. It is the persistently infected animal, or 'PI', that is by far the greater risk in turning a relatively minor pestvirus problem into substantial reproductive losses and other production losses.

Signs of Pestivirus

The main problem in combating pestivirus is that, in most cases, there are no signs beyond a small number of animals with ill thrift and/or reproductive failure. As a consequence, the signs are sometimes ignored on the basis that the odd animal not doing very well or having an occasional reproductive problem is normal. Other signs in cattle that are infected later in life, apart from reproductive losses, are relatively uncommon but include diarrhoea, excessive drooling and breathing difficulties. In even rarer cases, there can be ulcers around the mouth and muzzle and also the feet, so it can look similar to foot and mouth disease. There may even be an occasional death.

The classic sign that an animal is a 'PI' is ill thrift – a beast that just doesn't grow as well as its peers – although it is important to stress that some infected animals can grow normally into adulthood. These 'PIs' usually die by eighteen months of age.

Testing for Pestivirus

How you manage the risk will depend on whether your herd is already affected. The first step is to have your vet investigate any reproductive failures or ill thrift to determine whether pestivirus is the cause. That involves a blood test on a number of young animals.

Managing Pestivirus

If the test results are positive, you have various options and you should consult your vet for the best one in your specific circumstances. A strategy practised in some herds is exposing heifers to known 'PIs' well before mating, as this will cause most of them to become infected and thereby develop a long-lasting natural immunity. There are some potential downsides to this strategy. For example, there is no guarantee that all animals exposed will become infected and consequently immune, particularly if a single 'PI' is relied upon to infect a large number of other animals. Typically, an infection and immunity rate of 80 per cent by this method would be considered a good result. Also, the fencing and farm practices must be such that there is no chance of the 'PI' inadvertently mixing with cattle in early pregnancy. Another issue to consider is that mixing a possible 'PI' with young heifers may interfere with Bovine Johnes Disease control strategies you may already have in place. So you should discuss it with your vet before proceeding.

Culling the 'PIs' and vaccination of the herd is another option. Again there are some potential downsides to this. Vaccination is not 100 per cent effective, so good biosecurity and ongoing monitoring will still need to be maintained. If you decide to vaccinate, the programme will need to be ongoing for many years at least. If a vaccination programme successfully eradicates pestivirus from the property and the vaccination stops, there will be no immunity and, as a result, the proportion of susceptible animals in the herd will increase over time and the herd will need ongoing management as a closed herd.

Managing the Pestivirus Risk

If there are no signs of active pestivirus in the herd, you can minimise the risk of infection by keeping a closed herd or checking for signs of pestivirus frequently and having any suspicious cases checked promptly. Even if there are no signs of active pestivirus in the herd, vaccination may still be a good option. Because circumstances vary from property to property, there is no 'one size fits all' solution.

Artificial Breeding

The pestivirus status of both the donor and recipient animals should be identified before proceeding. It is recommended that both the donor and recipient animals should test antibody positive (*i.e.*, immune) four weeks before the programme.

The Risk Factors

By far the most likely way of infecting cattle is through a PI. This could be a PI animal or a pregnant female carrying a PI foetus. A PI can infect another animal with as little as 1 hour contact time, so events such as sales, shows, other temporary high stocking situations, fence breakthroughs or even over-the-fence contact with neighbouring cattle are risks. There have been reported cases of infection by contaminated semen and embryos, cattle trucks and even husbandry equipment. But these risks are quite low, compared with the risk via a PI. Infection via sheep, goats or alpacas is possible but highly unlikely.

FACIAL ECZEMA

Facial eczema (FE) is a type of sunburn (sometimes called photosensitisation) affecting exposed areas of pale skin of cattle. It is caused by a poisonous substance called 'sporidesmin' that causes liver damage. Sporidesmin is produced on pasture plants, including rye grass, by a fungus called *Pithomyces chartartum.* This fungus is widely distributed and occurs naturally within dead plant material at the base of standing pasture. FE has been recorded in sheep and cattle on mainland south eastern Australia. These cases appear to be rare, sporadic and vary between years. Although no cases of FE have been reported in Tasmanian sheep, the Department identified a number of suspect cases in Tasmanian dairy herds during autumn 2006. The disease is seasonally common in New Zealand.

Signs of Disease

The disease may be seen in stock between several days and several weeks following pick-up of sporidesmin from the pasture. The toxin is absorbed from the intestine and reaches the liver, where it causes severe damage to bile ducts and liver cells. All the outward signs of FE result from the liver damage caused by sporidesmin.

The signs of FE range from mild photosensitisation (sunburn) to severe jaundice and death, depending on the amount of sporidesmin consumed. Sunburn is the most consistent sign, and usually affects the exposed areas of the skin of the face, ears, teats, and vulva, and areas of skin lacking dark pigmentation, *i.e.* areas covered by white hair. The skin over these areas becomes reddened, and then goes crusty and dark. It eventually peels off leaving large raw areas, which are susceptible to infections. The sunburn is often accompanied by watery swelling of the underlying tissues. Jaundice (yellowing of mucous membranes) is often seen at this stage.

Affected animals lose weight rapidly. Most animals recover from the acute phase, but tend to be unthrifty, often taking many months to regain condition. Some never recover, and either die or are culled. In dairy cattle, the udder and teats are often severely affected, and milk production drops sharply. Loss of weight and general illness are often severe, and death, although uncommon, can occur up to months after the initial liver damage occurs.

Occurrence

Outbreaks of FE typically occur when weather conditions suitable for rapid fungus growth and spore production are combined with abundant dead, recently killed plant material, which favours fungal growth. The fungus requires warm, humid weather and light rain (or irrigation) for growth. This is most likely to be a problem in autumn when the summer has been hot and dry, the pasture well eaten back, and rains fall when the ground is still warm. In such conditions both pasture and grass grow rapidly. The fungus producing sporidesmin is normally not visible to the naked eye. It multiplies by producing millions of spores which are coated with the toxin sporidesmin. Freshly produced spores are the most toxic; if fungal growth stops after a change in the weather, the residual spores on the pasture lose their toxicity within one or two weeks.

The fungus will grow on most pasture plants, but it grows best on perennial ryegrass. It grows in the dead pasture litter at the base of the plants. When the fungus reaches toxic levels, animals grazing short pasture at high stocking rates are at greatest risk.

Prevention and Control

Although the basis of prevention of FE is stock management, one of the difficulties in preventing FE is predicting the occurrence of the disease. Identify potential problem pastures and deal with them before high risk periods. During high risk periods or during an outbreak, the following actions may help to minimise the intake of toxic pasture:

- Shift stock to the longest pasture possible, and try to avoid very close grazing.
- Avoid paddocks cut for hay or late-topped. These are likely to be more toxic because of greater quantities of pasture litter. If topping must be carried out, ensure topped material is removed.
- In general, paddocks sheltered by windbreaks or hills are more dangerous and should be avoided.
- It is believed that warmer northern slopes may carry higher spore numbers and should be avoided in favour of cooler southern slopes during outbreaks.
- Feed hay or other supplements to preserve ground feed and minimise close grazing of pasture. Don't push stock to eat into the base of the sward where spore concentration is highest.
- Summer-growing crops are generally safer than pastures, and stock should be given as much access to these as possible where they are available.
- On irrigated farms, if pasture is short and grazing pressure is heavy, farm irrigation may be valuable if used immediately.
- Alternate grazing between native and improved pastures if feasible.

Fungicides have been used in New Zealand where FE commonly occurs, but probably cannot be justified economically in Australia. High doses of zinc can be used to reduce liver damage and production losses, however this must be administered at the time of, or before, animals ingest sporidesmin. Daily drenching, in-feed and drinking water have been used to administer zinc. Slow-release intra-rumen zinc boluses are also used overseas, but are currently not available in Australia. There are potential side effects with prolonged zinc dosing and these should be discussed with your veterinarian. Monitoring of pastures by undertaking spore counts is used in some countries to provide an early warning system.

Treatment

If FE is suspected, a veterinary practitioner should be called. Although there is no primary treatment for FE, a veterinarian will be able to provide supportive treatments, such as antibiotics to control secondary infections and provide advice on longer term care of affected stock. Importantly, affected animals should be sheltered from direct sunlight if possible. In dairy herds, affected cows should be dried off and shifted to low-risk pasture to ensure recovery and satisfactory future production.

ENZOOTIC BOVINE LEUCOSIS (EBL)

EBL is a viral disease of cattle. In most cases, the disease will not progress beyond lymphocytosis (*i.e.* too many lymphocytes in the blood), in which case the affected cattle will not develop clinical signs, will not suffer and there will be no loss in production. However, in some cases, the disease will develop into cancer of the lymph nodes (lymphosarcoma) and, from there, the cancer spreads into internal organs. Currently, there is no effective treatment for EBL.

Species are Affected

Cattle. Dairy cattle are more often affected than beef cattle. There is no evidence of it naturally infecting other species. It does not affect humans and any virus in the milk is destroyed by the pasteurisation process.

EBL Present in Tasmania

The Tasmanian dairy industry and the Department of Primary Industries (now DPIPWE) have been managing an EBL eradication campaign in Tasmania since 1994. Over the past 12 years, surveillance has identified EBL-positive animals in just two Tasmanian herds. Both were animals born on the mainland and both properties were quarantined until the infected animals were culled and tests confirmed the herds EBL-free. Currently, there are no known EBL-positive herds in Tasmania. A survey of beef herds in Tasmania in 1999 found no evidence of the disease in beef cattle. In the period August to December 2009, Tasmania participated in a national EBL testing programme. All 442 of Tasmania's dairy herds were negative, which means Tasmania is considered to be EBL-free.

Significant for Tasmania

EBL is a notifiable disease. The cattle that are affected but do not develop clinical signs do not appear to suffer and there is no obvious loss of production. But cattle that do develop the clinical signs can suffer considerably and will eventually die. The disease, therefore, has some welfare and productivity consequences. There are increasing international restrictions on the trade of cattle, semen, ova and milk products from affected herds and regions. Many of our competitors in the world markets have either eradicated EBL and gained formal EBL-freedom status or are in the process of doing so. Without formal recognition of EBL Freedom, we may lose some market access or opportunities. Under a 2008 national agreement, the dairy industries in all states are working together to get Australia formally recognised as being EBL Free.

Clinical Signs

Most cattle with EBL will not progress beyond lymphocytosis and show no clinical signs – and indeed be healthy. But in some cases, the animal will become obviously ill as the cancer develops and then spreads from the lymph nodes to internal organs. The clinical signs will vary somewhat according to the internal organ affected. They may include paralysis (if the spine is affected), breathing difficulty and/or listlessness – and may show none of these signs until very late in the disease's progress. The first signs you are most likely to see are small lumps on the skin or in the lymph nodes just under the skin – most commonly, but not always, in the shoulder and neck area or above the udder. It is rare to see the signs of EBL in young cattle.

How is it Spread

It can be spread from dam to calf either in utero or via the milk. It can be spread from cow to cow by blood transfer. Risks include hyperdermic needles, dehorning equipment and rectal pregnancy tests where equipment is not changed or disinfected between animals.

EBL Eradication

While the Tasmanian eradication programme has been successful, a very small number of herds were still testing positive on the mainland. In October 2008, all the State DPIs and industry bodies agreed to support a national EBL eradication campaign to clear up the few remaining infections and then move towards formal OIE (World Animal Health Organisation) EBL Freedom status for Australia as a whole. The Tasmanian eradication campaign had been based on an intense run of bulk milk testing from 1994 to 2003. Each dairy herd was tested three times a year. Testing since 2003 has been less intense. Under the national EBL eradication programme, all states undertook an EBL testing programme with a target of achieving provisional EBL freedom by the end of 2009. Tasmania's EBL testing programme was completed by that date and the results showed that all 442 of Tasmania's dairy herds tested negative.

Under the testing programme, herds with less than 200 cows had one bulk milk test. Where a herd was larger than 200 cows, it was broken down into sub-samples of 200 cows. Essentially, the milk from 200 cows was pooled and then tested – this is known as an 'intensive milk test'. Once all states have completed their EBL testing programmes, and providing all results are negative, the Australian dairy herd will have provisional freedom status. The ultimate goal of full freedom from EBL will involve each herd having one bulk milk test in each of the next three years. Providing all results in this three year period are negative, formal EBL freedom will then be recognised internationally. The milk processors will be collecting the samples and forwarding them to the labs. As this is an Industry control programme, the milk processors will accept the cost of testing. It is then up to the processor to determine how to manage that cost. Tasmania does not have a farmer funded Industry Disease Compensation fund for the EBL eradication programme.

If the testing programme does identify an EBL positive herd in Tasmania in the future, DPIPWE will investigate the farm to identify the individual EBL infected animals and facilitate eradication of the disease.

Biosecurity Practices

The risk of introducing EBL into your herd is low and will get progressively lower as Australia moves towards EBL-free status. With all dairy herds around Australia being tested every year until 2012 and, so far, all test results coming back negative, the risk of you bringing EBL onto your property through cattle you have bought is very low. The biosecurity measures you should take to prevent EBL are what you should be doing anyway-avoid transferring blood between cattle during examination or treatment. Any equipment that is capable of carrying blood from one animal to another is a biosecurity risk. Equipment such as dehorning gear, nose tongs, oral speculums and other instruments should be cleaned and disinfected between each animal. Other equipment such as needles, rectal examination gloves etc. are disposable and should be properly disposed of and not be used on another animal. Although the risk of introducing EBL through the purchase of a beef bull is low, there is still a risk. This should be managed by getting any beef bulls tested before they enter the herd. EBL is known to occur in beef cattle in Northern Australia.

BRUCELLOSIS IN CATTLE

Whilst most farmers know brucellosis means trouble, many are unsure of the exact nature of the disease. Brucellosis is the name given to the disease caused by the *Brucella* family of bacteria. There are five Brucella bacteria each causing a different form of the disease.

- *Brucella abortus*-affects cattle, causing bovine brucellosis (contagious abortion)-sometimes affects horses, causing fistulous withers.
- *Brucella ovis*-affects sheep, causing ovine brucellosis.
- *Brucella melintensis*-mainly affects female goats, causing caprine brucellosis-can also affect female sheep.
- *Brucella suis*-affects pigs, causing swine brucellosis-it has also been isolated from horses.
- *Brucella canis*-affects dogs, causing canine brucellosis.

The *Brucella* diseases occur throughout the world and, excepting ovine brucellosis, are zoonotic, that is they can be spread from animals to humans. Brucellosis in humans caused by *Brucella abortus* was known as undulant fever in Australia, before this disease was eradicated. It is an occupational disease of people who work with animals, such as veterinarians, farmers and abattoir personnel.

In animals the *Brucella* bacteria localise and multiply in the reproductive organs. In males this often results in reduced fertility. Pregnant females can suffer abortion, stillbirth or early death of the offspring when the uterus becomes infected. The disease can spread to other animals if they eat infected afterbirth, fluids or any contaminated feed. *Brucella* bacteria can also localise in mammary glands, (infecting milk) and in limb joints (causing arthritis).

Brucellosis in Cattle

Bovine brucellosis or contagious abortion causes mass abortion in cattle herds. Most affected cows remain carriers and suffer continuing reproductive problems. In Australia, Tasmania led the way in the eradication of bovine brucellosis with a rigorous test and slaughter scheme and strict quarantine measures. Other States followed Tasmania's example and Australia as a whole is now declared free of the disease. This status is recognised internationally.

Eradication of bovine brucellosis has enhanced Australia's reputation in expanding export markets for cattle and beef products. To protect this reputation and to ensure that Tasmania remains free of this disease, any abortions in cattle should be investigated by a veterinary practitioner and serious outbreaks can be referred to the Department of Primary Industries and Water on 1800 675 888.

Other Forms of Brucellosis

None of the three forms of the disease as listed below occurs in Tasmania. Swine brucellosis is a disease that affects reproduction in pigs. Although abortions are unusual, stillbirths are common and young piglets born with the infection have a high mortality. The disease appears to be confined to the north of Australia, occurring mainly in Queensland. Canine brucellosis causes abortions and infertility in dogs. It does not occur in Australia but has been reported in all the other continents except Africa. Dogs from the UK must be tested for canine brucellosis and found negative before they can be imported into Australia.

Caprine brucellosis causes abortion and udder infection in goats and sheep. The disease does not occur in Australia but it is common in the Mediterranean region, Asia and Latin America. The bacterium responsible can also infect humans, causing Malta Fever. Human infection usually occurs from consuming contaminated milk, milk products or uncooked meat. Horses occasionally become infected with *Brucella abortus,* and *Brucella suis,* and the problem is then called fistulous withers. Chronic draining abscesses occur, usually in the withers region, and surgery may be necessary to completely clean up the infection. Because *Brucella abortus* is involved there is an added risk that the infection can be transferred to humans or other animals, especially cattle. In Australia, however, horses are free of *Brucella abortus* bacterium because of the eradication programme for bovine brucellosis.

4

Diseases and Disorders of Cattle

CONGENITAL DISORDERS

The cause of many congenital defects is unknown, but some are inherited. The most common inheritance patternis as a simple recessive trait. The defective calfreceives a recessive gene from its sire and one from itsdam. A few congenital defects are known to be causedby genes with incomplete dominance and a few arecaused by two or more sets of genes. Genetically caused congenital defects usually run infamilies. The parents of a genetically defective calf willgenerally have at least one ancestor in common. Whenmore than one genetically caused defective calf is bornin a herd in the same calving season, their dams areusually related (for example, half sisters) and are siredby the same bull. A change in the breeding programme isrequired to correct this situation.

Many congenital defects are caused by environmental factors. These include the level of nutrition, excess orshortages of certain nutrients, toxic plants or other toxic substances, infectious diseases, and extremes in temperature during pregnancy. Most environmentally caused congenital defects will occur during a short period of the calving season, from cows that were managed as a group. After proper diagnosis, a change in management is necessary to correct these conditions.

DIAGNOSING THE CAUSE

The cause of defects, the breeder must have good records and know why every calf dies. Breeding records which include sire and dam of each calf and breeding date are needed. Blood typing or DNA typing of the calf and possible parents can be used to help determine parentage. The calf must be alive and atleast one month old when the blood sample is obtained for blood typing. Management records should include which cows were in groups during each time period. Most breeders have a list of which cows are in each pasture. A date in and out of the pasture usually will help identify problems. Feed analysis reports, toxic plants present, and herd health and vaccination programmes are also of value.

Meaningful the cause of death is important in controlling diseases as well as congenital defects. The cause of some deaths will be obvious, others will be much more difficult. If the breeder does not know the cause.

Genetic Defects

Dwarfism. There are several types of dwarfism caused by both environment and genetics. Each of the three genetically caused dwarfisms discussed here are different traits caused by different sets ofgenes.

- Snorter dwarfism causes short, blocky appearance with deformed bone growth in the nasal passages which causes difficulty in breathing. Inherited as a simple recessive trait.
- Long head dwarfism causes small size but does not affect the bone growth in nasal passages. Inherited as a simple recessive trait.
- Compress dwarfism is inherited as incomplete dominance. An individual with one compress gene and one normal gene has an extremely compressed body conformation. The individual with two compress genes is a dwarf and the calf dies at or soon after birth.

Water head (internal hydrocephalus). Excess fluid is present in the brain. Calves are usually born dead or die shortly after birth.

Environmental factors can cause the disease, as well as being inherited as a simple recessive trait. Marble bone (osteopetrosis). The calves are usually born dead two to four weeks early. Bones are solid and do not contain marrow, making them very brittle and easily broken. Inherited as a simple recessive trait.

Hairlessness (hypotrichosis). Partial to almost complete lack of hair. Hair develops and is lost so an affected animal will vary somewhat in expression from month to month. Inherited as a simple recessive trait.

Rigid joints (arthrogryposis). Many environmentally caused forms appear but one form is inherited as a simple recessive trait. The joints of all four legs are fixed symmetrically and a cleft palate is present.

Extra toes (polydactyly). One or both front feet are usually affected, but all four may have the outerdew claw develop into an extra toe. Atleast two sets of genes are involved in the inheritance of this trait.

Mulefoot (syndactyly). The two toes are fused together to produce only one toe. The front feet are most often affected, but all four may be affected. These cattle cannot tolerate hot temperatures. Inherited as a simple recessive trait.

Weaver calf (progressive bovine my eloencephalopathy). Calves start developing a weaving gait at 6-8 months and get progressively worse until death at 12-20 months. Inherited as a simple recessive trait.

Photosensitivity (protoporphyria). Animals are sensitive to sunlight and develop scabs and open sores when exposed to sunlight. The liver is also affected and the animals may suffer from seizures. Inherited as a simple recessive trait.

Bulldog (achondroplasia). This trait is inherited as an incomplete dominant. The homozygous may be aborted dead at 6-8 months gestation, and has acompressed skull, nose divided by furrows and shortened upper jaw, giving the bulldog facial appearance. The heterozygous calf is small and heavy-muscled.

Double muscling. Animals are extremely heavily muscled. However, considerable variation exists in the expression of this trait. Inherited as a simple recessive trait.

Parrot mouth (brachygnathia inferior). One type of parrot mouth is inherited as a simple recessive trait. The more common cause of teeth and denture pads not meeting is a quantitative trait caused by several sets of genes. This can cause either an under or over shot jaw with varying degrees of expression.

Cryptorchidism. One or both testicles fail to descend into the scrotum. Inherited as a sex limited trait and probably involves at least two sets of genes.

Prolonged gestation. The fetus fails to trigger parturition. Parturition must be induced or the calf removed. The calf is often extremely large and of tendies. Inherited as a simple recessive trait.

White eyes (Oculocutaneous Hypopigmentation). Hair coat is a bleached colour and the iris is pale blue around the pupil with tan periphery. Inherited as a simple recessive trait.

Many other genetically caused undesirable traits are known. The beef cattle geneticist at your land grant university will have knowledge of most of them and will beable to help if a problem arises.

Many abnormal conditions are not genetically caused. Two headed calves and calves with extra legsare caused by mistakes in development and not thegenetic makeup of the individual or its parents. Freemartin heifers are caused by circulation of the malet win's hormones through the developing female fetus. Some hydrocephalus can be caused by BVD (bovinevirus diarrhea) infection during pregnancy. Crippled-calfdisease is caused by the cow eating lupines between days 40 and 60 of pregnancy. Flexed pasterns (contractedflexor tendons) is usually caused by a large fetus developing in a small uterus. However, both crippled calf and flexed pasterns can also be genetically caused, inherited as simple recessive traits.

CONTROLLING GENETIC DISEASES

The greatest control of genetic diseases is to avoid animals that carry these genes. Bulls or semen should be purchased from reputable breeders, produced by parents who are not known to carry undesirable genes. Long established inbred lines that have not recently produced genetic undesirables are usually quite safe. Commercial producers who use a crossbreeding system rarely have a problem. The elite purebred breeder or owner of Al bulls may wish to test for simply inherited traits before bulls or donor cows are heavily used. If the undesirable trait is dominant, no test is needed since the animal would show the trait even if only one dominant gene is present. If the trait is inherited as incomplete dominance, the individual that has only one undesired gene can usually be identified and testing is not needed. Testing is usually useful only when the trait is inherited as a simple recessive trait.

The slightest expensive test is to mate the animals to ones having that undesired trait. For example, if horns are not desired, the polled animal to be tested would be mated to horned animals to produce at least 7 calves (P>.99). If any horned calves are produced, the polled animal has one gene for horns. If the undesired trait is lethal, the dead animals cannot be used to make the test. If only one lethal trait is of concern, the test should be made using animals that have produced calves with this lethal trait. At least 16 calves should be produced from these matings (P>.99). If a calf is produced that has this lethal trait, the tested animal has one recessive gene for the trait. If the breeder is concerned about identifying all recessive traits, at least 36 progeny from sire-daughter or mother-son matings should be produced (P>.99). This test is time consuming and expensive and only truly outstanding animals will be able to pay for it. All calves from these matings must be observed very closely and all recessive traits recorded. The tested animal will have a recessive gene for any recessive traits observed.

What do Do with Carriers

The animal's desirable genes should be weighed against its undesirable genes. If the desirable genes can be found in other animals without the undesirable gene, carriers should be slaughtered and replaced. When the production traits are superior, these animals can be used in a cross breeding programme to produce beef. Heifers should not be kept for breeding. If the individual is extremely superior in production traits, a superior son can be produced that does not carry the undesirable gene. The outstanding carrier animal would be mated to a small group of very outstanding individuals. The best two to four sons produced would be selected and used in test matings to known carrier cows. The best one that does not carry the undesired gene would then be used and all carriers slaughtered. This would take several years and only truly superior individuals could justify such a procedure. In most cases, the animal that carries the undesirable recessive gene should not be used to produce breeding animals. Daughters should be worked out of the herd and replaced with superior animals that do not carry undesirable genes. Purebred breeders should work with their breed associations, extension and university personnel, and veterinarian to eliminate and avoid problems.

Ethical and Legal Considerations

Serious ethical and legal problems are involved in selling known carrier cattle or progeny of known carriers. A seed stock producer in this position should be completely honest with the buyer. It is doubtful that he should sell possible carriers, under any circumstances, to a youngster or to someone who is just getting started in business and may not have the knowledge to understand the consequences of using offspring from known carriers. Selling carriers without informing the buyer will ultimately reduce the confidence that buyers have in the breeder and may eventually reflect negatively on the entire breed.

GENETIC ABNORMALITIES IN BEEF CATTLE

Hereditary defects can cause abortion or be present at time of birth. They are uncommon but do occur in most breeds of cattle. Defects are abnormalities in skeleton, body form, and body functions. Abnormalities may result from genetic or environmental causes. When the environment is the cause, adjustments can reduce further economic losses. However, genetic (inherited) causes are much more complex and difficult to correct.

Environmental Causes

Environmental or non-genetic causes have the same economic results as genetic causes but are far easier to rectify. Simply correcting the environment will remove the problem. There are many environmental factors, including disease and diet. Certain conditions show that an abnormality is likely to be environmental in nature:

- The abnormality coincided with an environmental factor and was absent upon removal of the factor.
- The abnormality occurred in groups of non-related individuals.
- The symptoms are similar to those of an abnormality known to result from environmental factors.

Genetic Causes

Chromosomes inherited from parents determine an animal's genetic make-up. There are many genes in each chromosome. Genetic abnormalities occur when genes are missing, in excess, mutated or in the wrong location (translocation). A few genes can directly cause an abnormality, however, these are rare. Usually, these genes are recessive, meaning two must be present to cause an abnormality. Both parents must be carriers of the gene for a calf to be abnormal. In this case, only one of every four offspring will be abnormal. Two will be carriers and one will be normal. Certain conditions show that an abnormality is likely to have a genetic origin:

- The abnormality is more common in a group of related animals.
- The symptoms are similar to those of an abnormality identified through test matings. Study of an animal's chromosomes using blood samples can identify several genetic defects.

COMMON GENETIC DEFECTS

Hypotrichosis (Hairlessness)

Hairlessness occurs in several breeds of beef cattle. It expresses itself as complete or partial loss of hair. Calves are often born with no hair but will grow a short curly coat of hair with age. Affected individuals are prone to environmental stress (cold and wet) and skin infections are more prevalent. A recessive gene causes hairlessness.

Alopecia Anemia

This syndrome has recently been identified in the Polled Hereford breed. At the time of birth, alopecia anaemia may be mistaken for hairlessness. Affected calves are often small at birth, have a dirty-faced appearance, and have protruding tongue and eyes.

Hair is wiry, tightly curled or absent while wrinkled skin gives the appearance of advanced aging. Calves are lethargic, cannot tolerate stress and are very prone to disease. Few survive past six months of age. Malfunction of the skeletal structure results in reduced red blood cell production (anaemia). Alopecia anaemia occurs in families but the exact mode of transmission is unknown.

Translocations

A translocation occurs when part of a chromosome breaks off and attaches to another chromosome. The 1/29 translocation has been identified in the Simmental, Charolais and Blonde D'Aquitaine breeds. The 14/20 translocation occurs in most Continental breeds. Translocations affect fertility but no other production traits. Carriers of translocations have reduced conception rates and increased abortion rates. Blood analysis allows easy identification of carriers.

Beta-mannosidosis (Beta-man)

The Beta-man disorder is due to a recessive gene that produces a defective enzyme. The result is the birth of calves that never get up and eventually die. The syndrome occurs in the Salers breed and a blood test is available for identifying carriers.

Syndactyly (Mulefoot)

Syndactyly refers to the fusion of the two toes of the foot. Caused by a recessive gene, mulefoot most often affects the front feet. This condition occurs in the Aberdeen Angus breed.

Other genetic defects exist, most being of very low frequency.

What Should You Do?

When you suspect that you have a problem calf, consult your veterinarian and OMAFRA extension specialist. Investigate all symptoms and possible causes before concluding the problem is genetic or environmental. When the cause is genetic, contact the breed association and give them a full report of the findings. Progressive breed associations are working to reduce the frequency of genetic abnormalities within their breed. To avoid further abnormalities in your herd without culling female carriers, use non-carrier bulls unrelated to your herd. Practice no inbreeding within the herd. Crossbreeding to a different breed is another alternative.

CONGENITAL ERYTHROPOIETIC PORPHYRIA

Congenital erythropoietic porphyria is a rare hereditary disease of cattle, pigs, cats, and humans in which defective hemoglobin formation results in production of an excess of Type I porphyrins in the nuclei of developing normoblasts. The defect in cattle is inherited as a simple autosomal recessive and is usually confined to herds in which inbreeding or close line-breeding is practiced. The condition has been recognized in the USA, Canada, Denmark, Jamaica, England, South Africa, Australia, and Argentina. This broad geographic distribution indicates that the disease likely occurs worldwide and probably affects all meat-producing animals, especially cattle, swine, and sheep.

Heterozygous animals seem to be normal, but homozygous recessive animals are affected at birth with reddish brown discoloration of the teeth, bones, and urine that persists for the life of the animal. The inherited enzymatic defect causes deficient activity of uroporphyrinogen III synthase—an essential part of porphyrin-heme biosynthesis.

Uroporphyrinogen III cosynthetase is the enzyme that is deficient. The urine contains an excess of coproporphyrin I and uroporphyrin I; in affected animals, the colour is amber or reddish brown. Bones, urine, and teeth (especially the deciduous teeth) fluoresce pink when irradiated with near-ultraviolet light. Prolonged exposure to sunlight causes typical lesions of photosensitization with hyperemia, vesicle formation, and superficial necrosis of unpigmented portions of the skin. The severity of the skin lesions depends on the intensity of the solar radiation and the extent of cutaneous pigmentation occurring in specific families of animals. A normochromic, hemolytic anemia with macrocytes and microcytes and marked basophilic stippling develops. Splenomegaly eventually occurs. The texture of bones is not altered except in cases in which bones have increased fragility due to a diminished cortex. Affected animals are generally of medium to good condition unless solar injury has occurred. Some animals become progressively unthrifty unless protected from sunlight. A similar disease, bovine protoporphyria, causes photosensitivity only in Limousin cattle and humans.

In humans, a series of porphyrias caused by defective functions of enzymes in porphyrin-heme biosynthesis have been described and grouped according to their presenting clinical signs. These vary broadly and may include severe cutaneous lesions on exposed areas of the body, acute photosensitivity reactions, serious liver damage, and acute attacks of neurologic dysfunction. In animals, the recognized diseases are commonly classified as either congenital erythropoietic porphyria, congenital erythropoietic protoporphyria, or porphyria. It is likely that all of the syndromes described in humans also occur in animals and that a broader classification could be used.

The defect in pigs and cats is extremely rare and differs from the condition in cattle in that photosensitization is not a feature. In pigs and cats, the disease is transmitted as an autosomal dominant. In pigs, even with high levels of porphyrins in the blood, photodynamic dermatitis does not occur. The disease has been reported only in Denmark and

New Zealand; in cats, it has been recognized only in the USA. Diagnosis should be based on the excretion of abnormal uroporphyrins, the brown discoloration of the teeth (which fluoresce when irradiated with near-ultraviolet light), the appearance of discoloured urine, and hemolytic anemia.

The recessive genetic character is widely distributed in cattle, but the clinical condition is comparatively rare. Clinically normal heterozygotes have lower levels of uroporphyrinogen III cosynthetase than do normal animals, but laboratory identification of the carrier state is impractical due to the relatively low incidence of the disease and is not widely used. Morbidity can be controlled by keeping affected animals indoors and out of direct sunlight.

INTEGUMENTARY SYSTEM

Skin

Dermatitis is an inflammation of the skin. A bacterial infection is one cause of dermatitis. During warm, humid weather, the skin and haircoat is more susceptible to bacterial infection and the prevalence of skin diseases is highest. The most common sign is pruritus (itching). This can be followed by skin lesions that progress from reddening and thickening of the skin to bumps, blisters, and crusts or scales. Other causes of dermatitis include viruses, parasites, fungi, and allergens. Pyoderma is dermatitis characterized by the presence of purulent exudate (pus). Dermatitis can develop into pyoderma due to the invasion of pus-forming bacteria. These infections can be superficial or deep pustules with draining tracts. Bacterial dermatitis and pyoderma are commonly associated with skin allergy and mange conditions.

Dermatophytosis, or ringworm, is a result of a pathogenic fungus. This fungus infects the skin of dogs, cats, horses, cattle, pigs, humans, sheep, and goats. The normal habitat is in the skin but can survive in dark humid environments of soil, bedding, carpet, furniture, tack, blankets, brushes, and clippers. Transmission of ringworm occurs through direct contact with infected animals and humans or contaminated environment. The fungus is transmitted through skin contact from a carrier dam to her nursing young. The most susceptible hosts appear to be the young and they often display the characteristic lesions. The fungal infection may not be evident until several months after exposure. The cutaneous disease begins as focal alopecia (hair loss). These round areas of hair loss become scaly with circumscribed edges that may be raised and reddened. Pruritus may or may not be present.

Use direct microscopic examination of skin scrapings and skin fluorescent examinations with a ultraviolet lamp (Wood's lamp) to make ringworm diagnosis. Confirm the diagnosis using culture techniques. Since spontaneous recovery after several months is common, the primary objective of topical or oral therapy is to prevent spread of the lesions and spread of infection to other animals and humans.

Dermatophilosis, or rain gall, is a result of a fungus (*Dermatophilus* spp.). This disease is common in horses, cattle, sheep, and goats that live in warm, humid, damp climates. During the rainy season, biting flies may help transmit the disease from infected animals and from wet contaminated soils by acting as a mechanical vector. The cutaneous disease is an exudative dermatitis with scabs. Typical lesions are raised, crusty lumps covered with hair that can be pulled off. Removal of the crust with a tuft of hair (paintbrush lesions) leaves a bare spot. These lesions commonly develop on the lower legs, chest, back, and hips. Use cultures, biopsies, and scrapings to make a definitive diagnosis of this fungal disease. Warts are fibrous tumors of the skin and occasionally of the mucous membranes of animals (especially cattle, dogs, rabbits) and humans. They can be caused by many strains of viruses. The virus is transmitted by direct contact and possibly by arthropods. The cauliflower-type growths occur primarily on the head, neck, and shoulder, in the mouth, and on the vulva and penis.

Pox diseases cause skin lesions by replication through poxviruses in the skin. Animals acquire the virus through the skin or by biting arthropods. Bumps, blisters, pustules, and crusts are the types of skin lesions present in the course of the disease. The pox diseases are named after the affected animals, such as fowlpox, swinepox, and cowpox.

Arthropod parasites are external parasites, or ectoparasites. Their presence, or the dermatitis they cause, is referred to as an infestation instead of an infection. Therefore, external parasites infest an animal. Parasitic infestations of the skin affect the health of animals by causing tissue damage, blood loss, and annoyance. Annoying pests interfere with the animal's ability to eat and sleep, which may result in weight loss. In addition to the skin diseases directly caused by arthropods, many ectoparasites are vectors of infectious diseases, transmitting disease agents from carrier animals to other susceptible animals.

Some flies, such as houseflies, do not suck blood but annoy animals. Other flies, such as horseflies, deer-flies, stableflies, and hornflies, are blood-suckers and cause anemia, as well as, annoyance. Blood-sucking flies, mosquitoes, and gnats aid the transmission of diseases, such as anaplasmosis, bluetongue, leukosis, equine infectious anemia, and heartworms.

Heelflies have larval stages, called cattle grubs that migrate through the body and emerge through the skin on the backs of cattle. Large numbers of cattle grubs may cause migratory damage to internal tissues and the hide. Ticks are subdivided into two groups: hard ticks and soft ticks. The hard ticks attach and feed on animals by sucking blood for several days; many types serve as vectors of diseases. Hard ticks help transmit anaplasmosis and Lyme disease to other animals. Soft ticks common in fowl are intermittent feeders. The immature stages of spinose ear tick, a soft tick, develop in the external ear canal of animals, especially cattle, but the adult ticks are free-living.

Dogs and cats are commonly infested with fleas. Fleas are blood-suckers and can be vectors of the tapeworm, called the flea tapeworm. Fleas are extremely annoying to pets and may cause severe anemia. Lice infestations of animals are more common during the cool and cold months of the year, especially in late winter and early spring. During this time animals are in close contact with one another, their skin has less oil, and lice reproduction is greater. Lice are more common on cattle, swine, and poultry than on other animals. Both biting lice and sucking lice annoy animals and cause skin allergies and hair loss. In large numbers, the sucking lice can cause anemia. Lousy is the condition of an animal with a lice infestation. Lice and their eggs are easily visible on animals with the naked eye.

The entire life cycle of mange mites is completed on or in the skin and ear mites in external ear canals of animals. Transmission occurs through direct contact. Mites infesting the skin of animals cause a condition called mange. Mange is more common in the winter and during times of stress. Mange is common in dogs and swine, occasionally in cattle, and rarely in other animals. Types of mange conditions with hair loss and dermatitis are sarcoptic mange, scabies, and red mange. Ear mites common in dogs and cats do not cause mange but do cause extreme annoyance. Microscopic examination of skin scrapings from infested animals reveals the presence of surface mites or burrowing mites and ear swabs the presence of ear mites.

Nematodes, or roundworms, infect the skin of animals. Examples of nematodes include habronema, on-chocerca, stephanofilaria, and dipetalonema. House-flies and stableflies help transmit habronema larvae that infect wounds and external mucous membranes of horses. They can cause excessive granulation (proud flesh), a condition called summer sores. Onchocerca larvae, transmitted by mosquitoes and gnats, can cause an allergic skin reaction on the face, neck, chest, and underline of horses. Hornflies transmit stephanofilaria to cattle and cause local circumscribed lesions on the underline. Fleas transmit dipetalonema to the skin of dogs but it causes no harm.

THE INTEGUMENTARY SYSTEM

The integumentary system, formed by the skin, hair, nails, and associated glands, enwraps the body. It is the most visible organ system and one of the most complex. Diverse in both form and function—from delicate eyelashes to the thick skin of the soles—the integumentary system protects the body from the outside world and its many harmful substances. It utilizes the Sun's rays while at the same time shielding the body from their damaging effects. In addition, the system helps to regulate body temperature, serves as a minor excretory organ, and makes the inner body aware of its outer environment through sensory receptors.

Design: Parts of the Integumentary System

Integument comes from the Latin word *integumentum,* meaning 'cover' or 'enclosure.' In animals and plants, an integument is any natural outer covering, such as skin, shell, membrane, or husk. The human integumentary system is an external body covering, but also much more. It protects, nourishes, insulates, and cushions. It is absolutely essential to life. Without it, an individual would be attacked immediately by bacteria and die from heat and water loss. The integumentary system is composed primarily of the skin and accessory structures. Those structures include hair, nails, and certain exocrine glands (glands that have ducts or tubes that carry their secretions to the surface of the skin or into body cavities for elimination).

Skin

Although the skin is not often thought of as an organ, such as the heart or liver, medically it is. An organ is any part of the body formed of two or more tissues that performs a specialized function. As an organ, the skin is the largest and heaviest in the body. In an average adult, the skin covers about 21.5 square feet (2 square meters) and accounts for approximately 7 percent of body weight, or about 11 pounds (5 kilograms) in a 160-pound (73-kilogram) person. It ranges in thickness from 0.04 to 0.08 inches (1 to 2 millimetres), but can measure up to 0.2 inches (6 millimetres) thick on the palms of the hands and the soles of the feet. The skin in these areas is referred to as thick skin (skin elsewhere on the body is called thin skin).

The Integumentary System: Words to Know

Apocrine sweat glands (AP-oh-krin): Sweat glands located primarily in the armpit and genital areas.

Arrector pili muscle (ah-REK-tor PI-li): Smooth muscle attached to a hair follicle that, when stimulated, pulls on the follicle, causing the hair shaft to stand upright.

Dermal papillae (DER-mal pah-PILL-ee): Finger-like projections extending upward from the dermis containing blood capillaries, which provide nutrients for the lower layer of the epidermis; also form the characteristic ridges on the skin surface of the hands (fingerprints) and feet.

Dermis (DER-miss): Thick, inner layer of the skin.

Eccrine sweat glands (ECK-rin): Body's most numerous sweat glands, which produce watery sweat to maintain normal body temperature.

Epidermis (ep-i-DER-miss): Thin, outer layer of the skin.

Epithelial tissue (ep-i-THEE-lee-al): Tissue that covers the internal and external surfaces of the body and also forms glandular organs.

Integument (in-TEG-ye-ment): In animals and plants, any natural outer covering, such as skin, shell, membrane, or husk.

Keratin (KER-ah-tin): Tough, fibrous, water-resistant protein that forms the outer layers of hair, calluses, and nails and coats the surface of the skin.

Lunula (LOO-noo-la): White, crescent-shaped area of the nail bed near the nail root.

Melanocyte (MEL-ah-no-site): Cell found in the lower epidermis that produces the protein pigment melanin.

Organ (OR-gan): Any part of the body formed of two or more tissues that performs a specialized function.

Sebaceous gland (suh-BAY-shus): Exocrine gland in the dermis that produces sebum.

Sebum (SEE-bum): Mixture of oily substances and fragmented cells secreted by sebaceous glands.

Squamous cells (SKWA-mus): Cells that are flat and scalelike.

Subcutaneous (sub-kew-TAY-nee-us): Tissues between the dermis and the muscles.

The skin has two principal layers: the epidermis and the dermis. The epidermis is the thin, outer layer, and the dermis is the thicker, inner layer. Beneath the dermis lies the subcutaneous layer or hypodermis, which is composed of adipose or fatty tissue. Although not technically part of the skin, it does anchor the skin to the underlying muscles. It also contains the major blood vessels that supply the dermis and houses many white blood cells, which destroy foreign invaders that have entered the body through breaks in the skin.

Epidermis

The epidermis is complete of stratified squamous epithelial tissue. Epithelial tissue covers the internal and external surfaces of the body and also forms glandular organs. Squamous cells are thin and flat like fish scales. Stratified simply means having two or more layers. In short, the epidermis is composed of many layers of thin, flattened cells that fit closely together and are able to withstand a good deal of abuse or friction. The epidermis can be divided into four or five layers. Most important of these are the inner and outer layers. The inner or deepest cell layer is the only layer of the epidermis that receives nutrients (from the underlying dermis). The cells of this layer, called basal cells, are constantly dividing and creating new cells daily, which push the older cells towards the surface. Basal cells produce keratin, an extremely durable and water-resistant fibrous protein.

Another type of cell found in the lower epidermis is the melanocyte. Melanocytes produce melanin, a protein pigment that ranges in colour from yellow to brown to black. The amount of melanin produced determines skin colour, which is a hereditary characteristic. The melanocytes of dark-skinned individuals continuously produce large amounts of melanin. Those of light-skinned individuals produce less. Freckles are the result of melanin clumping in one spot. The outermost layer of the epidermis consists of about twenty to thirty rows of tightly joined flat dead cells. All that is left in these cells is their keratin, which makes this outer layer waterproof. It takes roughly fourteen days for cells to move from the inner layer of the epidermis to the outer layer. Once part of the outer layer, the dead cells remain for another fourteen days or so before flaking off slowly and steadily.

Dermis

The dermis, the second layer of skin, lies between the epidermis and the subcutaneous layer. Much thicker than the epidermis, the dermis contains the accessory skin structures. Hair, sweat glands, and sebaceous (oil) glands are all rooted in the dermis. This layer also contains blood vessels and nerve fibres. Nourished by the blood and oxygen provided by these blood vessels, the cells of the dermis are alive. Connective tissue forms the dermis. Bundles of elastic and collagen (tough fibrous protein) fibres blend into the connective tissue. These fibres provide the dermis strength and flexibility.

The upper layer of the dermis has fingerlike projections that extend into the epidermis. Called dermal papillae, they contain blood capillaries that provide nutrients for the basal cells in the epidermis. On the skin surface of the hands and feet, especially on the tips of the fingers, thumbs, and toes, the dermal papillae form looped and whorled ridges. These print patterns, known as fingerprints or toeprints, increase the gripping ability of the hands and feet. Genetically determined, the patterns are unique to every individual.

Using Fingerprints to Identify Community

Fingerprints are unique to each individual and the patterns never change. People have long known about the distinctiveness of fingerprints, but their use in identifying people did not arise until the nineteenth century. It is generally acknowledged that English scientist Francis Galton (1822–1911) was the first person to devise a system of fingerprint identification. In the 1880s, Galton obtained the first extensive collection of fingerprints for his studies on heredity. He also established a bureau for the registration of civilians by means of fingerprints and measurements.

Galton's ideas were further developed by fellow Englishman Edward R. Henry (1850–1931). In the 1890s, Henry developed a more simplified fingerprint classification system. In 1901, he established England's first fingerprint bureau, called the Fingerprint Branch, within the Scotland Yard police force. Henry's system is still used today in Great Britain and the United States. Within the dermis are sensory receptors for the senses of touch, pressure, heat, cold, and pain. A specific type of receptor exists for each sensation. For pain, the receptors are free nerve endings. For the other sensations, the receptors are encapsulated nerve endings, meaning they have a cellular structure around their endings. The number and type of sensory receptors present in a particular area of skin determines how sensitive that area is to a particular sensation. For example, fingertips have many touch receptors and are quite sensitive. The skin of the upper arm is less sensitive because it has very few touch receptors.

Accessory Structures

The accessory structures of the integumentary system include hair, nails, and sweat and sebaceous glands.

Hair

Roughly 5 million hairs cover the body of an average individual. About 100,000 of those hairs appear on the scalp. Almost every part of the body is covered by hair, except the palms of the hands, the soles of the feet, the sides of the fingers and toes, the lips, and certain parts of the outer genital organs.

Each hair originates from a tiny tubelike structure called a hair follicle that extends deep into the dermis layer. Often, the follicle will project into the subcutaneous layer. Capillaries and nerves attach to the base of the follicle, providing nutrients and sensory information. Inside the base of the follicle, epithelial cells grow and divide, forming the hair bulb or enlarged hair base. Keratin, the primary component in these epithelial cells, coats and stiffens the hair as it grows upward through the follicle. The part of the hair enclosed in the follicle is called the hair root. Once the hair projects from the scalp or skin, it is called a hair shaft.

The older epithelial cells forming the hair root and hair shaft die as they are pushed upward from the nutrient-rich follicle base by newly formed cells. Like the upper layers of the epidermis, the hair shaft is made of dead material, almost entirely protein.

The hair shaft is divided into two layers: the cuticle or outer layer consists of a single layer of flat, overlapping cells; the cortex or inner layer is made mostly of keratin. Hair shafts differ in size, shape, and colour. In the eyebrows, they are short and stiff, but on the scalp they are longer and more flexible. Elsewhere on the body they are nearly invisible. Oval-shaped hair shafts produce wavy hair. Flat or ribbonlike hair shafts produce kinky or curly hair. Perfectly round hair shafts produce straight hair. The different types of melanin-yellow, rust, brown, and black-produced by melanocytes at the follicle base combine to create the many varieties of hair colour, from the palest blonde to the richest black. With age, the production of melanin decreases, and hair colour turns gray. Attached to each hair follicle is a ribbon of smooth muscle called an arrector pili muscle. When stimulated, the muscle contracts and pulls on the follicle, causing the hair shaft to stand upright.

Nails

Nails in humans correspond to the hooves of horses and cattle and the claws of birds and reptiles. Found on the ends of fingers and toes, nails are produced by nail follicles just as hair is produced by hair follicles. The nail root is that portion of the nail embedded in the skin, lying very near the bone of the fingertip. Here, cells produce a stronger form of keratin than is found in hair. As new cells are formed, older cells are pushed forward, forming the nail body or the visible attached portion of the nail. The free edge is that portion of the nail that extends over the tip of the finger or toe. Healthy fingernails grow about 0.04 inches (1 millimetre) per week, slightly faster than toenails. The nail body is made of dead cells, but the nail bed (the tissue underneath the nail body) is alive. The blood vessels running through the nail bed give the otherwise transparent nail body a pink colour. Near the nail root, however, these blood vessels are obscured. The resulting white crescent is called the lunula (from the Latin word *luna*, meaning 'moon').

Sweat Glands

More than 2.5 million sweat glands are distributed over most surfaces of the human body. They are divided into two types: eccrine sweat glands and apocrine sweat glands. Eccrine glands, the more numerous of the two types, are found all over the body. They are especially numerous on the forehead, upper lip, palms, and soles. The glands are simply coiled tubes that originate in the dermis. A duct extends from the gland to the skin's surface, where it opens into a pore. Eccrine glands produce sweat or perspiration, a clear secretion that is 99 percent water. Some salts, traces of waste materials such as urea, and vitamin C form the remainder (the salts give sweat its characteristic salty taste).

Depending on temperature and humidity, an average individual loses 0.6 to 1.7 quarts (0.3 to 0.8 liters) of water every day through sweating. During rigorous physical activity or on a hot day, that amount could rise to 5.3 to 7.4 quarts (5 to 7 liters).

Apocrine glands are found in the armpits, around the nipples, and in the groin. Like eccrine glands, apocrine glands are coiled tubes found in the dermis. However, they are usually larger and their ducts empty into hair follicles. Also, apocrine glands do not function until puberty. At that time, they begin to release an odourless cloudy secretion that contains fatty acids and protein. If the secretion of apocrine glands is allowed to remain on the skin for any length of time, bacteria that lives on the skin breaks down the fatty acids and protein for their growth, creating the unpleasant odour often associated with sweat. Apocrine glands are activated by nerve fibres during periods of pain and stress, but their function in humans is not well understood. Scientists theorize they may act as sexual attractants.

Sebaceous Glands

Sebaceous glands, also known as oil glands, are found in the dermis all over the body, except for the palms and soles. They secrete sebum, a mixture of lipids (fats), proteins, and fragments of dead fatproducing cells. The function of sebum is to prevent the drying of skin and hair. It also contains chemicals that kill bacteria present on the skin surface. While most sebaceous glands secrete sebum through ducts into hair follicles, some secrete sebum directly onto the surface of the skin. Arrector pili muscles, which contract to elevate hairs, also squeeze sebaceous glands, forcing out sebum.

FUNCTIONS OF INTEGUMENTARY SYSTEM

The integumentary system is essential to the body's homeostasis, or ability to maintain the internal balance of its functions regardless of outside conditions. The system works to protect underlying tissues and organs from infections and injury. It also prevents the loss of body fluids. Receiving about one-third of the blood pumped from the heart every minute, the skin and its glands help maintain normal body temperature.

The system also acts as a mini-excretory system, secreting salts, water, and wastes in the form of sweat. Cells in the skin utilize sunlight to create vitamin D, which is necessary for normal bone growth and function. Finally, the skin contains sensory receptors or specialized nerve endings that allow an individual to 'feel' sensations such as touch, pain, pressure, and temperature.

Protection

The outermost epidermal layer of the skin is a barrier between the internal environment of the body and the external world. Keratin, in abundance in this outer layer, waterproofs the body. Without it, handling household chemicals, swimming in a pool, or taking a shower (a necessary everyday activity) would be disastrous to the underlying cells of the body. Not only does keratin keep water out, it also keeps water in. Excessive evaporation or loss of body fluids would result in dehydration and eventual death.

WETTERHAHN'S DEADLY RESEARCH

Karen Wetterhahn (1948–1997) was a chemistry professor at Dartmouth College in Hanover, New Hampshire, where she conducted environmental research projects. During an experiment in August 1996, Wetterhahn spilled a tiny drop of dimethyl mercury (a highly toxic chemical) on her hand. Less than a year later, she was dead. Wetterhahn had been conducting research to determine the effects that heavy metals (metals such as mercury having a high specific gravity) produce on the environment. During her experiment, she was transferring some dimethyl mercury to a tube when she spilled a tiny amount. Although Wetterhahn was wearing latex gloves, the mercury permeated the thin latex and soaked into her skin, passing through its waterproof layers within seconds.

Dimethyl mercury is deadly. Once in the body, it seeps from the bloodstream into brain tissues, causing fatal damage to the central nervous system and the brain. Symptoms of mercury poisoning include loss of motor (movement) control, numbness in the arms and legs, blindness, hearing and speech loss.

Wetterhahn did not feel the effects of the mercury until six months after the accident. Within three months, she was dead. After her death, the U.S. Occupational Safety and Health Administration urged scientists to wear highly resistant laminate gloves (consisting of several bonded layers) under a pair of heavy-duty neoprene gloves when handling compounds such as dimethyl mercury. The thickness of the outer layer of the epidermis, combined with the toughness provided by keratin, also prevents microorganisms and viruses from entering the body.

In addition, sebum secreted by the sebaceous glands helps prevent microorganisms from living and growing on the skin surface. Since it is slightly acidic, sebum creates a condition in which many microorganisms cannot exist. Sebum serves a further protective function by keeping the skin and hair moist; dry skin would crack, allowing viruses and bacteria to enter. If the protective outer layer of the skin is broken because of an injury and microorganisms enter the body, the many blood vessels in the dermis help prevent the microorganisms from reaching internal tissues.

As an immune response, the vessels dilate or expand. This increases the amount of blood flowing to the area, which in turn brings in more white blood cells and other protein factors to battle the infection. Even though the skin forms a protective barrier, it is still slightly permeable or allows certain substances to pass through it. Vitamins A, D, E, and K all pass through the skin and are absorbed in the capillaries in the dermis. Steroid hormones such as estrogen and chemicals such as nicotine also pass through and are absorbed. With this in mind, medical researchers have developed therapeutic patches that are attached to the skin to deliver chemicals or medication (nicotine patches for those individuals trying to quit smoking are an example).

Nails protect the exposed tips of fingers and toes from physical injury. Fingernails also aid the fingers in picking up small objects. Hair serves a protective function, although it is limited. On the head, hair protects the scalp from damaging ultraviolet (UV) radiation from the Sun, cushions the head from physical blows, and insulates the scalp to a degree. On the eyelids, eyelashes prevent airborne particles and insects from entering the eyes. Hairs in the nostrils and the external ear canals perform a similar function.

When stimulated by cold or an emotion such as fear, the arrector pili muscles contract, pulling hair follicles upright. In animals (and in our evolutionary ancestors, who had much more body hair), this action adds warmth by adding a layer of insulating air to the fur. In present-day humans, who have very little body hair, this action seems to serve no purpose other than to create dimples or 'goose bumps' in the skin.

The body is protected against the Sun's harmful UV radiation by melanin, produced by melanocytes in the epidermis. Melanin accumulates within the cells of the epidermis. It then absorbs UV radiation before that radiation can destroy the cells' DNA or deoxyribonucleic acid (large, complex molecules found in the nuclei of cells that carries genetic or hereditary information for an organism's development). Increased exposure to the Sun causes melanocytes to increase their production of melanin. The temporary result is that the skin becomes darker or tanned and is able to withstand further exposure to UV rays. The protection afforded by melanin, however, is limited. Prolonged or excessive exposure to UV radiation eventually damages the skin. It causes elastic fibres in the dermis to clump, and the skin takes on a leathery appearance. Overexposure can also result in melanoma, a tumor composed of melanocytes.

Body Temperature

Normal internal body temperature averages approximately 98.6°F (37°C). The heat-regulating functions of the body are extremely important. If the internal temperature varies more than a few degrees from normal, life-threatening changes take place in the body. Eccrine glands play an important part in maintaining normal body temperature. When the temperature of the body rises due to physical exercise or environmental conditions, the hypothalamus (region of the brain containing many control centres for body functions and emotions) sends signals to the eccrine glands to secrete sweat. When sweat evaporates on the skin surface, it carries large amounts of body heat with it and the skin surface cools.

Because blood carries heat (a form of energy), blood flow is another regulator of body temperature. Under warm conditions, the hypothalamus signals blood vessels in the dermis to dilate or expand. This increases blood flow (and carries excess heat) to the body's surface. Like a radiator, the skin then gives off heat to the surrounding environment. During cold conditions, the hypothalamus signals eccrine glands to stop secreting sweat. It also signals blood vessels in the dermis to constrict or close, which reduces blood flow to the skin surface. As a result, heat is kept within the core of the body.

Excretion and Vitamin D Formation

Excretion is a very minor function of the skin. Sweat does contain salt and urea (a compound produced when the liver breaks down amino acids), but the amounts of these wastes are slight. The kidneys are mainly responsible for removing waste products from the blood.

SANDBLASTING YOUR FACE

For years, workers have cleaned old stone and concrete structures by blasting their surfaces with a spray of fine sand. In the late 1990s, dermatologists and beauty salon owners in the United States began using a similar technique to remove the signs of aging on people's faces. The new treatment, already used in Europe since the early 1990s, is called microdermabrasion. A machine blows tiny sterile sand crystals onto the skin of the face, then suctions them off. The crystals rub off the top layer of the skin, helping remove wrinkles.

The procedure is relatively painless and quick. However, its effects are not permanent, and it only removes fine lines. Deep lines around the mouth, crow's feet around the eyes, and deep lines on the forehead remain, although they are softened. As explained earlier, too much sunlight is harmful to the body. A limited amount, however, is beneficial. In the lower layers of the epidermis, cells contain a form of cholesterol (fatlike substance produced by the liver that is an essential part of cell membranes and body chemicals). When exposed to UV radiation, that cholesterol changes into vitamin D, which the body uses to absorb calcium and phosphorus from food in the small intestine. Those two minerals are then used to build and maintain bones and teeth, among other functions.

Sensory Reception

The main function of the sensory receptors in the dermis is to provide the brain with information about the external world and its effect on the skin. Thus, they alert the body to the possible tissue-damaging effects of extreme heat or cold or something that is pressing hard against the skin. They also transmit pleasant sensations, such as a gentle breeze blowing across the face or the soft caress of a loved one. The receptors differ in their sensitivity. Touch receptors are the most sensitive, responding to the slightest contact. Found mainly in the fingers, tongue, and lips, they number about 500,000.

Pain receptors, however, do not react unless the stimulus is strong enough. Located all over the body, pain receptors number between three and four million. Their high numbers indicate their importance to the body. Receptors send their information to the brain to be interpreted. The brain then directs the body to respond, whether to remove itself from the situation or remain. Sensation, therefore, is a function of the brain and the nervous system.

AILMENTS: INTEGUMENTARY SYSTEM

Unlike some other body systems, the integumentary system quickly shows when it is afflicted by an aliment or malady. Over one thousand different aliments can affect the skin. The most common skin disorders are those caused by allergies or bacterial or fungal infections. Burns and skin cancers, although less common, are more dangerous. In some cases, they can be lethal.

Acne

Acne is a skin disease marked by pimples on the face, chest, and back. The most common skin disease, acne affects an estimated 17 to 28 million people in the United States. Although it can strike people at any age, acne usually begins at puberty and worsens during adolescence. At puberty, increased levels of androgens (male hormones) cause the sebaceous glands to secrete an excessive amount of sebum into hair follicles. The excess sebum combines with dead, sticky skin cells to form a hard plug that blocks the follicle. Bacteria that normally lives on the skin then invades the blocked follicle. Weakened, the follicle bursts open, releasing the sebum, bacteria, skin cells, and white blood cells into the surrounding tissues. A pimple then forms.

Treatment for acne depends on whether the condition is mild, moderate, or severe. The goal is to reduce sebum production, remove dead skin cells, and kill skin bacteria. In very mild cases, keeping the skin clean by washing with a mild soap is recommended. In other cases, medications applied directly to the skin or taken orally may be prescribed in combination with gentle cleansing.

Athlete's Foot

Athlete's foot is a common fungus infection in which the skin between the toes becomes itchy and sore, cracking and peeling away. Properly known as tinea pedis, the infection received its common name because the infectioncausing fungi grow well in warm, damp areas such as in and around swimming pools, showers, and locker rooms (areas commonly used by athletes). The fungi that cause athlete's foot are unusual in that they live exclusively on dead body tissue (hair, the outer layer of skin, and nails). Researchers do not know exactly why some people develop the condition and others do not. It is known that sweaty feet, tight shoes, and the failure to dry feet well after swimming or bathing all contribute to the growth of the fungus.

Symptoms of athlete's foot include itchy, sore skin on the toes, with scaling, cracking, inflammation, and blisters. If the blisters break, raw patches of tissue may be exposed. If the infection spreads, itching and burning may increase. Athlete's foot usually responds well to treatment. Simple cases are treated with antifungal creams or sprays. In more severe cases, an oral antifungal medication may be prescribed.

Burns

There are few threats more serious to the skin than burns. Burns are injuries to tissues caused by intense heat, electricity, UV radiation (sunburn), or certain chemicals (such as acids). When skin is burned and cells are destroyed, the body readily loses its precious supply of fluids. Dehydration can follow, leading to a shutdown of the kidneys, a life-threatening condition. Infection of the dead tissue by bacteria and viruses occurs one to two days after skin has been burned. Infection is the leading cause of death in burn victims. Burns are classified according to their severity or depth: first-, second-, or third-degree burns. First-degree burns occur when only the epidermis is damaged. The burned area is painful, the outer skin is reddened, and slight swelling may be present. Sunburns are usually first-degree burns. Although they may cause discomfort, these minor burns are usually not serious and heal within a few days.

Second-degree burns occur when the epidermis and the upper region of the dermis are damaged. The burned area is red, painful, and may have a wet, shiny appearance because of exposed tissue. Blisters may form. These moderate burns take longer to heal. If the blisters are not broken and care is taken to prevent infection, the burned skin may regenerate or regrow without permanent scars. Third-degree burns occur when the entire depth of skin is destroyed. Because nerve endings have been destroyed, the burned area has no sensitivity. The area may be blackened or gray-white in colour. Muscle tissue and bone underneath may be damaged. In these serious to critical burns, regeneration of the skin is not possible. Skin grafting—taking a piece of skin from an unburned portion of the burn victim's body and transplanting it to the burned area—must be done to cover the exposed tissues. Third-degree burns take weeks to heal and will leave permanent scarring.

Dermatitis

Dermatitis is any inflammation of the skin. There are many types of dermatitis and most are characterized by a pink or red rash that itches. Two common types are contact dermatitis and seborrheic dermatitis. Contact dermatitis is an allergic reaction to something that irritates the skin. It usually appears within forty-eight hours after touching or brushing against a substance to which the skin is sensitive. The resin in poison ivy, poison oak, and poison sumac is the most common source of contact dermatitis. The skin of some people may also be irritated by certain flowers, herbs, and vegetables. Chemical irritants that can cause contact dermatitis include chlorine, cleaners, detergents and soaps, fabric softeners, perfumes, glues, and topical medications (those applied on the skin). Contact dermatitis can be treated with medicated creams or ointments and oral antihistamines and antibiotics.

ARTIFICIAL SKIN

Artificial skin, the synthetic or manmade equivalent of human skin, was first developed in the 1970s. Since then, the lives of many severely burned people have been saved through the use of artificial skin. In the 1970s, John F. Burke, chief of trauma services at Massachusetts General Hospital in Boston, and Ioannis V. Yannas, chemistry professor at Massachusetts Institute of Technology in Cambridge, teamed up to develop some type of human skin replacement. In their research, the two men found that collagen fibres (protein found in human skin) and a long sugar molecule (called a polymer) could be combined to form a porous material that resembles skin. They then created a kind of artificial skin using polymers from shark cartilage and collagen from cowhide.

Burke and Yannas soon discovered that artificial skin acts like a framework onto which new skin tissue and blood vessels grow. As the new skin grows, the cowhide and shark substances from the artificial skin are broken down and absorbed by the body. Researchers used their artificial skin on their first patient, a woman who had suffered burns over half her body. After peeling away her burned skin, Burke applied a layer of artificial skin and, where possible, grafted or added on some of her own unburned skin. Three weeks later, the woman's new skin, the same colour as her unburned skin, was growing at an amazingly healthy rate.

With continued research and development, synthetic skin may become a more common treatment for burns and other serious skin disorders. Seborrheic dermatitis, known commonly as seborrhea, appears as red, inflamed skin covered by greasy or dry scales that may be white, yellow, or gray. These scaly lesions appear usually on the scalp, hairline, and face. Dandruff is a mild form of seborrheic dermatitis. Medical researchers do not know the exact cause of this skin disease. They believe that a high-fat diet, alcohol, stress, oily skin, infrequent shampooing, and weather extremes (hot or cold) may play some role. The disease may be treated with special shampoos that help soften and remove the scaly lesions. In more severe cases, medicated creams or shampoos containing coal tar may be prescribed.

Psoriasis

Psoriasis is a chronic (long-term) skin disease characterized by inflamed lesions with silvery-white scabs of dead skin. The disease affects roughly four million people in the United States, women slightly more than men. It is most common in fair-skinned people. Normal skin cells mature and replace dead skin cells every twenty-eight to thirty days. Psoriasis causes skin cells to mature in less than a week. Because the body cannot shed old skin as rapidly as new cells are rising to the surface, raised patches of dead skin develop. These patches are seen on the arms, back, chest, elbows, legs, folds between the buttocks, and scalp. The cause of psoriasis is unknown. In some cases, it may be hereditary or inherited. Attacks of psoriasis can be triggered by injury or infection, stress, hormonal changes, exposure to cold temperature, or steroids and other medications. The treatment for psoriasis depends on its severity. Steroid creams and ointments are commonly used to treat mild or moderate psoriasis. If the case is more severe, these medications may be used in conjunction with ultraviolet light B (UVB) treatments. Strong medications are reserved for those individuals suffering from extreme cases of psoriasis.

Skin Cancer

Skin cancer is the growth of abnormal skin cells capable of invading and destroying other cells. Skin cancer is the single most common type of cancer in humans. The cause of most skin cancers or carcinomas is unknown, but overexposure to ultraviolet radiation in sunlight is a risk factor. Basal cell carcinoma is the most common form of skin cancer, accounting for about 75 percent of cases. It is also the least malignant or cancerous (tending to grow and spread throughout the body). In this form of skin cancer, basal cells in the epidermis are altered so they no longer produce keratin. They also spread, invading the dermis and subcutaneous layer. Shiny, dome-shaped lesions develop most often on sunexposed areas of the face. The next most common areas affected are the ears, the backs of the hands, the shoulders, and the arms. When the lesion is removed surgically, 99 percent of patients recover fully.

Squamous cell carcinoma affects the cells of the second deepest layer of the epidermis. Like basal cell carcinoma, this type of skin cancer also involves skin exposed to the sun: face, ears, hands, and arms. The cancer presents itself as a small, scaling, raised bump on the skin with a crusting centre. It grows rapidly and spreads to adjacent lymph nodes if not removed. If the lesion is caught early and removed surgically or through radiation, the patient has a good chance of recovering completely.

Malignant melanoma accounts for about five percent of all skin cancers, but it is the most serious type. It is a cancer of the melanocytes, cells in the lower epidermis that produce melanin. In their early stages, melanomas resemble moles. Soon, they appear as an expanding brown to black patch. In addition to invading surrounding tissues, the cancer spreads aggressively to other parts of the body, especially the lungs and liver. Overexposure to the Sun may be a cause of melanomas, but the greatest risk factor seems to be genetic. Early discovery of the melanoma is key to survival. The primary treatment for this skin cancer is the surgical removal of the tumor or diseased area of skin. When the melanoma has spread to other parts of the body, it is generally considered incurable.

Vitiligo

Vitiligo is a skin disorder in which the loss of melanocytes (cells that produce the colour pigment melanin) results in patches of smooth, milky white skin. This often inherited disorder affects about 1 to 2 percent of the world's population. Although it is more easily observed in people with darker skin, it affects all races. It can begin at any age, but in 50 percent of the cases it starts before the age of twenty. Medical researchers do not know the exact cause of the disorder. Some theorize that nerve endings in the skin may release a chemical that destroys melanocytes. Others believe that the melanocytes simply self-destruct. Still others think that vitiligo is a type of autoimmune disease, in which the body targets and destroys its own cells and tissues. Vitiligo cannot be cured, but it can be managed. Cosmetics can be applied to blend the white areas with the surrounding normal skin. Sunscreens are useful to prevent the burning of affected areas and to prevent normal skin around the patches from becoming darker.

Warts

Warts are small growths caused by a viral infection of the skin or mucous membrane. The virus infects the surface layer. Warts are contagious. They can easily pass from person to person. They can also pass from one area of the body to another on the same person. Affecting about 7 to 10 percent of the population, warts are particularly common among children, young adults, and women. Common warts include hand warts, foot warts, and flat warts. Hand warts grow around the nails, on the fingers, and on the backs of the hands. They appear mostly in areas where the skin is broken.

Foot warts (also called plantar warts) usually appear on the ball of the foot, the heel, or the flat part of the toes. Foot warts do not stick up above the surface like hand warts. If left untreated, they can grow in size and spread into clusters of several warts. If located on a pressure point of the foot, these warts can be painful. Flat warts are smaller and smoother than other warts. They grow in great numbers and can erupt anywhere on the body. In children, they appear especially on the face.

Many nonprescription wart remedies are available that will remove simple warts from hands and fingers. Physicians use stronger chemical medications to treat warts that are larger or do not respond to over-the-counter treatments. Freezing warts with liquid nitrogen or burning them with an electric needle are advanced treatment methods.

TATTOOS: BODY ART AND MUTILATION

Tattoos are relatively permanent marks or designs made on the skin. Tattoo comes from the Tahitian word *tattau,* meaning 'to mark.' The process of tattooing is accomplished by injecting coloured pigment into small deep holes made in the skin. The modern method of tattooing employs an electric needle to inject the pigment. People have been decorating their bodies with pictures of animals, flowers, supernatural creatures, and various designs for thousands of years. Egyptian mummies dating from 3035 b.c. have been discovered with ornate designs of flowers tattooed on their skin. Many ancient cultures believed that a tattoo of an animal could capture the mystical spirit of that animal and magically link the wearer to the animal depicted. While many cultures have revered tattoos, many others have considered them vulgar and offensive. For as long as people have applied tattoos to their skin, they have sought ways to remove them.

In modern times, tattoos can be removed medically through one of four ways. If the tattoo is small, it can be surgically cut off and the skin sewn back together. In a method called dermabrasion, the tattoo is 'sanded' with a rotary abrasive instrument until the layers of skin peel. Another method that uses abrasion is called salabrasion. In this procedure, which is centuries old, salt water is applied to the tattoo and then it is vagourously rubbed with some sort of sanding device until the tattoo pigments are dispersed. All three of these methods leave some sort of scarring, but the last method, laser surgery, does not. Pulses of light from a laser are directed onto the tattoo, breaking up its pigments. The pigments are then removed over the next few weeks by the body's defence cells.

KEEPING THE INTEGUMENTARY SYSTEM HEALTHY

The epidermis thins as basal cells divide less and less. The dermis also thins and its elastic fibres decrease in size. As a result, the skin becomes weaker and starts to sag, forming wrinkles. Melanocytes decrease production of melanin, and the skin becomes pale and hair turns white. Sebaceous glands also decrease production of sebum, causing the skin to become dry and scaly. Blood supply to the skin is reduced and body temperature cannot be regulated as well. Finally, the skin takes longer and longer to repair itself. Although there is no way to avoid aging of the skin, there are ways to decrease the effects of aging. The loss of elasticity in the skin is speeded up by sunlight. The skin should be shielded from the Sun through the use of sunscreens, sunblocks, and protective clothing. Sunburns are never healthy and should always be avoided. This will also help reduce the risk of skin cancer.

As in all other body systems, the following play a part in keeping the integumentary system operating at peak efficiency: proper nutrition, healthy amounts of good-quality drinking water, adequate rest, regular exercise, and stress reduction. Hair loss and graying are both genetically controlled, but stress can add to both conditions. Exercise and relaxation techniques are proven ways to reduce stress. Proper daily cleansing of the skin is highly recommended. However, harsh detergents and scrubbing will not make the skin cleaner. In fact, they can injure the skin and cause excessive drying. Greater benefits can be gained by cleaning the skin with gentle soaps or lotions, then applying an appropriate moisturizer to all areas of the body.

RESPIRATORY DISEASES OF CATTLE

Respiratory disease is among the most economically important diseases of cattle in production on a worldwide basis. Allergic rhinitis is an uncommon disease of cattle that, when chronic, may lead to granuloma formation. The etiology is an allergic reaction to pollen or fungal spores. Signs are seasonal and occur under warm, moist conditions; they include rhinorrhea, sneezing, and a sudden onset of dyspnea. In the chronic stage, multiple granulomas may form on the mucosal surface of the nasal cavity. Cytologic examination of nasal discharges may reveal eosinophils. Treatment should focus on removing the allergen or removing the animal from the allergen. Treatment with corticosteroids to block the hypersensitivity reaction is a consideration.

SINUSITIS

Etiology

Sinusitis in cattle typically involves the frontal or maxillary sinus. Frontal sinusitis is usually associated with dehorning and maxillary sinusitis with infected teeth. Numerous bacteria have been isolated from sinusitis infections in cattle.

Clinical Findings

Frontal sinusitis may occur immediately after dehorning while the site is still open or months later after the dehorning site has healed. The condition is most often unilateral. Signs may include anorexia, pyrexia, unilateral or bilateral nasal discharge, changes in air flow through the nasal passages, and foul breath. Head carriage may be abnormal. In longstanding cases of frontal sinusitis, there may be distortion of the frontal bone, exophthalmos, and neurologic signs.

Diagnosis

Diagnosis can usually be made on the basis of clinical signs. Percussion may reveal a dull sound over the affected sinus. Radiographs may reveal fluid in the sinus, the presence of dental disease, or bone lysis. Cytology of aspirated material from the affected sinus may reveal purulent material.

Treatment

Sinusitis is treated by draining the affected sinus. Trephine sites should be reviewed for appropriate anatomic landmarks. If an infected tooth is the cause of maxillary sinusitis, the tooth can be repelled through a sinusotomy site created with a trephine. Once drainage has been established, the sinus can be lavaged daily with antiseptic solutions. Treatment with parenteral antibiotics is indicated if systemic signs are present. NSAID can be given for pain relief, if needed. The prognosis is guarded.

Control

The best control method is to dehorn calves at a young age using a closed dehorning technique. If this is not possible, close attention should be paid to disinfection of surgical instruments between animals, dust control, and fly control.

TRACHEAL EDEMA SYNDROME OF FEEDER CATTLE

Tracheal edema syndrome is characterized by extensive edema of the mucosa and submucosa in the dorsal membrane of the lower trachea. The etiology is unknown. Proposed causes include respiratory viruses and bacteria, trauma to the trachea from feed bunks, passive congestion and edema from excessive fat accumulation in the thoracic inlet, hypersensitivity reactions, and mycotoxins. The condition occurs in heavy feeder cattle in the later two-thirds of the feeding period throughout North America but may be most severe in the summer in southern plains (USA) feedlots. Onset is sudden and appears to be associated with an increase in respirations stimulated by hot weather or exercise. The initial signs are a loud inspiratory noise (stridor) and the onset of dyspnea. Forced movement causes the respiratory distress to worsen. The cattle become cyanotic and typically collapse and die of asphyxiation in <24 hr. Usually, only 1 or 2 animals per pen are affected.

In the acute form, necropsy lesions include edematous and/or hemorrhagic thickening of the submucosa and mucosa of the dorsal trachea extending from the midcervical area to the thoracic inlet. There is extensive hemorrhage in the trachea but no lung lesions. In the chronic form, lesions consist of hyperemia of the caudal third of the trachea with mucopurulent exudate in the trachea. In fatal cases, the lesion becomes completely obstructive. Movement and handling of affected cattle should be limited. Antibiotics and corticosteroids are recommended for the acute form. Tracheostomy may be required in severe cases. Providing shade and cooling with fans or water sprays is recommended. Animals that recover are prone to relapse and should be sent to slaughter.

BOVINE RESPIRATORY DISEASE COMPLEX

Bovine respiratory disease (BRD) has a multifactorial etiology and develops as a result of complex interactions between environmental factors, host factors, and pathogens.

Environmental factors (*e.g.*, weaning, transport, commingling, crowding, and inadequate ventilation) serve as stressors that adversely affect the immune and nonimmune defence mechanisms of the host.

In addition, certain environmental factors (*e.g.*, crowding and inadequate ventilation) can enhance the transmission of infectious agents among animals. Many infectious agents have been associated with BRD. An initial pathogen (*e.g.*, a virus) may alter the animal's defence mechanisms, allowing colonization of the lower respiratory tract by bacteria.

BACTERIAL PNEUMONIA

Etiology

Mannheimia haemolytica, serotype 1 is the bacterium most frequently isolated from the lungs of cattle with BRD. Although less frequently cultured, Pasteurella multocida is also an important cause of bacterial pneumonia.

Histophilus somni is being increasingly recognized as an important pathogen in BRD; these bacteria are normal inhabitants of the nasopharynx of cattle. When pulmonary abscessation occurs, generally in association with chronic pneumonia, Arcanobacterium pyogenes is frequently isolated.

Under normal conditions, *M haemolytica* remains confined to the upper respiratory tract, in particular the tonsillar crypts, and is difficult to culture from healthy cattle. After stress or viral infection, the replication rate of *M haemolytica* in the upper respiratory tract increases rapidly, as does the likelihood of culturing the bacterium. The increased bacterial growth rate in the upper respiratory tract followed by inhalation and colonization of the lungs may occur due to suppression of the host's defence mechanism related to environmental stressors or viral infections. It is during this log phase of growth of the organism in the lungs that virulence factors are elaborated by *M haemolytica,* such as an exotoxin that has been referred to as leukotoxin.

The interaction between the virulence factors of the bacteria and host defences results in tissue damage with characteristic necrosis, thrombosis, and exudation and the development of pneumonia.

The pathogenesis of pneumonia caused by *P multocida* is poorly understood. This organism may opportunistically colonize lungs with chronically damaged respiratory defences, such as occurs with enzootic calf pneumonia or existing lung lesions of feedlot cattle, and cause a purulent bronchopneumonia.

H somni may invade the lung and cause pneumonia following damage to the respiratory defences. This organism is capable of systemic spread from the lung to the brain, myocardium, synovium, and pleural and pericardial surfaces; often death can occur later in the feeding period from involvement of these additional organ systems.

Clinical Findings

Clinical signs of bacterial pneumonia are often preceded by signs of viral infection of the respiratory tract. With the onset of bacterial pneumonia, clinical signs increase in severity and are characterized by depression and toxemia. Fever (104-106°F [40-41°C]); serous to mucopurulent nasal discharge; moist cough; and a rapid, shallow respiratory rate may be noted. Auscultation of the cranioventral lung field reveals increased bronchial sounds, crackles, and wheezes. In severe cases, pleurisy may develop, characterized by an irregular breathing pattern and grunting on expiration. The animal will become unthrifty in appearance if the pneumonia becomes chronic, which is usually associated with the formation of pulmonary abscesses.

Lesions

M haemolytica causes a severe, acute, hemorrhagic fibrinonecrotic pneumonia. The pneumonia has a bronchopneumonic pattern. Grossly, there are extensive reddish black to grayish brown cranioventral regions of consolidation with gelatinous thickening of interlobular septa and fibrinous pleuritis. There are extensive thromboses, foci of lung necrosis, and limited evidence of bronchitis and bronchiolitis. *P multocida* is associated with a less fulminating fibrinous to fibrinopurulent bronchopneumonia. In contrast to *M haemolytica, P multocida* is associated with only small amounts of fibrin exudation, some thromboses, limited lung necrosis, and suppurative bronchitis and bronchiolitis.

H somnus infection of the lungs results in purulent bronchopneumonia that may be followed by septicemia and infection of multiple organs. Occasionally, *H somni* is associated with extensive pleuritis. Pulmonary abscessation can occur as the pneumonia becomes chronic. Abscesses develop in ~3 week but do not become encapsulated until 4 week. Arcanobacterium pyogenes is frequently cultured from these abscesses.

Diagnosis

Generally, neither serologic testing nor direct bacterial detection are performed, and diagnosis relies on bacterial culture. Because the bacteria involved are normal inhabitants of the upper respiratory tract, the specificity of culture can be increased by collecting antemortem specimens from the lower respiratory tract by tracheal swab, transtracheal wash, or bronchoalveolar lavage. Lung specimens can be collected for culture at postmortem. If possible, specimens for culture should be collected from animals that have not been treated with antibiotics to permit determination of antimicrobial sensitivity patterns.

Treatment

Early recognition by trained personnel skilled at detecting the early symptoms of disease and treatment with antibiotics are essential for successful therapy. Antibiotics effective against the 3 gram-negative bacteria most often involved in BRD should be selected. Responses to treatment should be monitored and periodic culture and sensitivity should be performed to aid in the selection of antibiotics. Long-acting antibiotics have been specifically developed for treating bacterial pneumonia in cattle. It is important that antibiotic therapy extend beyond apparent recovery to avoid relapses.

Mass medication in feed or water is of limited value because sick animals do not eat or drink enough to achieve inhibitory blood levels of the antibiotic, and many of these oral antibiotics are poorly absorbed in ruminants. NSAID have been shown to be a beneficial ancillary therapy in treating bacterial pneumonia. If pulmonary abscessation has occurred, it is difficult to achieve resolution with antimicrobials and culling of the animal should be considered.

Control

General principles of control are discussed under enzootic pneumonia of calves and shipping fever pneumonia. The value of M haemolytica and P multocida bacterins is questionable, and some reports indicate they may even exacerbate the disease. Newer vaccines, which include live culture and subunit vaccines (leukotoxin), show much more promise for disease prevention. Vaccination should be done 3 week before transport to the feedlot and can be repeated on arrival. In dairy calves, vaccination of the dam may be of benefit by providing passive immunity to the calf. H somni bacterins are available, and there is some evidence that they are effective in control of BRD.

MYCOPLASMAL PNEUMONIA

The exact role of mycoplasmas and ureaplasmas in BRD requires better definition. Mycoplasmas can be recovered from the respiratory tract of nonpneumonic calves, but the frequency of isolation is greater in those with respiratory tract disease. Mycoplasmas commonly recovered from the lungs of pneumonic calves include *Mycoplasma dispar, M bovis,* and *Ureaplasma* spp. *M bovis* has been associated with otitis media in young calves and polyarthritis in feedlot cattle. Experimental infections usually result in inapparent to mild signs of respiratory disease. This does not preclude a synergistic role for mycoplasmas in conjunction with viruses and bacteria in BRD. Lesions include focal pulmonary abscessation and necrosis with histologic lesions of peribronchial and peribronchiolar lymphoid cuffing and alveolitis. Culture of these organisms requires special media and conditions; growth of the organisms may take up to a week. Mycoplasmas are sensitive to several antibiotics, including the tetracyclines and macrolides.

CHLAMYDIAL PNEUMONIA

Chlamydial agents have been implicated in a number of diseases of cattle, including pneumonia. Only mild clinical signs and lesions of bronchopneumonia have been produced by experimental infections. A synergism between Chlamydia and *Mannheimia haemolytica* has been demonstrated experimentally. Because this pathogen is infrequently tested for, its overall importance remains undetermined. The organism can be tested for by staining sections of lung lesions with Gimenez stain or by fluorescent antibody. Isolation requires inoculation of yolk sacs of embryonating chicks. Chlamydial agents are sensitive to tetracyclines.

CONTAGIOUS BOVINE PLEUROPNEUMONIA

This highly contagious pneumonia is generally accompanied by pleurisy. It is present in Africa, the Iberian peninsula, and parts of India and China; minor outbreaks occur in the Middle East. The USA has been free of the disease since 1892, the UK since 1898, and Australia since 1973.

Etiology

The causal organism is *Mycoplasma mycoides mycoides* small colony type. Susceptible cattle become infected by inhaling droplets disseminated by coughing in affected cattle. Goats and sheep are not important in the epidemiology. Septicemia produces lesions in the kidneys and placenta, which can be sources of infection. Transplacental infection of the fetus can occur. Viability of the organism in the environment is poor. The incubation period varies, but most cases occur 3-8 week after exposure. In some localities, susceptible herds may show up to 100 per cent morbidity, but much lower infection rates (~10 per cent) associated with clinical signs are more common. Mortality is likely to be ~50 per cent. Of recovered animals, 25 per cent may become carriers with chronic lung lesions in the form of sequestra of variable size. Because carriers may not be detectable clinically or serologically, they constitute a serious problem in control programmes. Breed susceptibility, management systems, and general health of the animal are important factors that influence the infection.

Clinical Findings

In acute cases, signs include fever up to 107°F (41.5°C), anorexia, and painful, difficult breathing. In hot climates, the animal often stands by itself in the shade, its head lowered and extended, its back slightly arched, and its elbows turned out. Percussion of the chest is painful; respiration is rapid, shallow, and abdominal. If the animal is forced to move quickly, the breathing becomes more distressed and a soft, moist cough may result. The disease progresses rapidly, animals lose condition, and breathing becomes very laboured, with a grunt at expiration. The animal becomes recumbent and dies after 1-3 wk. Chronically affected cattle usually exhibit signs of varying intensity for 3-4 week, after which the lesions gradually resolve and the animals appear to recover. Subclinical cases occur and may be important as carriers.

Lesions

The thoracic cavity may contain up to 10 L of clear yellow or turbid fluid mixed with fibrin flakes, and the organs in the thorax are often covered by thick deposits of fibrin. Varying amounts of one or both lungs may be involved, the affected portion being enlarged and solid. On section of the lung, the typical marbled appearance of pleuropneumonia is evident due to the widened interlobular septa and subpleural tissue that encloses gray, yellow, or red consolidated lung lobules. Microscopically, this is a severe, acute, fibrinous pneumonia with fibrinous pleurisy, thrombosis of pulmonary blood vessels, and areas of necrosis of lung tissue; the interstitial tissue is markedly thickened by edema fluid containing much fibrin. In chronic cases, the lesion has a necrotic centre sequestered in a thick, fibrous capsule, and there may be fibrous pleural adhesions. Organisms may survive in these sequestra, and the animals become carriers.

Diagnosis

Diagnosis is based on clinical signs, complement fixation test, and necropsy. Confirmation is by histopathology, detection of organisms in pleural fluid using darkfield microscopy, isolation of the organism from lung or pleural fluid, or demonstration of specific antigens in lung tissue by immunodiffusion or immunofluorescence and hyperimmune antigalactan serum. Subclinical disease is detected by complement fixation test. As soon as an outbreak is suspected, slaughter and necropsy of presumptively infected cattle is advisable.

Control

The disease is reportable by law in many countries from which it has been eradicated by slaughter of all infected and exposed animals. In countries where cattle movement can readily be restricted, the disease can be eradicated by quarantine, blood testing, and immunization with attenuated vaccine (*e.g.*, T1/44 strain). Where cattle cannot be confined, the spread of infection can be limited by vaccination. Tracing the source of infected cattle detected at abattoirs, blood testing, and imposition of strict rules for cattle movement also can aid in control of the disease in such areas. Treatment is recommended only in endemic areas because the organisms may not be eliminated, and carriers may develop. Tylosin (10 mg/kg, IM, bid for 6 injections) is reported to be effective.

VIRAL RESPIRATORY TRACT INFECTIONS

Etiology

Parainfluenza-3 virus (PI-3) is an RNA virus classified in the paramyxovirus family. Infections caused by PI-3 are common in cattle.

Although PI-3 is capable of causing disease, it is usually associated with mild to subclinical infections. The most important role of PI-3 is to serve as an initiator that can lead to the development of secondary bacterial pneumonia.

Clinical Findings and Lesions

Clinical signs include pyrexia, cough, serous nasal and lacrimal discharge, increased respiratory rate, and increased breath sounds.

The severity of signs worsens with the onset of bacterial pneumonia. Fatalities from uncomplicated PI-3 pneumonia are rare.

Lesions include cranioventral lung consolidation, bronchiolitis, and alveolitis with marked congestion and hemorrhage. Inclusion bodies may be identified. Most fatal cases have a concurrent bacterial bronchopneumonia.

Diagnosis

Diagnostic procedures for PI-3 are similar to those for bovine respiratory syncytial virus.

Treatment and Prevention

Treatment focuses on the antimicrobial therapy directed towards bacterial pneumonia. NSAID are also a therapeutic consideration.

PI-3 vaccines are available and are almost always combined with bovine herpesvirus 1 (infectious bovine rhinotracheitis). Modified live and inactivated vaccines are available for IM administration. Vaccines containing temperature-sensitive mutants for intranasal administration are also available.

BOVINE RESPIRATORY SYNCYTIAL VIRUS

Etiology

Bovine respiratory syncytial virus (BRSV) is an RNA virus classified as a pneumovirus in the paramyxovirus family. This virus was named for its characteristic cytopathic effect—the formation of syncytial cells. In additional to cattle, sheep and goats can also be infected by respiratory syncytial viruses.

Human respiratory syncytial virus (HRSV) is an important respiratory pathogen in infants and young children. Antigenic subtypes are known to exist for HRSV, and preliminary evidence suggests that there may be antigenic subtypes of BRSV. BRSV is distributed worldwide, and the virus is indigenous in the cattle population.

BRSV infections associated with respiratory disease occur predominantly in young beef and dairy cattle. Passively derived immunity does not appear to prevent BRSV infections but will reduce the severity of disease. Initial exposures to the virus are associated with severe respiratory disease; subsequent exposures result in mild to subclinical disease. BRSV is an important virus in the bovine respiratory disease complex because of its frequency of occurrence, predilection for the lower respiratory tract, and ability to predispose the respiratory tract to secondary bacterial infection. In outbreaks, morbidity tends to be high, and the case fatality rate can be 0-20 per cent.

Clinical Findings and Lesions

Fever (104-108°F [40-42°C]), depression, decreased feed intake, increased respiratory rate, cough, and nasal and lacrimal discharge are common. Dyspnea, possibly with open-mouthed breathing, may become pronounced in the later stages of the disease. Subcutaneous emphysema may occur. Secondary bacterial pneumonia is a frequent occurrence. A biphasic disease pattern has been described but is not consistent. Gross lesions include a diffuse interstitial pneumonia with subpleural and interstitial emphysema along with interstitial edema. These lesions are similar to and must be differentiated from other causes of interstitial pneumonia. Bronchopneumonia of bacterial origin is usually present. Histologic examination reveals syncytial cells in bronchiolar epithelium and lung parenchyma, intracytoplasmic inclusion bodies, proliferation and/or degeneration of bronchiolar epithelium, alveolar epithelialization, edema, and hyaline membrane formation.

Diagnosis

A diagnosis of BRSV requires laboratory confirmation. BRSV is a difficult virus to detect, although chances of isolation may improve when sampling animals that are in the incubation or acute phases of infection. An antigen detection enzyme immunoassay is useful in detecting BRSV antigen and establishing a diagnosis. Other procedures that have proved useful in detection of BRSV antigen are fluorescent antibody and immunoperoxidase staining.

Paired serum samples can be used to establish a diagnosis. However, the antibody titer of animals with well-developed clinical disease may be higher in the acute sample than in the sample taken 2-3 week later because the antibody response often develops rapidly, and clinical signs follow virus infection by up to 7-10 days. Single serum samples with high antibody titers from a number of animals in a respiratory outbreak may be useful in making a diagnosis if coupled with clinical signs. Calves that become infected with BRSV in the presence of passively derived antibody may not seroconvert.

Treatment and Prevention

Treatment focuses on antimicrobial therapy to control secondary bacterial pneumonia. There is no specific treatment for the viral interstitial pneumonia. Supportive therapy and correction of dehydration may be necessary. There are anecdotal reports of treatment with antihistamines and/or corticosteroids being of benefit. Most cases will recover in several days without treatment. General control and prevention are discussed under enzootic pneumonia of calves and shipping fever pneumonia. Inactivated and modified live vaccines are available and may serve to reduce losses associated with BRSV.

BOVINE HERPESVIRUS 1

Etiology and Epidemiology

Bovine herpesvirus 1 (BHV-1) is associated with several diseases in cattle: infectious bovine rhinotracheitis (IBR), infectious pustular vulvovaginitis (IPV), balanoposthitis, conjunctivitis, abortion, encephalomyelitis, and mastitis. Only a single serotype of BHV-1 is recognized; however, three subtypes of BHV-1 have been described on the basis of endonuclease cleavage patterns of viral DNA—BHV-1.1 (respiratory subtype), BHV-1.2 (genital subtype), and BHV-1.3 (encephalitic subtype). BHV-1.3 has been reclassified as a distinct herpesvirus designated BHV-5.

BHV-1 infections are widespread in the cattle population. In feedlot cattle, the respiratory form is most common. The viral infection alone is not life-threatening but predisposes to secondary bacterial pneumonia, which may result in death. In breeding cattle, abortion or genital infections are more common. Genital infections can occur in bulls (infectious pustular balanoposthitis) and cows (IPV) within 1-3 days of mating or close contact with an infected animal. Transmission can occur in the absence of visible lesions and through artificial insemination with semen from subclinically infected bulls. Cattle with latent BHV-1 infections generally show no clinical signs when the virus is reactivated, but they serve as a source of infection for other susceptible animals.

Clinical Findings

The incubation period for the respiratory and genital forms is 2-6 days. In the respiratory form, clinical signs range from mild to severe, depending on the presence of secondary bacterial pneumonia. Clinical signs include high fever, anorexia, coughing, excessive salivation, nasal discharge that progresses from serous to mucopurulent, conjunctivitis with lacrimal discharge, inflamed nares (hence the common name 'red nose'), and dyspnea if the larynx becomes occluded with purulent material. Nasal lesions consist of numerous clusters of grayish necrotic foci on the mucous membrane of the septal mucosa, just visible inside the external nares. They may later be accompanied by pseudodiphtheritic yellowish plaques. Conjunctivitis with corneal opacity may occur as the only manifestation of BHV-1 infection. In the absence of bacterial pneumonia, recovery generally occurs 4-5 days after the onset of signs.

Abortions may occur concurrently with respiratory disease but may be seen up to 100 days after infection. They can occur regardless of the severity of disease in the dam. Abortions generally occur during the second half of pregnancy, but early embryonic death is possible.

In genital infections, the first signs are frequent urination, elevation of the tailhead, and a mild vaginal discharge. The vulva is swollen, and small papules, then erosions and ulcers, are present on the mucosal surface. If secondary bacterial infections do not occur, animals recover in 10-14 days. With bacterial infection, there may be inflammation of the uterus and transient infertility, with purulent vaginal discharge for several weeks. In bulls, similar lesions occur on the penis and prepuce.

BHV-1 infection can be severe in young calves and cause a generalized disease. Pyrexia, ocular and nasal discharges, respiratory distress, diarrhea, incoordination, and eventually convulsions and death may occur in a short period after generalized viral infection.

Lesions

In uncomplicated IBR infections, most lesions are restricted to the upper respiratory tract and trachea. Petechial to ecchymotic hemorrhages may be found in the mucous membranes of the nasal cavity and the paranasal sinuses. Focal areas of necrosis develop in the nose, pharynx, larynx, and trachea. The lesions may coalesce to form plaques.

The sinuses are often filled with a serous or serofibrinous exudate. As the disease progresses, the pharynx becomes covered with a serofibrinous exudate, and blood-tinged fluid may be found in the trachea. The pharyngeal and pulmonary lymph nodes may be acutely swollen and hemorrhagic. The tracheitis may extend into the bronchi and bronchioles; when this occurs, epithelium is sloughed in the airways. The viral lesions are often masked by secondary bacterial infections. In young animals with generalized BHV-1 infection, erosions and ulcers overlaid with debris may be found in the nose, esophagus, and forestomachs. In addition, white foci may be found in the liver, kidney, spleen, and lymph nodes. Aborted fetuses may have pale, focal, necrotic lesions in all tissues, which are especially visible in the liver.

Diagnosis

Uncomplicated BHV-1 infections can be diagnosed based on the characteristic signs and lesions. However, because the severity of disease can vary, it is best to differentiate BHV-1 from other viral infections by viral isolation. Samples should be taken early in the disease, and a diagnosis should be possible in 2-3 days.

A rise in serum antibody titer also can be used to confirm a diagnosis. It is not possible to detect a rising antibody titer in abortions, because infection generally occurs a considerable length of time before the abortion, and titers are already maximal. BHV-1 abortion can be diagnosed by identifying characteristic lesions and demonstrating the virus in fetal tissues by virus isolation, immunoperoxidase, or fluorescent antibody staining. Gross and microscopic lesions detected shortly after death may help to establish a diagnosis.

Treatment and Control

Antimicrobial therapy is indicated to prevent or treat secondary bacterial pneumonia. General recommendations for control are discussed under shipping fever pneumonia. Immunization with modified live or inactivated virus vaccines generally provides adequate protection against clinical disease. Both IM and intranasal modified live vaccines are available, but the IM types may cause abortion in pregnant cattle. The intranasal vaccines can be used in pregnant cattle. The IM vaccines are easier to use and often are the vaccines of choice in feedlots. Breeding and replacement heifers and bulls should be immunized when 6-8 mo old, before breeding, and yearly thereafter. Some recommend that young bulls not be vaccinated because they may be discriminated against when sold for breeding if they have antibody titers. Feeder calves should be immunized 2-3 week before entry into the feedlot. Eradication of the virus is possible by serologic testing and either culling reactors or running a strict 2-herd system. To aid in eradication, deletion mutant vaccines have been developed that permit discrimination between antibody produced in response to the vaccine and antibody produced in response to natural exposure.

BOVINE VIRAL DIARRHEA VIRUS

Bovine viral diarrhea virus (BVDV) is an RNA virus classified as a Pestivirus in the family Flaviviridae. The role of BVDV in BRD has been controversial, but appears to be that of a virus capable of inducing immunosuppression, which allows for the development of secondary bacterial pneumonia. Seroconversion to BVDV has been reported to be predictive of the occurrence of respiratory disease in feedlot calves, and BVDV has been reported to be the virus most frequently associated with multiple viral infections of the respiratory tract of calves.

Treatment for BVDV infection is supportive and includes antimicrobials to prevent or treat bacterial pneumonia. General principles of control are discussed under enzootic pneumonia of calves and shipping fever pneumonia. Inactivated and modified live vaccines are available for IM administration. Recently, vaccines containing both the type I and type II genotypes have become available. Modified live vaccines can induce immunosuppression and should be used with caution in highly stressed cattle. Modified live BVDV vaccines are not approved for use in pregnant cattle.

OTHER BOVINE RESPIRATORY VIRUSES

Several other viruses may potentially be involved in BRD. Bovine herpesvirus-4 has been implicated in several diseases, including BRD. Bovine adenovirus has been associated with a wide spectrum of diseases, with bovine adenovirus type 3 being the serotype most often associated with BRD. Two serotypes of bovine rhinovirus have been recognized to cause respiratory tract infections in cattle. Other viruses reported to be associated with BRD include bovine reovirus, enterovirus, and coronavirus.

There is growing evidence that bovine coronavirus may have a more important role in BRD than previously recognized. These viruses have a role similar to the other viruses previously discussed in that, in combination with other stressors, they can serve as initiators of bacterial pneumonia. Vaccines are not available for prevention of these viral respiratory diseases.

Enzootic Pneumonia of Calves and Shipping fever Pneumonia

Enzootic pneumonia and shipping fever pneumonia share many similarities in their respective etiologies and pathogeneses and general measures for control and prevention.

ENZOOTIC PNEUMONIA OF CALVES

Enzootic pneumonia of calves refers to infectious respiratory disease in calves. The term 'viral pneumonia of calves' is sometimes used but is not preferred based on the current understanding of etiology and pathogenesis. Enzootic pneumonia is primarily a problem in calves <6 mo old with peak occurrence from 2-10 week, but may be seen in calves up to 1 yr of age. It is more common in dairy than in beef calves and is a common problem in veal calves. It is also more common in housed calves than those raised outside. Peak incidence of disease may coincide with decline of passively acquired immunity. Morbidity rates may approach 100 per cent; case fatality rates vary but can reach 20 per cent.

Etiology

The etiology is similar to that for BRD complex in general. The pathogenesis involves stress and possibly an initial respiratory viral infection followed by a secondary bacterial infection of the lower respiratory tract. Stress results from environmental and management factors, including inadequate ventilation, continually adding calves to an established group, crowding, and nutritional factors such as poor-quality milk replacers. Partial or complete failure of passive transfer of maternal antibodies is an important host factor related to development of disease. Any of several viruses may be involved, and a variety of bacteria may be recovered from affected calves. Mycoplasmal and bacterial agents including Pasteurella multocida, Mannheimia haemolytica, and Mycoplasma bovis represent the most frequently isolated pathogenic organisms. The individual viral and bacterial etiologies, clinical signs, lesions, and treatment are discussed under viral respiratory tract infections and bacterial pneumonia.

Control and Prevention

When calves of varying ages are placed in communal pens, control of enzootic pneumonia is difficult. The severity of the pneumonia may be decreased by improved husbandry, proper housing, adequate ventilation, and good nursing care. Prevention begins with vaccinating the cows against specific respiratory viruses and bacteria 3-4 week prepartum to improve the quality of colostral antibodies. Calves should receive good quality colostrum at 8-10 per cent of body wt in the first 12 hr after birth. Newborn dairy calves should be housed individually in hutches or stalls and fed whole milk or a high-quality milk replacer with a fibre content of <0.25 per cent until 8-12 week old. Calves should be vaccinated against respiratory viruses 3-4 week before the first grouping, although in some situations, the presence of passive immunity may interfere with an active immune response. Calves should be of similar age when assembled into groups and the group should be limited to <10. As calves mature, groups can become larger as the size of the herd, facilities, and available labour dictate. An 'all in/all out' management style should be practiced when establishing and terminating a group. At minimum, newly purchased calves should be isolated before introduction to an existing group. Newborn beef calves and their dams should be moved from concentrated calving areas as soon as the calf is nursing well and is strong enough to travel.

SHIPPING FEVER PNEUMONIA

Shipping fever pneumonia is a respiratory disease of cattle of multifactorial etiology with Mannheimia haemolytica and, less commonly, Pasteurella multocida or Histophilus somni, being the important infectious agents involved. Shipping fever pneumonia is associated with the assembly into feedlots of large groups of calves from diverse geographic, nutritional, and genetic backgrounds. Disease is typically seen in feeder calves 7-10 days after assembly in a feedlot. Morbidity can approach 35 per cent; mortality is 5-10 per cent.

Etiology

The pathogenesis of shipping fever pneumonia involves stress factors, with or without viral infection, interacting to suppress host defence mechanisms, which allows the proliferation of commensal bacteria in the upper respiratory tract. Subsequently, these bacteria colonize the lower respiratory tract and cause a bronchopneumonia with a cranioventral distribution in the lung. Multiple stress factors are believed to contribute to the suppression of host defence mechanisms. Transportation over long distances serves as a stressor; it may be associated with exhaustion, starvation, dehydration, chilling and overheating depending on weather conditions, and exposure to vehicle exhaust fumes. Additional stressors include passage through auction markets; commingling, processing, and surgical procedures on arrival at the feedlot; dusty environmental conditions; and nutritional stress associated with a change to high-energy rations in the feedlot. The individual viral and bacterial etiologies, clinical signs, lesions, and treatment are discussed under viral respiratory tract infections.

Control and Prevention

Prevention of shipping fever pneumonia should focus on reduction of the stressors that contribute to development of the disease. Cattle should be assembled rapidly into groups, and new animals should not be introduced to established groups. Auction markets and mixing of cattle from different sources should be avoided if possible. Transport time should be minimized, and rest periods, with access to feed and water, should be provided during prolonged transport. Calves should be weaned 2-3 week before shipment, and surgical procedures should be performed in advance of transport. Cattle should be processed within 48 hr after arrival at the feedlot. A rest period of 6-12 hr after transport may allow for rehydration and return of cortisol to levels that will have less impact on the immune response to vaccination. Adaptation to high-energy rations should be gradual as acidosis, indigestion, and anorexia may inhibit the immune response. Vitamin and mineral deficiencies should be corrected. Dust control measures should be used. Metaphylaxis with long-acting antibiotics given 'on arrival' for cattle at high risk for developing shipping fever pneumonia has been shown to significantly reduce morbidity and improve rate of gain.

The administration of viral respiratory vaccines on entry to the feedlot has been historically controversial, especially with modified live vaccines. These vaccines have been reported to increase the mortality associated with shipping fever pneumonia. Continuous improvements in modified live vaccine production, and the fact that these vaccines do not require a booster, have made them preferred over killed vaccines for on-arrival processing. When possible, vaccinations for the viral and bacterial components of shipping fever pneumonia should be given 2-3 week before transport and can be repeated on entry to the feedlot.

INTERSTITIAL PNEUMONIA

This classification represents a group of respiratory diseases that are characterized by an acute onset of respiratory distress and a combination of lung lesions that include pulmonary edema and congestion, interstitial emphysema, alveolar epithelialization, and hyaline membrane formation.

Acute bovine pulmonary emphysema and edema (ABPEE) is one of the more common causes of acute respiratory distress in cattle, particularly adult beef cattle, and is characterized by sudden onset, minimal coughing, and a course that ends fatally or improves dramatically within a few days.

It is a disease involving groups of cattle; morbidity may be >50 per cent, although usually only a small minority develops severe respiratory distress. Typically, ABPEE occurs in fall, 5-10 days after change to a better, often lush, pasture. A similar condition has been reported on a wide variety of grasses, alfalfa, rape, kale, and turnip tops.

Etiology

Metabolites of the naturally occurring amino acid L-tryptophan probably are responsible for many outbreaks. In the rumen, L-tryptophan is degraded to indoleacetic acid, which can be converted to 3-methylindole by some ruminal microorganisms. 3-methylindole is absorbed into the bloodstream and is the source of the pneumotoxicity after metabolism by the mixed function oxidase system, which is very active in the lungs. Apparently, the level of L-tryptophan in crops is most likely to be high in lush, rapidly growing pastures, particularly (but not exclusively) in the fall.

Clinical Findings

ABPEE is most common in heavy beef cows but may occur in either sex and in dairy or beef cattle under similar management conditions. Nursing calves are unaffected. Outbreaks usually develop within 5-10 days of a change to better grazing and rarely occur in animals that have been on a field >3 wk. Mild cases may go unnoticed. Cattle are subdued but still alert; there is tachypnea and hyperpnea, but auscultation is usually unrewarding. Such cattle usually recover spontaneously within days.

Severely affected cattle show extensive respiratory distress with mouth breathing, extension of the tongue, and drooling. A loud expiratory grunt is common, but coughing is unusual. In the early stages, auscultation reveals surprisingly soft respiratory sounds. Mild exercise increases dyspnea and may precipitate death.

If death does not occur, the animals improve dramatically and resume eating by the third day. At this stage, auscultation reveals harsh respiratory sounds and, in some animals, dorsal (emphysematous) crackles. Some cattle have subcutaneous emphysema extending along the back from the withers. Full clinical recovery may require 3 wk.

Lesions

In affected cattle that have died or been slaughtered in extremis, the lungs are heavy and do not collapse normally. They are widely affected with various degrees of firmness; there is extensive edema and emphysema, often with the formation of large air-filled bullae in interlobular and subpleural regions. Submucosal hemorrhages are often present on the larynx and in the trachea and larger bronchi. Histologically, the lesion is characterized by congestion, alveolar edema, hyaline membrane formation, and areas of early alveolar epithelial hyperplasia of type II pneumocytes; occasionally, areas of bronchiolar necrosis may be found. The emphysema is often dramatic and is limited to interstitial fascia where it is accompanied by edema.

In animals that are slaughtered after 3 days of illness, the lungs are still heavy and do not collapse normally. They are pinkish gray and of increased firmness; edema and emphysema are inconspicuous or absent. Histologically, widespread alveolar epithelial hyperplasia characteristic of a diffuse, acute, proliferative alveolitis is seen.

Diagnosis

Diagnosis is based on history, signs, and lesions. Because the syndrome is not specific with regard to cause, evidence must be obtained from management factors such as change in pasture.

Treatment

Severely affected animals have so little pulmonary reserve that any driving or handling must be done with caution to prevent immediate deaths. Removal of cattle from the offending pastures may not prevent the development of new cases for the next 4-7 days. No treatment has been identified that will reverse the fully developed lesions of ABPEE.

Control

One approach to control is dietary management, including the following options: 1) avoiding pastures likely to induce

ABPEE, 2) feeding hay before turn out on pasture and limiting exposure time on suspect pastures, 3) limiting grazing time and gradually increasing exposure to the pasture over time, 4) using pastures before they become lush, 5) delaying use of lush pastures until after a hard frost, 6) initially grazing pastures with less susceptible stock (cattle <15 mo of age or sheep), or 7) using strip grazing. A medical approach to control involves feeding monensin or lasalocid, which inhibit the bacteria that convert L-tryptophan to 3-methylindole. Treatment with monensin can be started 1 day before introduction to pasture, whereas lasalocid requires a 6-day pretreatment period. These drugs are of no benefit after onset of clinical signs.

ANAPHYLAXIS

Anaphylaxis or Type I hypersensitivity reactions in cattle can result in an atypical interstitial pneumonia. The lung is a major target organ in cattle for Type I hypersensitivity. Clinical signs are those of acute respiratory distress. Cattle that die of anaphylaxis may have lesions consistent with those described for atypical interstitial pneumonia. Treatment is the administration of epinephrine; supportive treatment includes anti-inflammatory therapy with corticosteroids or NSAID. If pharyngeal or laryngeal edema is present, a tracheostomy may be indicated.

HYPERSENSITIVITY PNEUMONITIS

A condition that appears to be similar to farmer's lung disease in humans occurs in both acute and chronic forms in adult cattle. The human and bovine forms of the disease may coexist on problem farms due to common exposure to dust from moldy hay.

Etiology

The disease occurs when sensitized individuals inhale antigens from thermophilic actinomycetes, commonly the spores of Micropolyspora faeni. The actinomycetes proliferate in vast numbers in hay, grain, or other vegetable material that has overheated to ~150°F (65°C) after damp storage (30-40 per cent moisture content). Dust that contains large numbers of spores is released when this moldy hay is shaken. The small size (1 μm) of the spores allows them to reach the smallest airways and alveoli to provoke a reaction that has been termed a 'hypersensitivity pneumonitis'; this is considered to be predominantly a Type III hypersensitivity reaction, although a Type IV hypersensitivity component is suspected.

Affected herds exist in areas where significant rainfall usually occurs during the haymaking season, suggesting that a clinical problem may arise only after repeated sensitization and challenge from the spores. Clinical disease tends to arise during the latter half of the winter feeding period and usually only when moldy hay is fed indoors. Under such circumstances, serum antibodies (usually detected by immunodiffusion) to *M faeni* are widespread among adult cattle by the end of each winter feeding period, and many apparently normal cattle are seropositive. By contrast, few adult cattle are seropositive on other farms on which 'good' hay or grass silage is fed.

Clinical Findings

Cattle may succumb to the acute form of the disease over a period of weeks. Usually, only severe acute cases are noticed. There is respiratory distress, anorexia, and agalactia in animals >5 yr old; coughing and pyrexia also occur, and adventitious sounds are occasionally heard on auscultation. Death is rare. The chronic disease usually has a higher morbidity; in most instances, the signs are weight loss, poor production, and persistent coughing. Affected cattle are fairly bright and eat reasonably well, but tachypnea, hyperpnea, and coughing are widespread. Auscultation may reveal cranioventral crackles and sometimes, in more severe cases, scattered rhonchi. Exercise intolerance may be seen, and congestive cardiac failure can develop if pulmonary fibrosis is widespread.

Lesions

The macroscopic lesions are often unremarkable; usually, there is mild peripheral lobular overinflation with diffusely scattered, small, gray, subpleural spots. Although transient pulmonary edema may be a feature of severe acute cases, the histologic lesions that are consistently found are interalveolar cellular infiltration, epithelioid granulomata, and bronchiolitis obliterans. In some chronic cases, small foci of alveolar epithelial hyperplasia and metaplasia with interstitial fibrosis are found. These areas may extend to include most, if not all, of the lung substance to produce cases clinically indistinguishable from diffuse fibrosing alveolitis. Circumstantial evidence suggests that some cases of diffuse fibrosing alveolitis are the end stage of hypersensitivity pneumonitis.

Treatment and Control

Because it is often impossible to completely shield cattle from further challenge, most recover only partially after dexamethasone treatment (1 mg/5-10 kg body wt). However, improvement is usually marked when cattle are turned out in the spring. Prevention is difficult in areas where hay is likely to be wet during the curing process and it is not possible to alter the feeding regimen.

DIFFUSE FIBROSING ALVEOLITIS

Diffuse fibrosing alveolitis is a chronic, progressive respiratory disease of undetermined cause and possibly of multiple etiologies. A proportion of affected cattle are seropositive for precipitating antibodies to Micropolyspora faeni, and this condition may represent the end stage of hypersensitivity pneumonitis. Other than the respiratory signs, the animals appear alert and maintain a good appetite until the onset of heart failure in the terminal stages. Signs include coughing, increased respiratory rate, dyspnea, and weight loss. Necropsy findings include right ventricular hypertrophy, interalveolar fibrosis, obliteration of the alveolar spaces, alveolar hyperplasia, bronchitis, and bronchiolitis. There is no treatment.

ACUTE RESPIRATORY DISTRESS SYNDROME OF FEEDLOT CATTLE

An acute respiratory distress syndrome has been described in feedlot cattle with clinical signs and pathologic findings of an atypical interstitial pneumonia. The syndrome occurs sporadically and the etiology remains undefined. Bovine respiratory syncytial virus, abnormal production of 3-methylindole in the rumen, dusty conditions, and pre-existing lesions of chronic cranioventral bacterial pneumonia have been suggested as causes or contributing factors. Clinical signs include respiratory distress characterized by tachypnea and dyspnea, and affected cattle may be found dead if clinical signs are unobserved. Lesions are those of atypical interstitial pneumonia with prominent emphysema and edema in the lungs. Treatment protocols have not been defined, and thus would be symptomatic and supportive. Management strategies suggested include vaccinating for bovine respiratory syncytial virus, controlling dust in the feedlot, and avoiding abrupt dietary changes.

4-Ipomeanol Toxicity (Moldy Sweet Potato) and Perilla Ketone Toxicity (Purple Mint Toxicity)

Clinicopathologic syndromes indistinguishable from acute bovine pulmonary emphysema and edema occur after ingestion of either moldy sweet potatoes infested with Fusarium solani, or the wild mint Perilla frutescens. Moldy sweet potato toxicity is caused by the ingestion of a furanoterpenoid toxin produced by sweet potatoes (Ipomoea batatus) in response to infestation with the fungus F solani; the end result is production of the pneumotoxin 4-ipomeanol. Perilla ketone toxicity is caused by ingestion of the leaves and seeds of the plant P frutescens (purple mint), which contains a pneumotoxin and is found in the southeastern USA. The pathogeneses of both these conditions are similar to that of ABPEE, as is approach to treatment.

GENETIC ASPECTS OF CARDIOVASCULAR DISEASES IN ANIMALS

When the incidences and types of cardiovascular disease present in various species, breeds, and strains, or families of animals are compared, certain differences are apparent. It is often difficult, however, to separate hereditary from environmental influences. Studies of vascular disease in zoo animals have shown that changing environmental conditions can alter the incidence of certain types of lesions in various species. Species differences, however, in resistance to diet-induced atherosclerosis appear to be genetically determined. The prevalence and types of congenital cardiac malformations appear to differ from species to species, but further systematic study is required. Arterial blood pressure is higher in the giraffe and turkey than in other species, and normal variants in cardiac rhythm are characteristic of the dog, horse, and mole.

Relatively high incidences of specific cardiovascular diseases are found in certain breeds of animals. The White Carneaux, Autosexing King, and Silver King breeds of pigeons have a high incidence of atherosclerosis. Congenital heart disease appears to be more common in purebred than in mongrel dogs, and an unusual aggregation of cases of subaortic stenosis in the Boxer and German Shepherd breeds has been found. In a survey of heart disease in dogs, the prevalence of chronic congestive heart failure in the male Cocker Spaniel greatly exceeded that in the male and female of all other breeds. Arterial blood pressure is higher in Broad Breasted Bronze turkeys than in the Jersey Buff breed. This is associated in the former breed with a relatively high incidence of spontaneous aortic rupture.

The occurrence of cardiovascular disease is unusually high in certain families and strains of animals. Among swine, litter and strain differences in serum cholesterol levels and in susceptibility to atherogenic diets occur. The White Carneaux breed of pigeons is actually a highly inbred strain with a remarkable predisposition to the development of atherosclerosis. Strains of chickens and rats with high incidences of interventricular septal defects have been developed by selective breeding. The familial occurrence of congenital heart disease in dogs and swine has been observed, and an inherited vascular anomaly in cattle has been described. Through selective breeding of laboratory rodents, strains with various types of cardiomyopathies have been developed. Certain diseases thought to be similar to the heritable disorders of connective tissue in man have been identified in domestic species. The level of arterial blood pressure is a heritable characteristic, and strains of rabbits, rats, and chickens with relative hypertension have been produced by selective breeding. Many of these observations indicate the importance of inheritance in determining susceptibility to various types of acquired cardiovascular disease. Genetic factors appear to operate in determining the occurrence of certain congenital malformations. Breeding experiments provide the most convincing evidence of genetic influence on the development of specific cardiovascular lesions. This experimental approach holds the greatest promise for furthering knowledge and understanding of the role of inheritance in the etiology of disease of the heart and blood vessels.

FUNCTION OF THE CARDIOVASCULAR SYSTEM

By circulating blood throughout the body, the cardiovascular system functions to supply the tissues with oxygen and nutrients, while removing carbon dioxide and other metabolic wastes. As oxygen-rich blood from the heart flows to the tissues of the body, oxygen and other chemicals move out of the blood and into the fluid surrounding the cells of the body's tissues. Waste products and carbon dioxide move into the blood to be carried away. As blood circulates through organs such as the liver and kidneys some of these waste products are removed. Blood then returns to the lungs (or gills, in the case of fish), receives a fresh dose of oxygen and gives off carbon dioxide. Then the cycle repeats itself. This process of circulation is necessary for continued life of the cells, tissues, and ultimately the whole organism. Up and down the evolutionary ladder, there are different forms of cardiovascular systems with different levels of efficiency, but they all perform this same basic function.

MAMMALIAN ANATOMY AND PHYSIOLOGY

The cardiovascular systems of mammals, birds, amphibians, reptiles, and fish are all slightly different. The following is an overview of the main components of the mammalian system – the heart and blood vessels.

Heart

The heart is composed of cardiac muscle that differs slightly from the skeletal and smooth muscle found elsewhere in the body. This special type of muscle adjusts the rate of muscular contraction, allowing the heart to maintain a regular pumping rhythm. The main parts of the heart are the chambers, the valves, and the electrical nodes.

Heart Chambers: There are two different types of heart chambers. The first is the atrium (plural is atria), which receives blood returning to the heart through the veins. The right atrium pumps blood to the right ventricle, and the left atrium pumps blood into the left ventricle. This blood is then pumped from the atrium into the second chamber called the ventricle. The ventricles are much larger than the atria and their thick, muscular walls are used to forcefully pump the blood from the heart to the body and lungs (or gills).

Valves: The valves found within the heart are situated between the atria and ventricles, and also between the ventricles and major arteries. These valves are opened and closed by pressure changes within the chambers, and act as a barrier to prevent the backflow of blood. The characteristic '*lub-dub, lub-dub*' heart sounds heard through a stethoscope are the result of vibrations caused by the closing of the respective valves.

Electrical Nodes: There are two different electrical nodes, or groups of specialized cells, located in the cardiac tissue. The first is the sinoatrial (SA) node, commonly called the pacemaker. The pacemaker is embedded in the wall of the right atrium. This small patch of tissue experiences rhythmic excitation and the impulse rapidly spreads throughout the atria, causing a muscular contraction and the pumping of blood from the atria to the ventricles. The other node, the atrioventricular (AV) node, relays the impulse of the SA node to the ventricles. It delays the impulse to prevent the ventricles from contracting at the same time as the atria, thus giving them time to fill with blood. The cycle of contraction of the heart muscle is called a heartbeat, the rate of which varies greatly between organisms. The following table gives the average heart rates of some common mammals.

Table 4.1 : Heart Rates Comparison (beats/minute)

Organism	*Average Rate*	*Normal Range*
Human	70	58-104
Cat	120	110-140
Cow	65	60-70
Dog	115	100-130
Guinea Pig	280	260-400
Hamster	450	300-600
Horse	44	23-70
Rabbit	205	123-304
Rat	328	261-600

Vessels

A vessel is a hollow tube for transporting something, like a garden hose transporting water. A blood vessel is a hollow tube for transporting blood. There are three main types of blood vessels:

- Arteries
- Capillaries
- Veins.

These main blood vessels function to transport blood through the entire body and exchange oxygen and nutrients for carbon dioxide and wastes. The arteries carry blood away from the heart, and are under high pressure from the pumping of the heart.

To maintain their structure under this pressure, they have thick, elastic walls to allow stretch and recoil. The large pulmonary artery carries unoxygenated blood from the right ventricles to the lung, where it gives off carbon dioxide and receives oxygen.

The aorta is the largest artery. It carries oxygenated blood from the left ventricle to the body. The arteries branch and eventually lead to capillary beds.

The capillaries make up a network of tiny vessels with extremely thin, highly permeable walls. They are present in all of the major tissues of the body and function in the exchange of gases, nutrients, and fluids between the blood, body tissues, and alveoli of the lungs.

At the opposite side of the capillary beds, the capillaries merge to form veins, which return the blood back to the heart. The veins are under much less pressure than the arteries and therefore have much thinner walls.

The veins also contain one-way valves in order to prevent the blood from flowing the wrong direction in the absence of pressure. The pulmonary vein returns oxygenated blood from the lungs to the left atria.

The vena cava returns blood from the body to the right atria. The blood that is returned to the heart is then recycled through the cardiovascular system.

COMPARATIVE ANATOMY

Mammals and Birds

Mammalian and avian hearts have four chambers – two atria and two ventricles. This is the most efficient system, as deoxygenated and oxygenated bloods are not mixed. The right atrium receives deoxygenated blood from the body through both the inferior and superior vena cava. The blood then passes to the right ventricle to be pumped through the pulmonary arteries to the lungs, where it becomes oxygenated. It returns to the left atrium via the pulmonary veins, this oxygen-rich blood is then passed to the left ventricle and pumped through the aorta to the rest of the body. The aorta is the largest artery and has an enormous amount of stretch and elasticity to withstand the pressure created by the pumping ventricle. The four-chambered heart ensures that the tissues of the body are supplied with oxygen-saturated blood to facilitate sustained muscle movement. Also, the larger oxygen supply allows these warm-blooded organisms to achieve thermoregulation (body temperature maintenance).

Amphibians and Reptiles

Amphibians and reptiles, by contrast, have a three-chambered heart. The three-chambered heart consists of two atria and one ventricle. (The crocodile is sometimes said to have a four-chambered heart. The separation of the ventricles is not complete, however, because a hole remains in the septum (wall) that divides the two chambers.) Blood leaving the ventricle passes into one of two vessels. It either travels through the pulmonary arteries leading to the lungs or through a forked aorta leading to the rest of the body. Oxygenated blood returning to the heart from the lungs through the pulmonary vein passes into the left atrium, while deoxygenated blood returning from the body through the sinus venosus passes into the right atrium. Both atria empty into the single ventricle, mixing the oxygen-rich blood returning from the lungs with the oxygen-depleted blood from the body tissues. While this system assures that some blood always passes to the lungs and then back to the heart, the mixing of blood in the single ventricle means the organs are not getting blood saturated with oxygen. This is not as efficient as a four-chambered system, which keeps the two circuits separate, but it is sufficient for these cold-blooded organisms.

The heart rate of amphibians and reptiles is very dependent upon temperature. For example, Table 4.2 gives the approximate heart rate of a crocodile at the indicated temperatures. Notice that the higher the temperature, the faster the heart beat.

Table 4.2. Average Heart Rate of Crocodiles at the indicated Temperature

Temperature (Celsius)	*Average Rate (beats/minute)*
10 C	1-8
18 C	15-20
28 C	24-40
>40 C	Irreversible cardiac damage

Fish

Fish possess the simplest type of true heart – a two-chambered organ composed of one atrium and one ventricle. A rudimentary valve is located between the two chambers. Blood is pumped from the ventricle through the conus arteriosus to the gills. The conus arteriosus is like the aorta in other species.

At the gills, the blood receives oxygen and gets rid of carbon dioxide. Blood then moves on to the organs of the body, where nutrients, gases, and wastes are exchanged. There is no division of the circulation between the gills and the body. That is, the blood travels from the heart to the gills, and then directly to the body before returning to the atrium through the sinus venosus to be circulated again.

The heart rates of fish fall within the wide range of 60-240 beats per minute, depending upon species and water temperature. The fish's heart rate will be slower at lower temperatures.

ULTRASONOGRAPHIC DIAGNOSIS OF THE BOVINE GENITAL TRACT DISORDERS

In bovine practice, ultrasonography has become an important diagnostic tool for evaluating the female reproductive system. Its importance in diagnosis lies in the non-invasiveness of the instrument.

In spite of its immense use in supplementing diagnosis during physiological states, its use in delineating different pathological conditions of the bovine genital tract continues to be less frequently described.

This study was conducted on clinical cases presented to the veterinary gynaecology and obstetrics outdoor to record the sonographic appearance during different pathological conditions of genital tract.

Materials And Methods

Cows presented to the veterinary gynaecology and obstetrics outdoor (n=85) with different pathological conditions were included in the present study. Transrectal sonographic examination was performed using a portable ultrasound machine (AGROSCAN linear, ECM 1"6 BD de la Republique, F 16000 Angouleme, FRANCE), with a linear array dual frequency probe (5.0/7.5 MHz). The images were saved in a multimedia kit attached to the instrument and subsequently transferred to the computer. Animals were examined by rectogenital palpation and ultrasonography was done later to confirm/potentiate the clinical diagnosis. After administration of an appropriate treatment sonography was done again to determine the effect of treatment.

5

Cattle Sympathetic and Behaviour

When moving cattle, it helps to know how they will react to various things. Understanding cattle behaviour can help you get the job done with fewer cowboys and less trauma for cattle. If you are patient, understanding and consistent, you can move cattle with little stress and minimal effort. Whether moving cattle on horseback or on foot, use their behaviour patterns to your advantage, paying particular notice to their flight zone-their bubble of security. Each animal has its own space in which it feels safe and unthreatened. If you come closer than that imaginary boundary, the animal will move away from you.

This bubble is much larger for the wilder, suspicious animal than for a gentle, trusting individual. Wild cattle have a much wider flight zone than tame ones who have been handled frequently and quietly. A wild cow that rarely sees humans may not let you get within 50 yards.

Watch for Signals

Cattle that are excited have a larger flight zone than they do when they are calmer. If you are trying to move cattle without stressing them, pay close attention to the flight zone and stay in tune with the animals' signals and intentions. Approach quietly and slowly, giving the animal or herd time to see you and to realize you are not a threat. If the cattle are accustomed to you, speak to them so they know it is you. Cattle that know you may be more relaxed once they recognize you, whereas they might be more upset by strangers. Cattle have wide-angle vision and can see behind themselves without turning their heads, but they have a blind spot directly behind them and can be startled if you approach them the wrong way.

The direct calm cattle by approaching, but not entering, the bubble of security. One or two people can move a herd or get an individual into a corral using patience and common sense, giving the necessary room for them to move away from you — in the proper direction-while keeping the situation calm and controlled. Understanding the security bubble is one of the keys to easy handling. When you get too close, the animals move. When you retreat from this personal space, they slow down or stop. To move cattle quietly, walk or ride on the edge of this flight zone, pressing it to make them move away from you, and easing off to slow or stop them. When they move in the proper direction at the proper speed, ease up as a reward. Press closer only if they stop.

When working cattle in a small space-such as a corral, alleyway or barn-remember that confined animals may become more nervous. Their 'bubble' will be larger. If you get too close, they may become agitated, especially if you approach them head on. If an animal feels cornered, it won't stay calm. If you invade a cows security space when she feels cornered, she may panic, try to jump the fence or run back over you. If cattle in a corral or sorting alley start to turn back, give them space, back up and get out of their flight zone to allow them to calm down.

If moving a cow forward, approach her from the rear half of her body, behind the shoulder. If you approach ahead of the shoulder, she will turn away from you or back up, defeating your purpose. To keep a cow moving forward, stay off to the side, at the edge of her security bubble, at a position behind her shoulder. Don't follow directly behind a cow; you need to be a little to one side so she can see you. If you are in her blind spot, she will want to stop and turn around to face you.

Cattle don't like a possible threat that is out of their sight. They want to know where you are at all times, and they are much more comfortable about your presence if they can see you. If you approach a cow too closely in her blind area, she may kick you.

TIPS FOR MOVING CATTLE

Don't try to move cattle from the rear. They may run away or stop and turn. Move them at a slow walk and concentrate on moving the leaders. Where they go, the others will follow. Get the herd moving, then you can steer them in a certain direction. Approach at an angle to start them in the direction you wish them to go. Once the leaders are moving, move with them, just behind the leader's shoulder to keep her moving. The herd will tend to stay together if you work quietly. If not alarmed and upset, the tailenders usually follow the rest.

A Two-person Job

Two people can move a large herd efficiently; one can go alongside the leader while the other moves alongside the main herd in a position where cattle won't try to go between the front and rear person. Move up on them to encourage them to go forward in the proper direction. Keep the proper distance to get the proper response. If the herd slows too much, move closer so they will start moving again, then veer off at an angle to relieve the pressure on their security bubble so they'll be at ease and won't move too fast.

Flighty cattle require more 'playing room' than gentle cattle. You can't press too close or they may spook, causing the herd to split or stragglers to break off and go another direction. If working cattle in a corral or through a gate, use body position to keep the herd movement under control and travelling at a sensible speed. Cattle should be trained to respond to your movements so you are always in control.

Follow the Leader

If moving cattle a long way; they will travel better if you let them drift in a long string at their own speed. It is their natural inclination to follow a leader, single file. This will stress them least and avoid the problem of a big bunch milling around in a trail or roadway without leaders. It is easy to move cattle if they are trained to come when you call and to follow you. One or two people can round up and move a large herd a long way, even through difficult terrain, if the cattle know and trust you and realize you are moving them to new pasture.

With one person going ahead of them, calling, and one person behind to herd the stragglers, two people can move a lot of cattle easily. My daughter and I can move our whole herd (more than 300 animals, including cows and calves) several miles up a steep mountain through heavy timber when gathering them off the range in the fall or taking them to the next range pasture. One of us is positioned ahead of the herd, calling them. They trust us and know that every time we call them they are going to better pasture or home to the green fields. Cows that trust you will follow much more readily and eagerly than they will drive, with a lot less energy expended by both them and you.

The best way to move cows is patiently and slowly, especially with calves in the group or fat ones that tire easily. Never hurry them on a hot day. Allowed to go their own speed, and knowing they are going to new pasture, they'll climb a steep mountain willingly without the yelling and chasing that wears out cowboys, horses and cattle. There's a lot of truth in the old cowboy saying that the fastest way to move cows is slowly. If you pace cattle to their abilities, you get there faster and with much less stress than if you try to hurry them and they wear out and quit.

UNDERSTANDING EXPECTED PROGENY DIFFERENCES (EPDS)

The role of purebred breeders is to improve the genetic quality of the seedstock cattle they produce to sell to the commercial beef producers. Expected progeny differences (EPDs) are a valuable tool to aid purebred and commercial producers in the selection of potential breeding stock. Cattle producers must clearly define their breeding objectives and determine what sort of animal is needed to meet their production goals. The purpose of this educational lesson is to assist you in understanding EPDs and to utilize the information to select animals with the genetic transmitting ability to improve your calf crop, your cowherd and eventually your profits. The future of most cattle operations and the future of the beef industry are dependent on the ability to identify animals with superior genetics and use them wisely.

EPDs—What are They?

Expected Progeny Differences (EPDs) can indicate the genetic value of one specific animal compared to another specific animal of the same breed, regardless of the age or location of the herd. In other words, the EPD values for a Hereford bull may not be compared against the EPDs for an Angus or Limousin bull. Each individual member of a breed can have EPD values calculated for it. Purebred breeders report data to the National Herd Improvement Program for their breed to contribute to the breed's national database. Age and sex of a calf, or status as a parent are not limiting factors. EPDs are indicators of the relative genetic merit of beef cattle for various traits. Both purebred and commercial cattle producers can use this genetic merit comparison, but producers must first understand their implications and meanings. Expected Progeny Difference (EPDs) are calculated using performance record information, with a complex algebraic formula in the National Cattle Evaluation Computing Centers at the University of Georgia and Iowa State University.

An EPD value of +10 lb. for weaning weight in one breed may reflect an entirely different level of genetic merit than a +10 lb. weaning weight EPD in a different breed. EPDs are reported by each breed association as a plus (+) or minus (-) value in units consistent with the traits measured. Traits such as birth weight (BW), weaning weight (WW) and yearling weight (YW) are expressed in pounds, but EPDs for scrotal circumferences are in centimeters, EPDs for hip height are in inches and marbling is recorded in degrees. For example, a bull with an EPD The role of purebred breeders is to improve the genetic quality of the seedstock cattle they produce to sell to the commercial beef producers. Expected progeny differences (EPDs) are a valuable tool to aid purebred and commercial producers in the selection of potential breeding stock. Cattle producers must clearly define their breeding objectives and determine what sort of animal is needed to meet their production goals. The purpose of this educational lesson is to assist you in understanding EPDs and to utilize the information to select animals with the genetic transmitting ability to improve your calf crop, your cowherd and eventually your profits. The future of most cattle operations and the future of the beef industry are dependent on the ability to identify animals with superior genetics and use them wisely.

USING EXPECTED PROGENY DIFFERENCES (EPDS)

Example: Assume Cameron the Bull has a birth weight (BW) EPD of +5 lbs. and Caleb the Bull has a birth weight (BW) EPD of –1.5 lbs. If these bulls were bred to an identical set of cows (in terms of genetics and environment) you would expect a difference of 6.5 lbs. in the average birth weight of their progeny. Therefore, from a practical standpoint, if selecting one of these bulls to breed to a set of heifers (with birth weight begin the major management concern) Caleb the Bull would be the sire of choice.

Accuracy values of EPDs

When EPDs are calculated there are some degree of probability that the estimate is correct and a chance that it is not. Don't panic! This is where Accuracy (ACC) values come into play. Each breed association reports an Accuracy figure (ACC) for each individual estimate, which is the amount of relative confidence you can place on the reliability of the EPD. The (ACC) value is the amount of relative information used to estimate the EPD. Accuracy (ACC) values can range from 0.0 to +1.0. Values closer to 1.0 represent greater reliability in the EPD represented.

Bulls without progeny will not have as high an Accuracy (ACC) value as bulls with progeny. As the number of progeny records are recorded, so will the reliability of the estimate. A young bull's EPD for weaning weight Accuracy (ACC) is around.35. As more progeny records become available, the Accuracy value will increase. Accuracy above 0.76 indicate that the EPDs for that particular animal are reliable with little change to be expected in the estimate. The accuracy values for EPDs (*for traits with moderate heritabilites*) can be classified into 3 basic categories.

Important are Carcass EPDs

Carcass EPDs are measures of genetic differences in carcass merit and are of vital importance if you would like to improve your end product. You can use carcass EPDs the same way you use any other EPDs.

For example, if you use a bull that is +. 30 for marbling, what percentage of my calves will grade USDA Choice? *The answer is nobody knows.* It depends upon the average marbling ability of your cowherd, and how the +.30 bull compares with the bull you used before. So let's put the question another way. Suppose you have been using *John the Bull* who has a +.0 for marbling. *John the Bull's* steer calves have averaged a marbling score of 4.8. This is 80 points into the Select grade (a marbling score of 5 would be low Choice). Now suppose you like *Wayne the Bull* who has a marbling score of +. 30. If you bred *Wayne the Bull* to the same cows that were mated to *John the Bull*, the *Wayne*-sired steers should have an average marbling score of 5.10, which is.10 into the small marbling range or low Choice. In other words, by using *Wayne the Bull* rather than *John the Bull*, you should be able to move the average marbling score of your herd from 4.8 to 5.10, or from Select to Low Choice.

GENETIC VALUE OF EXPECTED PROGENY DIFFERENCES

Expected progeny differences (EPDs) provide estimates of the genetic value of an animal as a parent. Specifically, differences in EPDs between two individuals of the same breed predict differences in performance between their future offspring when each is mated to animals of the same average genetic merit. EPDs are calculated for birth, growth, maternal, and carcass traits and are reported in the same units of measurement as the trait (normally pounds). EPD values may be directly compared only between animals of the same breed. In other words, a birth weight EPD for a Charolais bull may not be directly compared to a birth weight EPD of a Hereford bull (unless an adjustment is made to account for breed differences).

EPDs are reported by most major beef breed associations, and are calculated using complex statistical equations and models. These statistical models use all known information on a particular animal to calculate its EPD. This information includes performance data (*i.e.*, weight records) on the animal itself, information from its ancestors (sire and dam, grandsire, great grandsire, maternal grandsire, etc.), collateral relatives (brothers and sisters), and progeny (including progeny that are parents themselves). In short, virtually all performance data that relate to the animal of interest are used to calculate its EPD. These performance records are adjusted for such factors as age and sex of the animal, and age of the dam prior to inclusion in EPD databases.

These adjustment factors allow performance records to be fairly compared in the analysis. Additionally, genetic merit of mates is accounted in evaluating progeny information. Therefore, progeny records are not influenced by superior or inferior mates. The statistical analysis used for EPD calculation also accounts for the effects of environment (nutrition, climate, geographical location, etc.) that exist between herds. These environmental effects can be estimated due to the widespread use of artificial insemination.

Through AI, the same bull can be used in several herds across the country. These common sires create genetic links between herds with differing environments and serve as the foundation for evaluation of performance data and EPD calculation across herds. For these reasons, animals with published EPDs within a breed may be directly compared regardless of their age and origin. Finally, the genetic relationships that exist between various traits are also considered in the EPD calculations

GROWTH AND MATERNAL EPDS

EPDs are most useful to directly compare individuals for a trait of interest. An example set of growth and maternal EPDs for two hypothetical bulls. In this example, assume that the two bulls were each mated to the same set of cows.

Table 5.1

	Birth Weight EPD	*Calving Ease EPD*	*Weaning Weight EPD*	*Yearling Weight EPD*	*Maternal Milk EPD*	*Maternal WW EPD*
Bull A	+5	+0	+20	+40	+15	+25
Bull B	+1	+5	+10	+20	+10	+15

Birth Weight EPDs

The difference in the birth weight EPD value between Bull A and Bull B is 4 pounds (5-1 = 4). Therefore, Bull A would be expected to sire calves that average 4 pounds heavier at birth than calves sired by Bull B. It is important to recognize that EPDs predict the expected difference in performance, not the actual performance. In other words, the EPDs for Bulls A and B suggest there will be 4 pounds difference in birth weight in their progeny when we mate them to a comparable set of cows. EPDs do not predict what the actual birth weight of the calves will be. Research has documented that most calving difficulty is caused by heavy calves at birth. Birth weight EPDs are the most accurate indicators of genetic differences for birth weight. Therefore, considerable emphasis should be placed on birth weight EPDs when selecting bulls for use on heifers.

Calving Ease EPDs

Some breed associations publish calving ease EPDs (Gelbvieh and Simmental most notably). This EPD predicts the ease with which a bull's calves are born to first-calf heifers. Calving ease EPDs are reported as deviations in percentage of unassisted births. In the above example, if Bulls A and B were mated to the same set of heifers, we would expect the heifers bred to Bull B to have 5 per cent more unassisted births.

In other words, we would expect fewer calving problems when Bull B was mated to heifers. Calving ease EPDs consider differences between animals in calf birth weights and actual observed levels of calving difficulty. The calving ease EPD directly predicts calving ease and should be used (when available) as the primary tool for avoiding dystocia problems in the cowherd.

Weaning and Yearling Weight EPDs

Weaning and yearling weight EPDs are indicators of the genes for growth that will be passed from an animal to its progeny. Weaning weight EPDs predict the average difference in weaning weight of a bull's progeny compared to progeny of another bull. This weaning weight difference is predicted for a standard weaning age of 205 days. We would expect calves sired by Bull A to weigh 10 pounds more at weaning than calves sired by Bull B. This difference in weaning weight is attributed solely to differences in genes for growth passed from the bulls to their offspring. The effect of milking ability of the cow is not predicted by this EPD. Rapid early growth is an important selection criteria for cow-calf producers since feeder cattle are sold by the pound.

Yearling weight EPDs predict the average difference in weight of a bull's progeny at a year of age (365 days). Using the EPDs for Bulls A and B above, we would expect calves sired by Bull A to be 20 pounds heavier at a year of age on the average than calves sired by Bull B. Yearling weight EPDs are the most useful indicators of growth rate of slaughter progeny in the feedyard.

Maternal Milk EPDs

Milk EPDs are expressed slightly differently from birth and growth EPDs. Milk EPDs reflect the milking ability of an animal's daughters. This difference in milking ability is expressed as additional pounds of calf weaned by a bull's daughters. Considering the milk EPDs for Bulls A and B, we would expect daughters of Bull A to wean calves that are 5 pounds heavier at weaning than calves out of daughters of

Bull B. This difference is due to the superior milk production of daughters sired by Bull A. Milk EPDs are reflected in weaning weight of a bull's grandprogeny (calves by his daughters).

Milk EPDs are important in bull selection when replacements will be retained in the herd. Optimum milk EPDs need to be determined that match the feed resources and environment of the operation. In other words, more milk is not necessarily better as heavier milking cows may require more nutritional inputs to maintain body condition and reproductive efficiency. Breed needs to be an important consideration when evaluating milk EPDs. Very high milk EPDs for bulls in breeds noted for heavy milking ability may not be advantageous.

Maternal Weaning Weight EPDs

Maternal weaning weight EPD is sometimes referred to as the total maternal EPD or the combined maternal EPD. The meaning is the same, but different terminology for the same EPD is used by different breeds. Maternal weaning weight EPD predicts the total difference in weight of a bull's daughters' calves at weaning. A portion of this difference in weight comes from the milking ability of the bull's daughters (milk EPD), and a portion comes from the genes for growth passed from the bull to his daughters and then on to their calves. Like milk EPDs, maternal weaning weight EPDs are expressed in the weaning weight of a bull's grandprogeny. By definition, maternal weaning weight is equal to the milk EPD + 1/2 the weaning weight EPD. For Bull A in the above example, maternal weaning weight EPD = 15 + (1/2 × 20) = 25. In this case, we would expect daughters of Bull A to wean calves that are a total of 10 pounds heavier at weaning (25-15 = 10) than daughters of Bull B. A portion of this weight advantage is due to the superior milking ability of Bull A's daughters, and a portion is due to superior growth genes for weaning weight passed on by Bull A.

Although maternal weaning weight EPDs can be calculated when milk and weaning weight EPDs are known, most breed associations publish this EPD as well. Like the milk

EPDs, maternal weaning weight EPDs are important when daughters will be retained in the herd. This EPD is the best predictor of how daughters of a bull will perform for calf weaning weight.

There are several other traits for which EPDs are available. These EPDs are not available in all breeds:

Scrotal Circumference EPDs: This EPD is expressed in centimeters and predicts difference in scrotal size that will be passed on to progeny. Bulls with larger scrotal circumference EPDs would be expected to sire daughters that reach puberty at an earlier age, and therefore have earlier calving dates. Scrotal circumference is also an indicator of the quantity of semen produced by bulls.

Gestation Length EPDs: This EPD predicts difference in gestation length (in days) for progeny of a bull. Bulls with lower gestation length EPDs are expected to sire calves that are born earlier (on the average). Shorter gestation lengths have been associated with slight decreases in birth weights and an associated improvement in calving ease. Those breeds that report EPDs for both calving ease and gestation length generally include effects of gestation length in calving ease EPD.

Stayability EPDs: This EPD predicts the probability that a bull's daughters will remain in the herd for a set period of time (commonly six years). This EPD is expressed as a percentage. Bulls with higher stayability EPDs will have an increased likelihood of their daughters remaining in the herd. Stayability EPDs are an indicator of the longevity of a bull[1]s daughters.

Mature Daughter Weight EPDs: Expressed in pounds, this EPD predicts the difference in mature weight of a sire's daughters.

Mature Daughter Height EPDs: This EPD is expressed in inches, and predicts the mature frame size of a sire's daughters

CARCASS EPDS

As a result of an increased emphasis on the end product by the beef industry, breed associations have placed considerable emphasis on providing EPDs for carcass traits.

These EPDs may be used to make desired directional change in carcass traits. Carcass trait EPDs are expressed at a constant slaughter age endpoint, usually around 480 days of age. Carcass trait EPDs are not available for all breeds, or for all bulls within a breed. As emphasis on carcass traits continues to increase, more data will become available for carcass trait EPD calculations.

Data utilized for the calculation of carcass EPDs are derived from two sources-1) slaughter steer and heifer progeny, and 2) ultrasound scan data from primarily yearling bull and heifer progeny. Breed associations may publish carcass EPDs utilizing data from one or both of these sources. Research has demonstrated that EPDs generated from slaughter data vs. ultrasound data are very similar. Therefore, EPDs generated from either source can be effectively used for selection. An example comparison of carcass trait EPDs for two bulls is shown below (Table 5.2)

Table 5.2

	Carcass Weight EPD	*Marbling EPD*	*% Intra-muscular Fat EPD*	*Ribeye Area EPD*	*Fat Thickness EPD*	*% Retail Product EPD*
Bull A	+20	+.20	+.15	+.50	-.04	+.5
Bull B	+10	+.00	+.00	+.25	+.00	-.3

Carcass Weight EPDs

Carcass weight EPDs predict differences in progeny carcass weight (pounds). In the above example, Bull A should produce calves that have carcasses that are 10 pounds heavier than calves sired by Bull B. Carcass weight is an indicator of the total amount of retail product in a carcass, but is a poor indicator of carcass composition (quality and cutability).

Marbling and % Intramuscular Fat EPDs

Marbling EPDs reflect genetic differences in marbling potential passed from a sire to his offspring. These values are expressed as a numerical marbling score. Table 5.3 relates quality grade and numerical marbling score Table 5.3 :

Table 5.3. Quality Grade and Numerical Marbling Score

Quality Grade	*Numerical Score*	*% Intramuscular Fat*
Prime+	10.0-10.9	
Prime"	9.0-9.9	> 12.2%
Prime-	8.0-8.9	9.9-12.1%
Choice+	7.0-7.9	7.7-9.8%
Choice"	6.0-6.9	5.8-7.6%
Choice-	5.0-5.9	4.0-5.7%
Select	4.0-4.9	2.3-3.9%
Standard	3.0-3.9	< 2.3%

This table indicates that a 1.0 unit change in numerical marbling score is equal to a change of a full quality grade (4.5 = Select vs. 5.5 = Choice-). In the example, Bull A would sire slaughter progeny with superior marbling scores compared to Bull B (marbling EPD +.20 vs. +.00). Higher marbling EPDs increase the likelihood of a bull's progeny attaining higher quality grades. In a similar fashion, EPDs generated from ultrasound scan data reflect differences in chemical fat content within the ribeye muscle (intramuscular fat). Research has shown a strong relationship between marbling score and % intramuscular fat. Therefore, selection for higher % intramuscular fat EPDs would be expected to increase marbling scores and associated quality grade in slaughter progeny.

Ribeye Area EPDs

Ribeye area EPD is expressed in square inches. Again using the example, calves sired by Bull A would be expected to have ribeyes that are .25 square inches larger than calves sired by Bull B. Ribeye area is an objective assessment of muscling, and an indicator of total muscle in the carcass or live animal. Ribeye area has been shown to have a positive influence on percentage of carcass retail product. Therefore, bulls with larger ribeye area EPDs will sire calves with more muscle and a higher percentage of carcass retail product.

Fat thickness EPDs

Fat thickness EPDs are expressed in inches, and predict

differences in carcass fat thickness between the 12th and 13th rib. For the two bulls in the example, Bull A should sire calves that have .04 inches less carcass fat cover (at a constant slaughter age) compared to calves sired by Bull B. Fat thickness is the primary indicator of saleable product in the carcass, and is also the primary factor affecting USDA beef carcass yield grades (increased fat thickness is associated with less desirable yield grades). As fat thickness increases, the percentage of carcass retail product declines.

Percent Retail Product EPDs

Percent retail product EPDs predict differences in the yield of closely trimmed retail cuts from the carcass and are expressed on a percentage basis. Percent retail cuts is calculated from the same traits used in the USDA yield grade equation (carcass weight, ribeye area, fat thickness, and % kidney, pelvic, and heart fat). Sires with higher % retail product EPDs are expected to produce progeny with higher cutability and more desirable yield grades. Bull A should sire slaughter progeny whose carcasses will have .8% more retail product than progeny of Bull B (+.5 vs. -.3 % retail product EPD).

INTERPRETING AND USING EPDS

Breed Averages

In addition to directly comparing the EPDs of bulls, it is useful to understand where a particular bull ranks within a breed for traits of interest. This ranking will give a general idea as to the genetic merit of the bull compared to others within the breed. It is important to understand that the average EPD for any trait within a breed is not 0. One reason for this is genetic trend. Genetic trend refers to the improvement in genetics that has taken place over time within a breed due to selection. Over the years, breeders have selected for increased growth, milk production, etc. As this selection has occurred, the average EPDs for bulls within a breed for these traits has also increased and the average EPD for bulls of the most recent calf crop may be considerably larger than 0. Table 5.4. depicts average EPD values for bulls from the 2002 calf crop for several breeds:

Table 5.4: EPD Averages for Non-Parent Bulls-Spring

	CE	*BW*	*WW*	*Milk*	*YW*
Angus		+2.6	+33	+17	+62
Charolais		+1.7	+14.2	+8.8	+24.3
Gelbvieh	104	+1.3	+34	+17	+61
Hereford		+3.9	+34	+12	+57
Limousin		+1.4	+12.3	+4.5	+23.1
Red Angus		+0.4	+28	+14	+49
Simmental	+2.3	+3.3	+36.0	+8.1	+59.1

Consider a bull that has a yearling weight EPD of +25. If this bull is a Charolais, he is around breed average in genetic potential for yearling weight (Charolais breed average yearling weight EPD = +24.3). However, if this bull is an Angus, his yearling weight EPD would be 37 pounds below the current breed average (Angus breed average yearling weight EPD = +62). In this case, a yearling weight EPD of +25 would be interpreted quite differently for a Charolais bull vs. an Angus bull. This demonstrates one reason why EPDs cannot be directly compared between bulls of different breeds. Also, it important to note that the EPDs in the above table do not reflect genetic differences for the traits between breeds, as the EPDs cannot be directly compared across breeds. These average breed values are not directly comparable due to the fact that each breed calculates its EPDs from its own data set. Since the data sets (performance records, pedigrees, etc.) are independent, there are few animals that would be found in more than one breed's records used to calculate EPDs. Without these ties, and without merging data from the different breeds into one data set, the calculated EPDs are not comparable across breeds. Due to genetic trend, the average EPD in each breed changes on a frequent basis. Therefore, it is important to utilize the most current breed averages as a basis of comparison. Current breed averages may be found in the sire summaries available from breed associations.

Breed Percentile Rankings

An understanding of where an animal ranks within its breed for a particular trait EPD is extremely valuable as a selection tool. Breed associations also publish percentile ranking tables in their sire summaries so that bulls can be specifically evaluated as to where their EPDs rank in the breed (top 10 per cent vs. bottom 20 per cent, etc.). Percentile rankings can be misleading if not used in the proper context. For example, a Simmental or Gelbvieh bull that ranks very high in the breed for milk EPD (top 10 per cent for example) may not necessarily be ideal in a commercial crossbreeding programme. A bull with breed average genetic merit for milk may produce daughters that are more optimum in their milk production, resulting in females that are potentially a more efficient match for feed resources and may maintain more optimum reproductive potential. Similar examples could be given for other traits. Perhaps most importantly, the general merit of the breed for each trait needs to be considered along with the rank of an individual bull within that breed.

Accuracy

Accuracy values are published for EPD values reported for an animal. Accuracy can be defined as the relationship between the estimated EPD of the animal and the 'true' EPD of the animal. This relationship is expressed as a number between zero and one. As the accuracy value approaches 1.0, the reported EPD is more likely to represent the true genetic merit of the animal and is less likely to change as more progeny records accumulate. Conversely, low accuracy values (closer to zero) indicate that the reported EPD is less reliable. Accuracy is primarily a function of the amount of information available to calculate an EPD for any given trait. Information, primarily in the form of performance records, is derived from several sources to estimate EPDs on a given animal. These sources include records on the animal itself, its sire and dam, collateral relatives, and progeny records. As the volume and quality of records used in the estimation of an EPD increase, so does the confidence we have that the EPD has been estimated correctly (accuracy).

Table 5.5. Accuracy Values

	Birth Weight EPD	*Accuracy*	*Possible Change*	*'true' EPD Range*
Bull A	+2.0	.25	+2.4	-0.4 to +4.4
Bull B	+2.0	.90	+1.2	+0.8 to +3.2

In Table 5.5 above, Bull A and B have identical Birth Weight EPDs, but differ considerably in their accuracy values. Bull A would be typical of a yearling bull, with his EPD derived from pedigree information and his own individual performance. Most yearling bulls will have accuracy values ranging from .10 to .35 for growth traits. Bull B would be typical of a sire with a large number of progeny who has probably been used by AI in several herds. A practical way to evaluate accuracy is to put it in the context of associated possible change. Possible change defines how much we might expect the current EPD to change (plus or minus) as more information is collected and used in the estimation of the EPD. For Bull A, an accuracy value of .25 for BW EPD is associated with a possible change of +2.4 pounds. From the definition of the possible change value, we expect there to be only one chance in three that the 'true' BW EPD is less than -0.4 pounds (the EPD minus the possible change) or greater than +4.4 pounds (the EPD plus the possible change). Bull B, with a higher accuracy value, has a much lower possible change (+1.2) and therefore smaller range. We expect his true EPD to be between +0.8 and +3.2 pounds. It is important to recognize that EPDs are our best estimates of an animal's genetic worth. We never know the 'true' EPD for any trait on any animal, although EPDs for bulls with high accuracies are expected to closely approach the 'true' value. Accuracy values, therefore, indicate how much we know about the animal's true genetic worth and how confident we can be in the estimated EPD.

Accuracy values can be used to manage risk in a breeding programme. If the two bulls were being considered for use on heifers, there would be much lower risk associated with the use of Bull B. Due to his higher accuracy value, it is less likely Bull B's 'true' EPD will turn out to be substantially higher than the reported value. Comparatively, Bull A has a larger possible change and there is more risk that his 'true' EPD could be higher than the reported value. This example illustrates a primary advantage of using high accuracy, low BW EPD sires through AI on heifers. Similar examples can be given for all EPD traits, and possible change values can be found in sire summaries of all breeds.

An important concept to understand is that EPDs, regardless of accuracy, are our most powerful tool to make genetic change in beef cattle. EPDs have been estimated to be several times more reliable than adjusted weight records, ratios, and visual appraisal. Even on young bulls with relatively low accuracy values, EPDs are our most objective indicator of the animal's genetic merit. For all practical purposes, high accuracy sires are available only through AI. Therefore, most natural service bull-buying decisions will be made using relatively low to moderate accuracy EPDs. Keep in mind when evaluating possible change that there is an equal chance that an EPD will go higher as opposed to go lower (or get 'better' vs. 'worse'). When evaluating young bulls, small differences in WW and YW EPD become less significant due to lower accuracy and higher possible change, permitting more overlap in the range of their 'true' EPDs.

A common misconception is that accuracy is an indicator of expected variation in a resulting calf crop. Accuracy and possible change are not related in any way to progeny variation. High accuracy EPD animals would not be expected to have any more or any less variation in their calf crop compared to low accuracy EPD animals.

CATTLE HANDLING AND WORKING FACILITIES

CATTLE HANDLING

You've heard of horse sense. Well, to get cattle to do what you want takes knowledge of animal behaviour, access to good facilities, and proper handling techniques. All of this together adds up to cow sense! Animal-related injuries to employees can be due to preoccupation, impatience, or anger by the animal or the handler! During these moments, a livestock handler really needs to understand animal behaviour. Well-designed facilities won't make up for a lack of cow sense at this point. Not understanding how cattle perceive their world can make for a long day for you — and your cattle. For example, a styrofoam cup that has fallen into the working alley can make cattle balk. A shadow or a flapping shirt on a post or some other distraction can prevent smooth cattle flow. If you are having trouble working a set of cattle, try looking at the world from their perspective.

How Cattle Perceive Their World?

Cattle really see the world differently. A cow may see more than you see and is often distracted by motion off to the side. However, she doesn't see the world as clear and sharply focused as humans see it, and it takes her more time to process what she has seen. Cattle have panoramic vision in excess of 300 degrees and only have a blind spot directly in the back of their heads. Human vision, by comparison, is roughly 180 degrees, and we have a much larger blind spot.

While their field of vision is practically unlimited, cattle have poor depth perception of nearby objects and have limited vertical vision. Cattle must lower their heads to focus on something on the ground because they only have about 60 degrees of vertical vision, compared to 140 degrees for humans. Due to their limitation in vertical vision and their lack of ability to focus quickly, a shadow on the ground appears to them to be a three-mile deep crevasse! Handlers can help reduce distractions and shadowing by taking these limitations into consideration and using a solid-sided working alley. Also, uniformity in colour of handling facilities will reduce balking. Curved, solidly enclosed, and well-lighted working facilities take advantage of these senses, along with the animal's strong desire to find an avenue of escape when confined.

Cattle also hear differently than humans. They can hear both lower volume and higher frequency sounds better than people. It may be the sound of your truck, with feed in it, more than the sight of the truck, that makes those cows 'come a runnin'. Cattle hear extremely well, but the trade-off is that they have less ability to locate the source of a sound. People can pinpoint where a sound came from within 5 degrees, whereas cattle can only isolate the source down to about 30 degrees. Be mindful of cattle with severe sight problems, such as an advanced case of cancer eye, as they will rely to a greater extent on their sense of hearing. Thus, they may suddenly swing around to investigate a noise.

Comfort/Flight Zone Affects Reactions

People and cattle have a comfort/flight zone that affects how we react. In many Western cultures, two feet is considered the comfort zone for conversing with another person. In some other Eastern regions of the world, six inches is considered normal. At parties, you might observe Western speakers backing up to seek their comfort zone and Eastern speakers following them to maintain their comfort zone. Also, consider that we typically turn and face someone who is talking to us.

Just as we have some predictable behaviours, so do cattle. Understanding this behaviour can be very useful in designing cattle-handling facilities. The flight zone (comfort zone) is the animal's personal space. The flight zone may be five to 25 feet for tame cattle or feedlot cattle and 300 feet for some wild cattle. The flight zone increases when the approach is from the head, and the flight zone also increases when cattle are excited. The flight zone decreases when animals are in a single file chute.

Cattle will normally move effectively if the handler works on the edge of the flight zone. Deep invasion of the flight zone can cause animals to panic. Position A is the location outside of the flight zone where animals will stop moving forward, and Position B, inside the flight zone, will cause the animal to move away from the handler.

Entering the Flight Zone

Livestock handlers need to understand the flight zone and the point of balance. The point of balance for cattle is typically at the shoulder. To make an animal move forward, the handler should stand behind the point of balance. To move the animal backward, the handler stands in front of the point of balance. The animal may try to turn if the handler enters the animal's blind spot. Therefore, don't walk directly behind an animal, but off to the side so you can be seen. Careful, quiet handling of cattle will help improve productivity. Stress imposed by handling and transport can have detrimental effects on weight gain, rumen function, reproductive function, and the immune system. Quiet handling reduces stress-related meat-quality problems such as dark cutters. The amount of stress imposed on an animal is an interaction involving previous experience and genetics.

How quiet your cattle are is at least partially a function of how they are worked. Cattle can remember rough handling. While most cattle will calm down when they are handled quietly, a small percentage of them may remain excited. Highly excitable cattle should be culled. To accurately cull for temperament, there should be a minimum of two observations. More than one evaluation is required to avoid culling a good animal that became excited because an animal next to it became agitated. A behaviour classification table helps in assessing which animals should be culled.

1 = Docile: Gentle; handles quietly; slightly elevated respiration.

2 = Restless: More active; elevated respirations but settles down after joining the group once again.

3 = Nervous: Constant movement; occasionally bumps fences and gates; settles down only after several minutes after returning to the group.

4 = Flighty: Agitated by handling and avoids handlers; bumps into gates and fences; always seems to watch handlers when approaching the group.

5 = Aggressive: Bumps gates and fences and might be willing to challenge handlers; attempts to jump fences and gates.

6 = Very Aggressive: Very aggressive towards handlers; jumps and bellows while in the chute. Exits chute frantically and may still exhibit aggressive behaviour.

If an animal becomes very excited, 20 to 30 minutes are required for its heart rate to return to normal. For this reason, many packers have 'standing' pens to allow cattle to calm down prior to harvest. Many practictioners of artificial insemination also try to sort cattle and let them relax prior to breeding.

Steps such as reducing yelling and minimizing electric prod usage should be considered. If a tool is needed, a stick with a plastic bag on the end or wands that rattle may be useful. Solid sides on chutes and crowd pens help keep animals calmer. Solid sides provide the most advantage when wild cattle are worked and have less effect on tame animals.

DEFENSIVE ANIMALS

Horses usually kick directly towards the rear. Cattle are 'round-house' punchers. Cows kick forward and out to the side. Cows also have a tendency to kick towards a side with pain. So, if a cow is suffering from mastitis in one quarter, consider approaching her from the opposite side of the affliction. Calves can kick directly backwards and can have a quick 'round-house' punch.

Cattle exhibiting maternal instincts are usually more defensive and difficult to handle. Removal from a familiar pasture or pen can cause animals to react unexpectedly. Shadows, yelling, and contrasts in lighting can further excite animals and make their behaviour unpredictable. Similar problems occur when animals are moved away from feed, separated from the herd, or approached by an unfamiliar person. It is usually easier to take two or three additional animals when you want to work only one of them. Never prod an animal when it has no place to go. Cattle that become upset during handling and/or that have a bad disposition may adopt a 'fight' rather than 'flight' behaviour. When entering an enclosed area with cattle, you should consider your escape routes — a fence, a tree, or a post.

Diseases

Handlers should also be concerned with disease transmission. Illnesses that can be transmitted back and forth between humans and animals include leptospirosis, rabies, brucellosis, salmonellosis, and ringworm.

A livestock producer can contract some illnesses through animal bites, handling an infected animal, or disposing of infected tissues. To reduce exposure to disease, use basic hygiene and sanitation practices, such as washing your hands after working with any animals. To Reduce Exposure to a Livestock Accident or Illness

- Understand animal behaviour.
- Provide proper and safe facilities.
- Protect against diseases by using good sanitation practices.
- Wear appropriate attire.

WORKING FACILITIES

CURVED WORKING CHUTES

A curved working alley takes advantage of an animal's natural behaviour to turn away from potential danger or unpleasant sites or sounds. Curved working facilities prevent the animal from seeing the squeeze chute or truck until they are almost upon it. A facility with solid sides is likely to require a catwalk.

Cattle like to follow each other. Each animal should be able to see the one ahead of it. Blocking gates in a chute need to be see-through gates, so cattle can see the animal ahead. If the animal views a dead-end, it will balk. Make single-file chutes at least 20 feet long. Uniform lighting can help avoid shadows. Cattle in the dark will move towards the light. If you are loading at night, use a frosted light in the truck or shine your flashlight into the truck. Avoid glare in their faces. Livestock tend to balk if they are forced to look into the sun. Position loading and squeeze chutes north and south for summer handling.

RESPONSE TO MOVEMENT OR STRANGE SIGHTS

A white styrofoam cup in the bottom of the working chute will cause the entire herd to balk. Cattle also balk at moving or flapping objects. Therefore, do not place your jacket on a strategic fence post in the working area. Use solid sides for the construction of crowding pens, single-file chutes, and loading chutes. Stand back from the head gate so that the cattle cannot see you or at least think they can escape past you.

Bruises

Bruises cost the cattle industry millions of dollars each year. A large loin bruise is a significant economic loss per animal. Bruised meat has to be trimmed off and cannot be used for human consumption. When cattle become excited, they are more likely to bump into gates, truck doors, and each other. Moving cattle at a slow walk will reduce bruises. Overloading trucks will greatly increase bruising. Although over crowding can increase bruising, having too few cattle can also increase bruising.

Table 5.6: Recommended Truck-Loading Densities.

Feed-Fed Steers or Cows, Average Weight *lbs.*	*Horned or Tipped or More Than 10% Horned or Tipped* *sq. ft.*	*Polled or Dehorned* *sq. ft.*
800	10.9	10.4
1,000	12.8	12.0
1,200	15.3	14.5
1,400	19.0	18.0

Bumping into a flat, wide surface is less likely to cause bruises compared to bumping into an elevated or sharp edge. Broken boards, protruding gate latches, and slick surfaces that allow falling will increase bruising. Consider regrooving concrete when it becomes too smooth. If you are getting reports of bruising, walk through your handling facility and look for the following situations.

BASIC CORRAL DESIGN

Working facilities are needed to carry out basic management practices. Some small producers feel that working facilities are too expensive, but without proper facilities, basic management practices are not done. Not doing basic management practices such as dehorning and castration can lead to economic losses as a result of discounts on your calves. Handling facilities also increase the safety for humans when working animals.

Planning

The goal is to develop a design that accommodates your cattle working needs while making safe and efficient use of available labour and reducing stress and bruising of animals.

Site Selection

Accessibility by people, trucks, and trailers is paramount for a working corral. This accessibility must be convenient even in adverse weather. Normally, the easiest place to pen cattle is along the fence, especially in a corner of a pasture. Ideally, this location would be where several pastures converge. The pasture fence in proximity to the corral may get additional pressure from cattle pushing on it. Therefore, larger posts and additional bracing may be needed in this part of the pasture fence.

Look for high, well-drained sites. Avoid locations with slopes of greater than 10 degrees (about two inches per foot). Build facilities near electric and water, if possible. However, avoid building adjacent to residences where dust, flies, noise, and odour might be grounds for a nuisance suit. Here is a checklist of items to consider when locating a cattle-handling facility. Basic Sections in a Well-Designed Working Facility:

- Holding pens
- Alley from pens to working area
- Crowding pen/tub
- Working alley
- Restraining area/squeeze chute
- Loading area.

HOLDING PENS

Keys to good holding-pen design are having enough pens to meet your needs, having them of sufficient size so animals cannot get past you, and having an easy animal flow to and from the working area. More than one pen will probably be needed so that you can sort cattle into groups. One of the most common flaws in existing corrals is having a holding pen that is too large. Cattle can easily get past you when you are trying to move them out. One of the easier 'refits' to an existing corral is splitting this large pen into two pens. This helps to address the other most common design flaw of existing corrals — not having enough pens for sorting.

Common design flaws of existing corrals are:

- Pens too large
- Inadequate number of pens for sorting
- Poor placement of gates
- Not enough gates
- Confusing animal flow to and from the working facility.

Smaller pens may be needed as hospital pens and to quarantine newly arrived animals. Provide a source of water and shade in one of the holding pens as a sick or quarantine area. You may want to take into account in what order you want to work cattle groups and thus this may affect pen placement. Keep in mind the fact that current pen placement affects possible corral expansion in the future.

Allow 20 square feet for each cow and 14 square feet for each calf. The area of a square or rectangular pen is equal to the length times the width. For example, a pen with an area measuring 30 feet by 40 feet equals 1,200 square feet. This will accommodate about 35 cows with calves. The following example illustrates how the value of 35 cows with calves was calculated:

20 sq. ft. per cow
+ 14 sq. ft. per calf
————————————
+ 34 sq. ft. for a cow with a calf
1,200 sq. ft. pen/34 sq. ft. = 35 cows with calves

Alley From Pens to Working Area

Typically, cattle are moved to the working area through an alley. This can be a common alley for cattle going to or returning from the working area. In larger operations, a second alley allows a continuous flow of cattle from the holding pens to the working area and back to their pens. Evaluate your corral design and determine if animal flow to and from the working facility is simple or confusing.

Holding-pen gates should be equal to or greater in length than the width of the alley. Alleys should be 10 to 12 feet in width. Wide alleys can be like large pens and allow cattle to escape past you.

Narrow alleys, less than 10 feet, may force animals to come through you, rather than go around you, if their desire to escape is great.

Notice in the examples here how the gates become a part of the fence and effectively direct flow of the animals to and from the working area. Cattle typically travel to corners. Therefore, gates should be located in corners rather than the middle part of a fence line.

Crowding Pen or Crowding Tub

Use a crowding pen to funnel cattle into the working alley and chute. Handle small groups in crowding pens, eight to 10, instead of 20. For construction with straight fences, build one side of the crowding pen straight. The other side should be at an angle of about 30 degrees. Make the large end of the funnel 8 to 12 feet wide. Although it is harder to build, a circular crowding area with solid sides works best. Pre-built crowding pens can be purchased from cattle-handling equipment vendors.

While there may be several gates in a corral that can benefit from being solid-sided, a gate in the crowding tub will benefit the most. A solid-sided gate will encourage animals to seek an alternative escape route — the working alley — rather than trying to turn around.

Rough concrete surfaces throughout a corral are ideal but may not be economically feasible. However, consider using concrete in the crowding tub, working alley, and restraining area.

Working Alley/Chute

Build working alleys at least 20 feet long. Shorter alleys cause delays in getting cattle to the working area. If you normally work cattle by yourself, an alley should be able to hold at least three animals for efficient labour utilization. Longer chutes can certainly be used. You may find spring loaded, back-stop gates useful to prevent cattle from backing up. The width depends on the size of the animal. Build alleys 22 to 26 inches wide for small-to medium-frame cows. Eighteen inches is wide enough for calves. Commercial working alleys may be adjustable. One idea to consider for constricting the width of a 'non-adjustable' alley is to hang a couple of plastic pipes in the alley when working calves.

Although they are harder to build, alleys with solid, sloping sides are better than those with vertical sides. A general recommendation is to build a five-foot-high alley 26 inches wide at the top and 16 inches wide at the bottom. Widths may need to be increased 2 to 4 inches for some large, exotic breeds.

Solid-sided working alleys can be built with wood or pipe frames covered with sheet metal or exterior plywood. Due to cost and ease of construction, straight alleys can be a reasonable choice for small herds. Emergency release panels, fences on hinges, could be considered if you are concerned about cattle getting down or falling backward. Pre-constructed, metal working alleys/chutes can be purchased from handling equipment vendors. These can also offer the option of being somewhat mobile.

Posts in the working alley receive a lot of pressure from the cattle. Use overhead crossbars to keep the posts in place and prevent them from bowing out. Further construction of overhead restrainers running parallel over the working alley will discourage rearing up or falling over backward in the working alley. Evaluate the height of the tallest animal you will work through a facility if your corral is to have overhead crossbars and restrainers. Cattle will move forward more easily in an alley with solid sides. Solid, curved chutes keep cattle from seeing the working area until they are a few feet away. Avoid sharp bends that look like a dead end to cattle.

Cattle tend to move uphill easier than downhill. If there is much slope, point the alley uphill. Cattle also tend to move best from dark areas to light areas. Facility layouts should be designed so that cattle do not look directly into the sun.

RESTRAINING AREA/SQUEEZE CHUTE OR HEADGATE

The simplest way to create a working area is to securely fasten a head gate to the end of the working chute. Insert pipes or posts behind animals to prevent backing. A squeeze chute is more expensive than a headgate but gives you more control over the animal. Many vendors sell head gates, squeeze chutes, and fence panels. While plans are available, it is difficult to build a head gate or chute that works as well as those that are commercially available. Some new designs allow easier access to the neck region. All injections should be in the neck region.

To save climbing over the fence, build an entrance gate behind the squeeze chute or at the rear of the animal. The gate should swing into the chute to block the next animal and create a cage to protect the person working the cattle.

Ideally, utilize a separate chute or breeding box for artificial insemination; this reduces the stress of the cow from her previous experiences in the working chute and headgate. The working chute is a common location for the use of electrical equipment.

To avoid exposure to electric shocks:

- Use a ground fault circuit interrupter with water heaters, clippers, and other equipment.
- Use moisture-proof electrical outlets in wet or damp areas.

Portable battery systems can be used as well. Boat batteries may have the most storage capacity.

LOADING CHUTE

Cattle can be loaded on stock trailers from the working chute. If pick-ups are used, a loading chute is required. Make sure the height of the chute fits your truck and that you can back the truck squarely against the chute. If you use more than one type of truck, build an adjustable loading chute. Do not exceed 3-1/2 inches of rise per foot of length.

A flooring of packed earth or gravel provides the best footing but is not adjustable. On wooden floored chutes, use cleats that are one inch to two inches in height. Space cleats six inches to eight inches apart from edge to edge. Build loading chutes 30 inches wide for cow-calf operations.

Materials

A layer of gravel in crowding and working chutes can prevent mud from becoming a problem. Concrete in heavy traffic areas is a good idea but only if it has a rough surface. Grooves one-inch deep and in an eight-inch diamond pattern improve footing. Use pipe or wooden gates that will not easily bend or break. Hang gates six to eight inches from the ground so they swing freely. Use latches that can be operated from either side. Plywood on some sorting and crowding tub gates can help prevent turning.

Build fence five-feet high for most cattle. Fences for holding pens do not have to be as strong as those in working areas. Wire panels are available from most farm supply centres. Install two-inch by six-inch rails on the inside at the top of the posts, bottom and middle. This type of fence is not strong enough for the crowding area and working chutes. The following are some simplified designs for smaller cow herds.

Table 5.6 : Corral and Working Facility Dimensions

	To 600 lb	*600-1,200*	*<1,200 and Cow-Calf*
Pen Space (sq ft/head)	14	17	20
Crowding Tub (sq ft/head)	6	10	12
Working Chute-vertical sides			
Width (inches)	18	20-24	26-30
Minimum Length (feet)	20	20	20
Working Chute-sloping sides			
Width at Bottom (inches)	13	15	16
Width at Top (inches)	20	24	28
Minimum Length (feet)	20	20	20
Working Chute Fence			
Height—minimum	45	50	60

Contd...

Depth of Posts—minimum	30	30	30
Corral Fence			
Height	60	60	60
Depth of Posts—minimum	30	30	30
Corral Fence			
Width (inches)	26	26	26-30
Length (minimum, feet)	12	12	12
Rise, in/ft	3½	3½	3½

Dimensions from *Corral and Working Facilities for Beef Cattle.*

UNDERSTANDING MOTIVATION OF CATTLE AND HORSES

Fear and aggression are often misinterpreted. Did the horse kick because he was fearful, or did he kick because he was aggressive or bad? Neurologically, fear and aggression are different emotions that may result in similar behaviours, such as kicking or pinning the ears back.

Determining which emotion motivates the kicking is important, because punishing a horse for kicking will make a fear-based behaviour worse. If kicking occurs during a training exercise, it is likely to be fear based. Fear is also the likely motivation if an animal becomes agitated when it is alone, tied up, or held in a squeeze chute.

Another factor is genetics. A horse or ox with a nervous, highstrung temperament is more likely to have fear-motivated behaviour than an animal with a calm, placid temperament. It is unfortunate that some breeders select for hot-blooded draft horses. This pattern of selection is likely to result in more problems with fear-motivated behaviour. An animal with a hot temperament is more likely to blow up when it is suddenly confronted with a scary novel experience.

Many people have said to me, 'My horse behaves well at home, but goes berserk at shows.' This behaviour occurs because shows have many scary things an animal never sees at home. A flighty horse must be accustomed to flags, balloons, and fast moving bikes long before he goes to a show. A safe way to introduce a horse to balloons and flags is to put them in a large pasture and allow the horse to explore them. A dangerous practice is to suddenly confront a horse that has a nervous flighty temperament with a scary object, such as a flag, when he is in a confined space where he cannot move away.

Flags and balloons are scary because they make rapid movements and have bright contrasting colours. Bikes are frightening because they move rapidly and can silently sneak up on the horse. If the horse is allowed to voluntarily approach these objects, however, they may become attractive.

ELIMINATING LEARNED BAD BEHAVIOUR

An animal often learns bad behaviours because people inadvertently reward the behaviour. One common problem behaviour is a horse pawing and striking the stall door at feeding time. The horse acts this way because he thinks it will speed up being fed. If feed is given while the horse is striking the stall door, his undesirable behaviour will be reinforced and rewarded. He learns to associate being fed with pawing the door. To eliminate the behaviour, drop feed into the manger at the precise instant the horse stops pawing at the door. The timing must be right so the horse will associate keeping his foot still with getting fed. To stop pawing behaviour, reward the horse for keeping his foot still.

True Aggression

True aggressive behaviour occurs when an animal views a person as a herd mate that needs to be dominated. This problem occurs especially with bulls. Castration will reduce aggression in adult animals and, if done at a young age, mostly eliminate it. In grazing animals, an orphan male raised away from its own species may be imprinted to people and think he is a person. The resulting behaviour is cute in a young animal, but when the male becomes fully mature he can be dangerous. At full maturity he may turn on his caretakers to prove that he is now the dominant male in the herd. Raising young bull calves in a social group helps prevent aggression towards people.

Young bulls and stallions must learn they are not people. Orphaned male grazing animals should be either castrated or placed in a social group with their own kind by 6 weeks of age. When they grow up with their own kind they learn who they are and any aggression is more likely to be directed towards their own kind.

The male aggression problem is not due to the animal being tame. It is due to mistaken identity. Social behaviour in grazing animals has to be learned. Grazing animals must learn the normal give and take of social behaviour. Horses or cattle that are reared alone will often be vicious fighters when mixed with other animals. A young stud colt reared alone may constantly fight other horses because he has never learned that once he has become dominant he doesn't need to keep fighting. Stallions will be easier to manage when they mature, if they are reared as young colts on a pasture full of other adult horses.

Instinctual Behaviour

Instincts or so-called fixed action patterns are behavioural patterns that are hard wired into an animal like a computer programme. These innate behavioural programmes are not dependent on learning. The behavioural programme runs when it is triggered by certain specific stimuli that animal behaviour specialists call sign stimuli.

Birds have many more instinctual behavioural patterns than mammals. The mating dance of birds is a good example of instinctual behaviour. In stallions and bulls the flehmen lip curl is an example of an instinct. Smelling a female in estrus will trigger it. Many reproductive behaviours are hard wired and instinctual. Pressing on a calf's forehead may trigger butting, which will become dangerous when he grows up. A calf should be stroked under the chin or on the withers to encourage it to take a submissive posture. Never play butting games with calves.

An instinctual behaviour often interacts with learned behaviour. Breeding behaviour is instinctual, but who is bred is learned. Ram lambs nursed by nanny goats will attempt to breed goats when they mature. To establish normal breeding behaviour, orphan animals should be reared in a pen with their own species. Bottle feeding a baby for a few weeks will usually not cause cattle to imprint to people if they are penned with their own species.

Understanding the motivating basis of a behaviour makes it easier to deal with that behaviour and improve an animal's performance. Punishing fear may make it worse, but some force may be required to stop true aggression. When dealing with aggression, imitate the animal's natural instinctual behaviour patterns. A bull that is ready to attack will make a broadside display to show how big he is, facing sideways towards the one he plans to dominate. The broadside threat is an innate instinctual aggressive threat behaviour. A bull that displays it towards people can be dangerous indeed. Some bulls will submit and move away when a person makes an imitation of the broadside threat by making themselves look big. If the bull will not submit and move away, he should be culled before he kills somebody. Any bull that charges people in an open pasture is potentially dangerous and should be culled. Aggression towards people must be prevented by rearing bulls in a social group.

Smaller animals, such as pigs and alpacas, that become aggressive may be dominated by using species typical aggressive patterns. I have successfully exerted dominance on more than one young pig by shoving on its neck with a board, in the same location where a dominant pig would bite. Rearing animals in social groups, however, is the best way to avoid problems of mistaken identity.

Exerting dominance over an animal does not mean beating it into submission. During training, all animals respond to positive reinforcement such as a feed treat, stroking, or a kind voice. Trainers should use positive reinforcements to train horses, cattle, and other animals to do tasks. Next time you watch a pulling contest, note how the loggers' horses usually pull better than horses that have been motivated to pull by whipping. Positive rewards make a better motivator than fear.

UNDERSTAND CATTLE'S GRAZING BEHAVIOUR

In order to optimize livestock production in grazing conditions, the animals must be able to graze the pasture effectively and efficiently. Having a good basic understanding of cattle grazing behaviour will help you to anticipate their impact on the pasture and ultimately help improve your grazing management skills. Cattle usually have anywhere from three to five large meals over the course of a day. The largest meals will occur early in the morning around sunrise and-again late in the day around sunset. During the daytime interval between those major meals they will consume a few other smaller meals. Overall they usually graze anywhere from six to 11 hours every day. The bulk of that grazing will be during daylight hours. Cattle do not generally spend a lot of time grazing at night. The exception to this is when daytime air temperature and humidity levels are high. At that point cattle may shift their daily grazing activities to include night grazing when the environmental conditions are less harsh.

The biting rate of cattle is an impressive 30 to 60 bites per minute. Variation in an animal's biting rate can be due to many factors, one of which is the condition of the pasture. In a pasture of short sparse forage cattle will take more bites, but they will be smaller bites. Whereas in a lush thick pasture the animal may take fewer bites, but each bite will contain more forage. This behaviour can also impact the total time they spend grazing each day. Where there is an ample supply of good quality forage, cattle will spend less total time grazing than when the quantity and/or quality of forage are inadequate. Cattle exhibit preferences for different parts of the plant based on their palatability. That extra time spent grazing when pasture conditions are less than favourable is because the cattle are spending extra time searching for the most palatable forage from what is available. So even though they appear to be grazing for a long period of time, their actual intake may not differ or may even be less than that of cattle in pastures of adequate forage availability that spent less time grazing.

Pasture condition will also impact how much time the animal spends ruminating each day. In general, cattle probably spend five to nine hours each day ruminating. Most ruminating occurs at night when cattle are bedded down, but cattle also ruminate between meals during the day. The more mature the forage is that is being consumed, the more time the animal must spend ruminating in order to breakdown that forage for further digestion. Eventually, daily intake may be restricted when mature forage is consumed due to the excessive amount of time necessary to ruminate that forage.

Since the biggest meals of the day are at dawn and dusk, this means that interrupting those meals will cause a change in the animals' natural grazing behaviour. If animals are being fed supplemental feed, think about what time of day that feed is offered. If it is early in the morning during one of their biggest grazing meals of the day they will stop grazing to consume the supplement. This will result in less time spent grazing. However if they are fed the supplement in the middle of the day or early afternoon, this will not interrupt the morning meal and they should still resume their large evening meal as normal. Interrupting the major grazing meals of the day may lead to a decrease in forage intake and animal performance.

Take the opportunity to watch your cattle during different times of the day and pick up on their customary behaviours. Also take note of how they behave when grazing during different times of the year, when grazing various types of forage, and when different supplemental feeds or hay are offered. Having the knowledge of what their routine behaviours are will help you determine how well they are responding when new or different management regimes are being implemented.

6

Reproductive Performance of Cattle

PRODUCTIVITY AND REPRODUCTION

The productivity of cattle largely depends on their reproductive performance. Cows that rarely deliver a live calf are not worth keeping. Poor reproductive performance is caused by:

- Failure of the cow to become pregnant, primarily due to anoestrus (prepubertal or postpartum);
- Failure of the cow to maintain the pregnancy; and
- Calf losses.

This monograph summarises knowledge of the reproductive biology of cows, with emphasis on *Bos indicus* types. After a brief introduction to the reproductive anatomy and endocrinology of the cow, subsequent chapters describe changes which occur at puberty, during the oestrous cycle, and at pregnancy; measures of reproductive performance; causes of infertility, and how these can be diagnosed and their effects minimised; the role of nutrition in cattle reproduction; lactational anoestrus and the effect of weaning; and herd health programmes. Data from Africa, Asia, America and Australia are presented. Where data from zebu cattle were not available, points are illustrated or emphasised using data on *Bos taurus* cattle, or other species.

This monograph is intended for field workers in agriculture and livestock production and health, particularly in Africa, who may not have access to current publications on this subject. However, it gives enough detail to be useful also to higher degree students and researchers. It is hoped that this review will stimulate more research, especially in Africa.

ANATOMY AND ENDOCRINOLOGY OF COW REPRODUCTION

Anatomy

The genital tract of non-pregnant cows normally lies in the pelvic cavity and consists of the vulva, vagina, cervix, uterus, Fallopian tubes (oviducts), ovaries and their supporting structures. Most of the reproductive structures can be palpated through the rectum; this is the basis of routine fertility work described in subsequent sections of this monograph. In general the reproductive tract of Bos indicus cattle is smaller than that of taurine cattle. The reproductive tract is supplied by blood from the utero-ovarian and uterine arteries, of which the middle uterine artery is the largest.

The uterus is a muscular organ consisting of a body, about 4 to 5 cm long, and two uterine horns (cornua), each 15 to 25 cm in length and 1 to 3 cm in diameter. The uterus is suspended by the broad ligament in a coiled or curled manner. Its size varies with breed, age, parity, pregnancy and disease. The cervix is a sphincter-like structure with a thick wall and a narrow lumen. This lumen is tightly closed, except during oestrus and at parturition, and the cervix forms a barrier between the uterus and the outside environment. The length of the cervix varies from 1.5 cm in heifers to 8 cm in multiparous cows of larger breeds. Interlocking ridges and complex folding of the lumen mucosa can hamper insertion of a pipette or tube for intra-uterine insemination or infusions.

The vagina extends backwards from the cervix and opens into the vulva. Its length varies with breed and stage of pregnancy. The vaginal epithelial cells near the cervix secrete mucus, especially around the time of oestrus. The ovaries are oval-shaped structures, 1 to 4 cm long and 1 to 3 cm in diameter; their size depends on the stage of the reproductive cycle. They are linked to the uterus by the Fallopian tubes which open anteriorly into the fimbriae-funnel-shaped structures close to, but not attached to the ovaries. The fimbriae guide unfertilized eggs from the ovary into the Fallopian tubes.

The ovary of a new-born heifer may contain up to 100,000 primordial follicles. However, only a few of these mature and release an ovum. From birth to shortly before puberty the primordial follicles are in a state of arrested development (dictyotene; the resting stage). Shortly before puberty, many primordial follicles start to grow and develop in response to hormone (gonadotrophin) stimulation. The presence of developing follicles indicates active gametogenesis and steroidogenesis. During each oestrous cycle, several follicles may develop to the Graafian stage, but usually only one reaches full maturity and ruptures to release the ripe ovum (ovulation): the others become atretic.

Ovulation involves changes in steroid, gonadotrophin and prostaglandin secretions along with alterations in ovarian neuromusculature, in particular the breakdown of the follicular wall, escape of the ovum and release of follicular fluid. The ovulation fossa formed after ovulation fills with blood to become the corpus haemorrhagicum and eventually the corpus luteum (yellow body), which protrudes from the surface of the ovary.

ENDOCRINOLOGY OF REPRODUCTION

The development of radio-immunoassay (RIA), competitive protein binding (CPB) and enzyme-linked immunosorbent assay (ELISA) methods since the 1960s has allowed rapid, accurate and sensitive measurement of the concentration of several pituitary, ovarian and adrenal hormones in blood, tissue, milk and urine. Ovarian tissue can now be studied in vitro. Cells can be broken down and the secretion and use of hormones by their organelles examined. The interrelations among hormones at various stages of the reproductive cycle in the female cow are therefore better understood, as are the physiological control mechanisms that govern reproductive function. The endocrine system comprises a series of ductless glands, each of which secretes one or several hormones that integrate body functions. Hormones are secreted directly into the blood and act on tissues elsewhere in the body.

The reproductive cycle of the cow is mainly coordinated by hormones produced by the hypothalamus, pituitary and ovary. Gonadotrophic releasing hormone (GnRH), secreted by the hypothalamus, stimulates the anterior pituitary to secrete two gonadotrophic hormones-follicle stimulating hormone (FSH) and luteinising hormone (LH). Both of these hormones control ovarian function: FSH initiates maturation of follicles, and LH induces ovulation and luteinisation of granulosa and thecal cells. The major hormones produced by the ovaries are oestrogens (primarily oestradiol-17 b), which are produced by the follicles, and progesterone, secreted by the corpus luteum. Oestrogens play important roles in oestrus manifestation, and progesterone in maintenance of pregnancy. Both regulate the reproductive cycle through a series of feedback mechanisms acting on the hypothalamus and pituitary glands. In addition to these hormones, prostaglandins, which are produced by several tissues, including the uterus, also control the cow reproductive cycle in various ways. Details of the functions of these hormones at puberty, during normal oestrous cycles, during pregnancy, and in the postpartum period are given in the following sections. Other hormones, produced by the thyroid, parathyroid and adrenal glands, the placenta and the pancreas are also important in regulating reproduction.

There are differences in the hypothalamic, pituitary and ovarian relationships in zebu and taurine cattle. These differences probably account for differences in fertility between the two species even when similarly fed and managed. This section highlights the endocrinology of reproduction in Bos indicus cattle. Data from taurine cattle and other species are used for emphasis and where information for zebu cattle is not readily available.

Endocrine Changes in the Prepubertal Heifer

Little information is available on the hormonal control of puberty in the zebu. Early studies tended to compare the endocrine patterns in heifers with those of more mature animals. It was originally thought that the pituitary of prepubertal animals was incapable of elaborating sufficient gonadotrophic hormones to stimulate the ovaries. This was based on observations, such as those by researchers among Boran zebus, that administering gonadotrophins stimulated follicular growth and ovulation. However, follicle growth starts soon after birth, as does the release of gonadotrophins, FSH and LH. The ovaries of 2-month old calves can respond to gonadotrophin therapy and calf follicles can secrete oestrogens. Prepubertal ovaries also respond when transplanted to mature animals and injecting oestradiol results in LH release in calves as young as 3 months old. The possible causes of sexual maturation at puberty appear to be an increase in pituitary hormones output culminating in increased size and activity of the ovaries, and maturation of the hypothalamo-pituitary axis, resulting in secretion of gonadotrophins.

Luteinising Hormone

LH levels fluctuate before puberty but tend to increase as puberty approaches. By taking samples more frequently from Angus heifers, Gonzalez-Padilla *et al.* (1975a) confirmed that prepubertal heifers do not lack LH as such, but there is no cyclic pattern to its release. Two LH peaks were observed prior to puberty, the first (priming) peak at 9 to 11 days before first oestrus. This diphasic profile was also observed among Brown Swiss heifers. In heifers attaining puberty at 10 months old, LH and FSH levels increased from birth to 3 months, declined to a nadir at 5-6 months and then increased to a second peak at about 9 months.

LH secretion in prepubertal heifers is probably suppressed through an inhibitory feedback (gonadostat) effect. The components of the endocrine system can apparently function soon after birth. LH is secreted from the pituitary gland and stimulates ovarian follicles to produce oestradiol-17 b. However, the hypothalamus-pituitary axis is highly sensitive to the negative feedback effect of oestradiol, and further LH release is inhibited. Ovariectomy of immature rats significantly increases the concentration of plasma LH and FSH. The same is true in the calf. The sensitivity of the hypothalamus-pituitary axis to oestradiol must thus decrease prior to puberty in the heifer. This allows LH to stimulate follicular growth and leads to increased oestrogen production and ovulation.

Oestradiol and Progesterone

There are few reports on the plasma concentration of oestradiol-17 b in prepubertal heifers. Glencross (1984), using a sensitive and fully validated radio-immunoassay, found that the plasma oestradiol-17 b levels of four British-Friesian heifers varied randomly within the range 1 to 4 ng/litre between 59 and 15 days before puberty. About 8 days prior to puberty, oestradiol-17 b levels increased significantly (P<0.02) to a mean of 6.3 ±1.3 ng/litre, comparable to the normal preovulatory peak in post-pubertal heifers. It was not clear, however, if this induced an LH surge and ovulation. Progesterone levels subsequently rose (P<0.001) to a peak of 1.0 ±0.1 m g/litre on the fourth day, indicating some luteinisation. After the return of the progesterone to basal levels, oestradiol-17 b again rose significantly (P<0.001) to a second peak of 9.0 ±1.0 ng/litre on the day of first oestrus. Following this second peak, concentration of progesterone in the plasma remained high and pregnancy was confirmed in three of the heifers. The second peak in oestradiol-17 b concentration had therefore been followed by ovulation. A third oestradiol-17 b peak (P<0.02) of 4.3 ±0.8 ng/litre occurred 4 days later, when progesterone levels were rising sharply due to the formation of a corpus luteum. The changes in oestradiol-17 b and progesterone on or after the day of first oestrus were similar to those observed in post-pubertal heifers and mature cows.

Studies among *Bos taurus* heifers showed that progesterone concentration is low through most of the prepubertal period with two rises before puberty. The first occurred between 18 and 11 days before the LH peak and was thought to be of adrenal origin. The second, from 9 days before until the day of the LH peak, was assumed to be of ovarian origin. Schams *et al.* (1981) also observed an increase in progesterone concentration for 8-12 days before first oestrus in four Brown Swiss heifers that attained puberty at about 10 months old. A fifth heifer, which showed first oestrus at 14 months, exhibited a progesterone secretion pattern resembling that of a normal corpus luteum during the 18 days before first oestrus. Prior to this rise, levels were elevated for 8 days, but only slightly. Similar elevations in progesterone concentration were reported by researchers who attributed them to small luteal tissues, deeply embedded in the ovary, which could not be palpated. This agrees with the scientists, who stated that, in general, there is no compelling evidence for a role of adrenal sex steroids in the onset of puberty. These initial rises in progesterone may establish a phasic pattern to LH release and/or sensitise the ovaries to LH as in some postpartum cows.

The observations have led to attempts to stimulate puberty. Most efforts have tried to simulate the transient rise in progesterone prior to first oestrus using implants or daily injections of progesterone combined with oestrogen or pregnant mare serum gonadotrophin. Generally the treatments have been more successful in animals approaching puberty.

Endocrinology of the Oestrous Cycle

The concentrations of the main reproductive hormones in the plasma change during the cow oestrous cycle. Hypothalamic GnRH induces the release of both LH and FSH from the pituitary. LH is released in pulses. Each LH pulse appears to be in response to a release of GnRH from the hypothalamus and LH secretion can be stimulated by GnRH injections. LH induces ovulation and luteinisation of the granulosa and thecal cells. It also appears to be the principal luteotrophic factor in the cow.

Luteinising hormone

LH concentration is low during most of the luteal phase of the oestrous cycle, with one pulse every 4 or more hours. It begins to rise a few days prior to oestrus. Pulse frequency increases to one or more per hour; pulse amplitude, however, falls. The large preovulatory LH peak or surge that occurs near the beginning of oestrus is preceded by a rise in the concentration of oestradiol one or 2 days before oestrus.

Scientists estimated the interval between oestrus onset and the LH surge to be 0.4 3.4 hours in Brahman cows, 6.8 ±2.1 hours in Brahman x Hereford cows and 5.3 ±1.3 hours in pure Herefords. Scientists recorded intervals of 2.0 ±1.3 in Brahman cows, 3.0 ±1.0 in Brahman × Hereford cows and 6.5 1.8 hours in Hereford cows. The preovulatory LH surge therefore seems to occur sooner after the onset of behavioural oestrus in zebu than taurine cows or their crosses. In addition, Randel (1976) estimated the interval between the LH surge and ovulation to be 18.5 ±3.1 hours in Brahman cows, 22.2 ±2.6 hours in Brahman x Hereford cows and 23.3 ±2.1 hours in Hereford cows. Zebu cows thus appear to ovulate sooner after the LH surge than Bos taurus cows

Oestradiol

Oestradiol-17 b is the principal biologically active oestrogen. Randel (1980) measured total serum oestrogen (TSO) from 72 hours before oestrus until 24 hours after oestrus in Brahman, Brahman x Hereford and Hereford heifers. TSO did not differ significantly between breeds prior to oestrus. The highest pro-oestrous TSO level occurred 24 hours before oestrus in Brahmans, 8 hours before oestrus in Herefords and 16 hours before oestrus in the crossbreds. The pattern was similar for the lowest levels after oestrus: 24 hours after oestrus TSO levels were lower in Brahmans than the other two genotypes ($P<0.05$) and these lower values coincided with ovulation. This finding agreed with data showing that Brahman cows tend to ovulate within 24 hours of the onset of heat, earlier than taurine cattle. Randel's (1980) data also indicate that the oestradiol surge has two peaks. The pre-oestrus rise in oestrogen mediates the LH release from the bovine pituitary, which in turn might stimulate the second oestradiol rise.

Researchers working with taurine cattle, found that oestradiol-17 b levels are low in peripheral plasma for most of the oestrous cycle and rise as the concentration of progesterone begins to fall, reaching a peak 3 to 4 days later. Probably the drop in progesterone concentration following luteal regression allows the preovulatory follicle to increase its secretion of oestradiol-17 b. In the Holstein heifers used the researchers, plasma oestradiol-17 b concentration was low at the start of luteal regression (2.2 ±0.5 pg/ml), increased to 3.8 ±0.6 pg/ml the next day and reached 6.6 ±0.9 pg/ml when the concentration of progesterone in the blood had fallen to a minimum. The highest concentration of oestradiol-17 b (10.1 pg/ml) was recorded one or 2 days after complete luteolysis. A similar trend was reported by Wettemann *et al.* (1972).

Scientists observed a second, postovulatory, peak in oestradiol 5 to 7 days after oestrus. The last authors observed this peak in non-pregnant cattle and those inseminated but failing to conceive. It appeared to be related to the presence of a large follicle. Its physiological significance is not clear but the follicle is not destined to ovulate.

Progesterone

Scientists using the ELISA method, found that the concentration of progesterone in the plasma of Ethiopian highland zebu cattle was less than 1.0 ng/ml from 2 days before oestrus to 3 days after oestrus. Scientists referred to this as the 'basal progesterone' period. Progesterone concentration gradually increased from 4 days after oestrus (the 'rising progesterone or early luteal' period), as the corpus luteum became functional. It reached a maximum of 8.0 to 10.0 ng/ml at 11 to 15 days after oestrus (the 'plateau progesterone' period) and then declined (the 'falling progesterone' period) to basal levels before the next oestrus and ovulation.

Researchers observed a drop in the concentration of progesterone in the blood of zebu cows about 13 days after oestrus. Similar observations were made by researchers in taurine cows. Researchers associated the decrease with mid-cycle follicle growth and development. They also found a small, but consistent, peak in progesterone concentration, 18-25 hours after the preovulatory LH surge, the time of ovulation. If consistent, this could be used to determine more precisely the time of ovulation.

The progesterone concentration was generally lower in Brahman and Brahman x Hereford crosses than in purebred Hereford heifers. Between-breed differences in progesterone concentration have sometimes been suspected to arise from differences in ovarian size. The exact relationship is, however, not clear. The lesser responsiveness of the ovaries of Brahman cows to gonadotrophic hormone during formation of a corpus luteum might also result in a smaller corpus luteum. Nevertheless, the corpora lutea of Brahman and Brahman x Hereford cows had similar total progesterone contents. The Brahman corpora lutea seemed to have compensated for the small size. In fact, the activity of 3 b-hydroxysteroid dehydrogenase, the enzyme responsible for converting pregnenolone to progesterone, was greater in corpora lutea from Brahman cows.

Prostaglandins

Oestrus usually occurs 1 to 5 days after the corpus luteum starts to regress. The regression of the bovine corpus luteum is brought about by the action of prostaglandin F_2 a (PGF_2 a). Researchers suggested that the variation in this interval is due partly to differences in the time ovulatory follicles take to develop and mature. Views on the growth, distribution and selection of follicles in the ovary differ. Numbers of follicles do not vary between stages of the cycle. In contrast, researchers suggested that antral follicles grow and regress throughout the oestrous cycle in two waves: the first ends around day 12 and is followed by atresia; the second culminates in oestrus.

There is little information about prostaglandin concentration in zebu cows. Studies in the buffalo showed increases in prostaglandin concentration in blood plasma and milk from 250 to 900 pg/ml over the 2 or 3 days prior to oestrus. Similar increases (150-750 pg/ml) were reported for the taurine cow.

Endocrinology of Pregnancy

When a cow conceives, plasma and milk progesterone

levels rise as in a normal oestrous cycle but instead of declining at about 15 to 18 days after oestrus, remain high for the rest of the gestation period, preventing further ovarian cycles. Working with Holstein heifers, Hansel (1981) noted that jugular plasma progesterone concentrations were higher ($P<0.05$) in pregnant than cyclic non-pregnant animals 10 days after oestrus, indicating that the bovine blastocyst is able to stimulate progesterone synthesis by as early as the 10th day after conception.

In a study of the blood progesterone levels during the gestation period of Ethiopian zebu cows, researchers observed a trend similar to that found in Haryana Zebu and Africander cows. Progesterone levels in Ethiopian zebu cows were high (over 5 ng/ml) until the last 12 to 18 days of pregnancy. This was followed by a decline to 3.7-8.2 ng/ml one to two days before parturition. Hashmat Shehata (1982) observed that progesterone levels declined to 1.2-2.0 ng/ml during the last 12-24 hours before calving and were less than 1 ng/ml 24-48 hours after delivery in local Egyptian cattle. The differences in progesterone concentration among the studies probably reflect breed and/or assay-technique variability.

Although the corpus luteum remains active throughout pregnancy its weight and progesterone content do not perfectly reflect changes in jugular plasma progesterone, indicating an extra-ovarian source. Abortion can be induced using prostaglandin F_2 a (PGF_2 a) prior to 120 days of pregnancy. After this time, both the placenta and adrenals can produce progesterone. Progesterone from these sources probably maintains pregnancy after mid-term ovariectomy. These sources probably also account for the low abortion rates after administering prostaglandins at 120 to 250 days of gestation, and the administration of PGF_2 a is not very successful until after 250 days of pregnancy Johnson, 1981).

Scientists reported that the level of unconjugated oestrogens was low (193 to 267 pg/ml) and fairly constant during pregnancy in Africander cattle. Between 2 and 6 days prior to delivery the level increased sharply to 271 to 523 pg/ ml. The upper limit is comparable to the 501 pg/ml obtained by researchers for Angus and Hereford beef cows. Two days after parturition the level stabilised at around 110 pg/ml, with little variation between individuals. Substantial amounts of oestrogens are also produced by the bovine placenta after 100 days of pregnancy.

Maternal Recognition of Pregnancy

The exact mechanisms involved in maternal recognition of pregnancy are not fully understood. However, it appears necessary that (i) corpus luteum function is maintained and (ii) the cyclic release pattern of LH must be terminated, prostaglandins must be stopped from reaching the corpus luteum, or some substance must be secreted to check the cyclic action of prostaglandins. It is suspected that interactions between the developing conceptus and maternal system are involved. The mechanisms regulating the establishment and maintenance of pregnancy in cattle must be understood before techniques can be developed to reduce the incidence of early embryonic mortality. Plasma progesterone levels are significantly ($P<0.05$) higher in pregnant than cyclic non-pregnant Holstein heifers by as early as 10 days after fertilisation. Researchers found that the bovine blastocyst can produce progesterone, some testosterone and limited amounts of oestradiol-17 b by day 13 to 16. Blastocysts 15-17 days old are also able to convert androstenedione to oestrogen in vitro. Oestrogens have a luteolytic action in the cow.

Homogenates of sheep embryos and sheep conceptus secretory proteins can extend corpus luteum function and cycle length when administered into the uterine lumen of cyclic ewes. Thus, in sheep the pre-implantation embryo appears to produce a luteotrophic substance that contributes to the maintenance of early pregnancy by directly stimulating progesterone secretion by the corpus luteum. In cattle too, scientists found that treating cycling Holstein cows with conceptus secretory proteins extended the life-span of corpora lutea and inter-oestrus interval. An evaluation of spontaneous prostaglandin response suggested that proteins synthesised and secreted by the bovine conceptus accommodate luteal maintenance during early gestation via an attenuation of prostaglandin production. In sheep and cows, oestrogen, which is luteolytic in the late luteal phase, may indirectly induce uterine prostaglandin synthesis. The role of the embryonic hormone, which the above substance appears to be, may be to counter the lytic action of the prostaglandins.

Endocrinology of the Postpartum Period

The interval between calving and conception depends on the reestablishment of normal ovarian cycles after calving, the occurrence of oestrous behaviour at the appropriate time in the cycle, and the pregnancy rate following service.

The interval between parturition and ovulation is characterised by sexual quiescence (postpartum anoestrus). The duration of this interval varies with breed, milk yield level, animal age, suckling or lactating status, nutritional level before and after calving, season and associated photo-periodism, climate, health status and calving difficulty. Of these factors, nutrition and suckling appear to be very important.

Researchers noted that pregnancy reduces the sensitivity of the pituitary to GnRH. Sensitivity of the pituitary to GnRH increases only gradually after calving. The resumption of ovarian cyclicity depends on the establishment of a pulsatile pattern of LH secretion. The observed delay is due, probably, to their being insufficient oestradiol to induce the pre-ovulatory LH surge.

Luteinising Hormone

Researchers estimated that a pulsatile pattern of LH secretion with a frequency of 0.25 to 1 per hour appears to be a prerequisite for the first ovulation postpartum. This results in gradually increasing LH concentration before the first LH surge. Hansel and Alila (1984) stated that the frequency of LH pulses is due to increased frequency of pulsatile releases of GnRH and that the factors affecting the duration of postpartum anoestrus also affect the time taken to establish the pulsatile pattern of LH release. Peters and Lamming (1986) thought that changes in gonadotrophin concentration may be brought about by changes in pituitary responsiveness to GnRH during the postpartum period. The time at which the pulsatile releases of LH appear and pituitary sensitivity increases varies among breeds and is also affected by suckling.

The exact mechanisms by which suckling interferes with the hypothalamus-hypophyseal axis are not well defined, but it is unlikely that teat manipulation alone can alter LH release patterns in the cow. Other factors, such as the presence of the calf or social interactions, might be necessary before teat stimulation has an effect. Suckling reduces the frequency and amplitude of LH release, pituitary sensitivity to GnRH and the pulsatile release of GnRH by the hypothalamus.

Suckling probably inhibits LH and GnRH release and their action rather than their synthesis. Both the hypothalamic concentration of GnRH and the pituitary concentration of LH are similar in milked and suckled cows. Suckling can also inhibit the positive effect of endogenous or exogenous oestradiol on the release of pituitary LH. Temporary weaning (48 hours) may, however, increase plasma LH concentration, but LH concentration falls to previous levels within 4 hours of calf return. Suckling delays LH release and reduces the amount of LH released in response to GnRH injection. Temporary calf removal can, however, enhance the total amount of LH released in response to GnRH injection.

Using suckled beef cows, researchers noted that the maximum magnitude and frequency of LH peaks occurred 10 to 33 days before the initial increase of plasma progesterone, *i.e.* when there was a marked development of large follicles and a large variation in oestradiol-17 b. These and similar observations have led researchers to (i) suggest that there might be a deficiency of GnRH during the early postpartum period and (ii) attempt to stimulate ovulation and ovarian cycles by repeated injections of GnRH in order to simulate the events of the preovulatory period.

Results from GnRH treatment have been inconsistent. The number of animals, whether milked or suckled, that respond positively to GnRH injection increases during the postpartum period. Suckled cows are, however, less likely to respond during the initial 15 days than milked cows. This difference diminishes during subsequent weeks. After this period the magnitude of GnRH-induced LH release appears to be directly proportional to follicular development.

Oestradiol

It is difficult to monitor pulses of oestradiol-17 b in the jugular vein. Peters and Lamming (1986) reported unpublished work in which cannulae were inserted into the posterior vena cava, anterior to the junction of the ovarian veins, of recently calved cows. Oestradiol-17 b pulses, both naturally occurring and induced by three-hourly injections of GnRH, were detected: similar pulses could not be registered in the jugular vein, although increases in oestradiol concentration were measured. It was concluded that the early postpartum cow is sensitive to GnRH-induced gonadotrophin release and responds by secreting oestradiol.

Progesterone

Two types of luteal activity have been observed in the postpartum cow. Fifty to 80 per cent of milked or suckled dairy cows exhibit an initial luteal phase in which increases in plasma progesterone concentration are of shorter duration and progesterone concentrations are lower than in the normal cycle. This is referred to as the short luteal phase and lasts 6 to 12 days. The second luteal phase lasts about 14 days and tends to have lower than normal progesterone levels. This dual progesterone pattern occurs even after GnRH challenge, early weaning or limited suckling with or without GnRH treatment.

Researchers thought that progesterone can be released from follicles that fail to ovulate. The short progesterone cycles are caused by shortage of LH or its receptor. However, no differences in plasma LH concentration are observed before or after an oestrus associated with a short cycle. The short life-span may be the result of short GnRH-induced LH surges. Alternatively, the amount of LH receptor and number of granulosa cells may not be sufficient to give optimum response to this luteotrophic stimulus.

The corpus luteum from a cow with regular cycles responds positively in vitro to LH addition but that a corpus luteum formed after GnRH injection does not. This may be due to luteal tissue of the latter being unable to recognise LH. It has been shown that the in vitro response of the postpartum corpus luteum during the first three cycles is related to the integrity of luteal tissue at the time of removal. These observations suggest that there may be premature luteolysis due to PGF_2 a synthesised after calving by caruncular uterine tissue. It has been suggested that oxytocin can increase production of PGFM (a metabolite of PGF_2 a) and lead to earlier luteolysis. Whatever the cause, the abnormal short cycles can result in increased early embryonic mortality.

In a study of 20 postpartum pluriparous Brahman cattle, Rutter and Randel (1984) reported a higher incidence of abnormal cycles after the first heat than the second (35 per cent vs 5 per cent; $P<0.05$). It was suggested that the higher incidence of abnormal luteal function following the first and second postpartum cycles contributes to lower conception rates in animals bred during the first or second postpartum heat.

PROCEDURES OF REPRODUCTIVE PERFORMANCE

Fertility is the ability of male and female animals to produce viable germ cells, mate, conceive and deliver normal living young. The lifetime productivity of a cow is influenced by age at puberty, age at first calving and calving interval. This chapter presents data on age at first calving, calving rate, number of services per conception, calving interval and other measures that can be used to estimate cow productivity.

AGE AT FIRST CALVING

First calving marks the beginning of a cow's productive life. Age at first calving is closely related to generation interval and, therefore, influences response to selection. Under controlled breeding, heifers are usually mated when they are mature enough to withstand the stress of parturition and lactation. This increases the likelihood of early conception after parturition. In traditional production systems, however, breeding is often uncontrolled and heifers are bred at the first opportunity. This frequently results in longer subsequent calving intervals. The average age at first calving in *Bos indicus* cattle is about 44 months, compared with about 34 months in *Bos taurus* and *Bos indicus* x *Bos taurus* crosses in the tropics. Heritabilities of age at puberty, at first conception and at first calving are generally low, indicating that these traits are highly influenced by environmental factors.

The effect of season on the reproductive performance of Brahman heifers that first conceived at between 15 and 37 months old in the Mexican Gulf coast. Of 111 heifers that first conceived at 15 to 24 months old, significantly more (P<0.001) did so during the dry season than during the wet season. However, among heifers that first conceived at more than 24 months old, most conceived during the rainy season and overall there was no significant difference between the percentage of heifers conceiving first during the rainy or dry season

The Nellore cows in Brazil that calved first in the dry season were younger than those that calved first in the rainy season. Researchers found that age at first calving in Brazilian Nellore heifers was significantly affected by year and month of birth: calves born from January to May tended to be younger at first calving than those born between June and December. Researchers also found a year-of-birth effect among Haryana, Gir and another unspecified zebu type cattle in Venezuela, as did scientists in Nagauri cattle in India. However, researchers found that neither month of birth nor breed significantly affected age at first calving.

Table 6.1 : Some Estimates of Age at First Calving in Bos Indicus Cattle

Breed	*Location*	*Estimate (months)*
Kenana	Sudan	23-58
Gobra	Senegal	31-40
Boran	Kenya	34
East African Zebu	Ethiopia	35.1 ±3.1
Red Sindhi	India	35.6
Sahiwal	India	35.8
Azaouak	Sahel	36-60
InduBrazil	South America	36.8
Brahman	Costa Rica	37-50
Tharparkar	India	37.2
Various zebu	Brazil	37.5-50
Sokoto Gudali	West Africa	38.6
N'Dama	West Africa	39.2
Nellore	Brazil	39.4 ±0.02
White Fulani	Nigeria	40.4 ±0.7
Nganda	Uganda	42
Zebu	Bangladesh	42-52
Haryana	India	42-56
East African Zebu	Uganda	43
Butana	Sudan	44
Deshi	India	45
Brahman	Mexico	45.9
Gir and Zebu	Venezuela	47 ±0.7
Nagori	India	47.43 ±1.06
Sahiwal	Pakistan	48.8 ±0.4
White Fulani	Nigeria	49.4
Sudan Fulani	Mali	49.5
Horro	Ethiopia	50
Haryana	India	50 ±0.5
Kenana	Sudan	50.1
Fulani	Niger	50.2 ±9.1
Haryana	India	51
Ankole	Uganda	51.3
Zebu	Uganda	51.7
Highland zebu	Ethiopia	53
Non-descript	India	58.6 ±1.0
White Fulani	Nigeria	60

Table 6.2 : Some Estimates of Age at First Calving among Bos Taurus and Bos Taurus × Bos Indicus Cattle in the Tropics

Breed	*Location*	*Estimate*
Jersey	India	27.5
Jersey	Egypt	28.4
Jersey	Ceylon	30.0
1/2 Jersey	Uganda	29.4
1/2 Jersey	India	31.7
1/2 Jersey	Rwanda	36.5
3/4 Jersey	Egypt	27.4
3/4 Jersey	India	39.5
Ayrshire	Iraq	35.0
Friesian	Nigeria	29.0
Friesian	India	30.1
Friesian	Uganda	40.0
F_1 Friesian × zebu	Ethiopia	29.1
1/2 Friesian	Nigeria	31.9
3/4 Friesian	Nigeria	30.0
Brown Swiss x zebu	India	37.2
Jamaica Hope	Jamaica	34.2
Costeno	Colombia	39.5
Blanco Orejine	Colombia	40.7
Bos taurus x *Bos indicus*	Ethiopia	35.5-40.3
Boran x Charolais	Kenya	34.0
Two breed cross	Various	33.8
3/4 Cross	Various	44.5
Bos taurus	Various	36.5

No significant difference in age at first calving (P>0.05) between Boran and Sahiwal heifers on a ranch in the Kenya Rift Valley, but researchers found that breed differences had a significant effect on age at first calving in Haryana, selected Haryana, Tharparkar and Sahiwal heifers in India. In an analysis of production data covering 14 years, scientists found that Gir heifers tended to be older than Nellore or InduBrazil heifers at first calving. Breed differences probably reflect differences in management conditions. The time taken by an animal to attain puberty and sexual maturity depends on the quality and quantity of feed available, which affects growth rate.

Scientists found a mean age at first calving of 50.2 ±9.1 months in 146 Fulani-type dams in Niger. None of the factors tested for in the least squares analysis (herd, season and year of birth of dam, sex of the calf) significantly affected this parameter. However, Saeed *et al.*, (1987) found that year of birth significantly (P<0.001) affected age at first calving in Kenana cattle in Sudan but that month of birth did not. Scientists observed a significant correlation (P<0.001, r =-0.52) between age at first calving and body weight at 3 years; heifers that weighed 10 kg more than average at 3 years old first calved 2 months earlier than average-weight heifers. There was no significant correlation between age at first calving and weight at 1, 2 or 4 years.

Table 6.3 : Some Estimates of Heritability of Age at Puberty, Age at First Conception and Age at First Calving

Cattle type	*Estimate*
Age at puberty	
Haryana crosses	0.4 ±0.21
Age at first conception	
Zebu	0.14 ±0.19
Guzerat	0.20
Age at first calving	
East African Zebu	0.08
Guzerat	0.15 ±0.18
Gir	0.15 ±0.24
Sahiwal	0.20
Gir	0.20 ±0.11
Zebu	0.24±0.30
Haryana	0.24 ±0.02
Small East African Zebu	0.25
Haryana	0.3 ±0.27
Haryana crosses	0.36 ±0.29

FERTILITY (CALVING) RATES

Estimates

Fertility in cattle is affected by environmental, genetic,

disease and management factors. These influence the reproductive process at ovulation, fertilization or implantation or during gestation and parturition. The commonest estimate of fertility rate is the percentage of mated or inseminated cows that become pregnant (pregnancy rate) or finally calve (calving rate). However, fertility can also be expressed in other ways. For example, Researchers referred to two measures of fertility: a general fertility rate, which is the ratio of calves born to females of breeding age, expressed as a percentage; and a specific fertility rate, which measures the number of births within a given group or the total fertility rates of females over their reproductive life. Net reproductive rate was given as the extent to which the female calves of one generation survive to reproduce themselves as they pass through calf-bearing age, expressed as the number of female calves that survive per 100 females of breeding age.

Fertility rates can also be estimated prior to calving as the percentage non-return rate. This is the number of cows bred that do not come back in heat and are thus assumed to have conceived. This value may be derived at 60, 90, 120, 145 or 200 days after mating. Where artificial insemination is employed, fertility rates can be expressed as the number of calves born per 100 inseminations. Progesterone assay now makes it possible to determine conception rates as early as 21 days after breeding. It is also ideal for estimating the magnitude of early embryonic losses.

Fertility rates in zebu cattle are generally low, particularly in animals raised traditionally under less-than-ideal management. For example, researchers estimated the calving rate of traditionally raised Tswana cattle in Botswana as 46.4 per cent, compared with 74.0 per cent for similar animals on a ranch. The higher calving rate on the ranch was probably due to the animals being better fed and managed than those under traditional management. Researchers calculated a calving rate of 67 per cent for White Fulani cattle raised on government ranches in Nigeria, compared with about 34-55 per cent for similar animals raised by local herders. Researchers reported a conception rate of 79 per cent in Ankole, Boran and an unspecified zebu-type cattle in western Uganda where feed and water were abundant and diseases were controlled.

Researchers studied reproductive performance in a herd of Nellore cattle in the Amazon over six mating seasons from 1968 to 1973. No animals were culled for reproductive reasons. Calves were weaned at 250 days old and breeding was between October and December each year. Overall calving rate was 59 per cent. The authors suggested that the low calving rate after the sixth mating opportunity (38 per cent) was due to the small number of cows presented for breeding, but it may also have been age-related. At this time, most cows would have been 9 to 10 years old, and fertility commonly decreases in cows of this age in the tropics. Cows calved irregularly and 33 per cent of those bred for the fifth time gave birth to only their third calf and 18 per cent to their second. In addition, several cows calved for the first time after the third, fourth or even fifth breeding opportunity. Although such cows would have been culled in a commercial livestock enterprise, traditional smallholders usually have only one or a few cows and cannot afford to cull extensively for infertility. Many keep their animals for long periods in the hope of eventually getting a calf. This practice is unsatisfactory because scarce feed resources are used by unproductive animals.

Table 6.4 : Some Estimates of Fertility (Calving) Rates among Some Bos Indicus Cattle in the Tropics

Breed	*Location*	*Estimates (%)*
Traditional management		
Nellore	Brazil	20-66.6
Fulani	Nigeria	34.2-54.5
Fulani	Nigeria	36
Native zebu	Botswana	36.2-51.9
Southern Darfur	Sudan	40.0
Guzerat	South America	42.2-100
Highland zebu	Ethiopia	46
Tswana	Botswana	46.4
Zebu	Malawi	52-69
Ranch/research station/migratory or improved pasture management		
Guzerat	Central America	32.5

Nellore	Central America	45.3
Boran	Tanzania	53-73
Africander	Zambia	54.2
Native zebu	Zambia	57.6
Nellore	Brazil	58.3-84.7
Azaouak	Sahel	58.8
Nellore	Peru	59 de
Dangi	India	60.5
Zebu	Cuba	61.18
Brahman	Costa Rica	62.8-81.7
Southern Darfur	Sudan	65.0
Boran	Zambia	66.0
Fulani	Nigeria	67
Zebu	Botswana	69-82
Angoni	Zambia	69.1
Zebu	Panama	72.1-90.6
Tswana	Botswana	74.0
Brahman	Mexico	75
Boran	Zambia	75.4
Zebu	Sudan	77.0
Various zebu	Uganda	79.0
Angoni	Zambia	82.5
Brahman	Mexico	85.5

Table 6.5 : Calving Rates of Nellore Cattle after Successive Mating Opportunities

Mating opportunity	*Number of females exposed*	*Percentage of females calving for the*						*Overall calving rate (%)*
		1st	*2nd*	*3rd*	*4th*	*5th*	*time*	
1	925	64						64
2	700	26	23					49
3	654	6	42	12				60
4	374	3	27	22	7			59
5	195	2	18	33	10	0		63
6	28	-	10	10	18	0		38
Total	2876							59

Effects of Age and Lactation

Analysing data found that fertility rate increased from 69 per cent in 2.5-year-old cows to a maximum of 82 per cent in 6-to 7 year-old cows and then declined. In Bolivia, also recorded an increase in pregnancy rate from 50 per cent in 3-year-old purebred Criollo and Criollo × zebu crossbreds to 75 per cent in 7-year-olds. Fertility then declined to 50 per cent among 12-year-olds. Causes of these age-related differences include lactational stress in young growing animals and the ability of older cows to gain bodyweight and condition quickly after calving

Lactation has a negative effect on cow bodyweight and thus indirectly affects animal reproduction. Researchers observed that cows grazing medium-or low-quality forage used body reserves to maintain milk yield in response to suckling. Such animals should be supplemented during lactation to increase their conception rates.

Effect of Breed

One of the few studies reporting extensively on the effect of breed on fertility in Africa was undertaken by Thorpe and Cruickshank (1980) in Zambia. They found that conception rate (averaging 82.5,78.1 and 75.4 per cent among 675 Angoni, 731 Barotse and 815 Boran cows, respectively) was significantly affected by year but not sire breed, although conception rate was higher in Angoni and Barotse cows when mated to bulls of their own breed. Evidence for dam breeds was also not conclusive. Among the Barotse, dry heifers had higher conception rates than lactating cows, whereas lactating Angoni and Boran cows had higher conception rates than dry cows. Perhaps the most significant observation among the Angoni and Barotse (but not the Boran) was that cows that calved early in the calving season were more likely to conceive during the following mating season than cows that calved late.

Effect of Bodyweight

The Barotse, Angoni and Boran cows that calved were marginally heavier at the beginning and end of the breeding season than cows that did not calve. This was consistent with the findings of in Africander, Tswana and Tuli cattle and in Nellore cattle. The heifers calving at the first and second opportunity averaged 272 ±33 kg liveweight, compared with 262 ±27 kg ($P<0.01$) for those failing to calve. The importance of cow bodyweight at time of breeding: Mashona cows that weighed 318-364 kg at mating had a calving rate of 87.5 per cent, compared with 45 per cent for cows weighing 237-273 kg.

Effects of Year and Season

Researchers attributed the significant effect of year on calving rate to differences between years in the quantity and quality of forage available.

Researchers found that calving percentage of Africander cross cows in South Africa was positively correlated ($r = 0.84$, $P<0.05$) with rainfall in the previous year, in an analysis of 18272 births from Nguni cattle in Swaziland.

Monthly calving frequency was correlated with previous monthly rainfall records but most of the variation was accounted for by rainfall 10 months earlier in both the highveld (79 per cent) and middleveld (50 per cent). Researchers also found direct linear correlations between conception rate in Brahman cows and precipitation, pressure and temperature. These findings further emphasise the importance of nutritional effects on fertility.

Genetic Effects

Heritability of fertility rate is low. It was estimated as 0.14 ±0.19 by Bastidas and Verde (1981) in Venezuela, while values of 0.25 and 0.15 for conception rate, and 0.09 and 0.11 for calving rate in Brahman heifers and older cows, respectively. Conception rates often exhibit substantial heterosis after crossbreeding.

Table 6.6 : Linear Correlations between the Seasonal Reproductive Performance of Brahman Cows and Climatic Factors

Variables	2	3	4	5
1. Conception	0.643	-0.751	0.827	0.324
2. Precipitation	-	-0.668	0.718	0.225
3. Pressure		-	-0.918	0.390
4. Temperature			-	0.161
5. Humidity				-

Source: Jochle (1972).

Researchers found a relationship between fertility rates and blood groups in 645 Haryana cows randomly mated over 4 years.

Cows with AA blood group had a significantly higher conception rate (67 per cent) than cows with AB (47.5 per cent) and BB (51.1 per cent) blood type. Type AA cows calved significantly earlier (41.2 months) than either the AB (44.5 months) or BB (44.7 months) animals.

It would be useful to investigate this further in animals from different populations, to find out if the phenomenon could be of use in identifying animals with higher inherent fertility.

NUMBER OF SERVICES PER CONCEPTION

The number of services per conception (NSC) depends largely on the breeding system used. It is higher under uncontrolled natural breeding and low where hand-mating or artificial insemination is used. A range of values for NSC is presented in Table 17. NSC values greater than 2.0 should be regarded as poor, and some of the factors contributing to high NSC values.

Researchers estimated the repeatability of NSC to be 19 per cent from 2152 records for Haryana cattle. The NSC was 2.81 ±0.03 and was significantly affected by herd, season, placenta expulsion time, lactation length and milk yield. Since heritability can be broadly estimated from repeatability, this study indicates that heritability of NSC is low and most of the variation in NSC is attributable to environmental factors.

Table 6.7 : Some Estimates of the Average Number of Services per Conception (NSC)

Breed	*Location*	*Estimates (NSC)*
InduBrazil	South America	1.4-1.6
Nagori	India	1.5 ±0.4
Dangi	India	1.65
Zebu	Ethiopia	1.74-1.8
East African Zebu	Ethiopia	2.0 ±1.2
Haryana	India	2.1-2.7
Various	India	2.1-3.6
Arsi	Ethiopia	2.4-2.6
Haryana	India	2.8

Researchers found a significant effect of parity on NSC in Sahiwal, Red Sindhi and Tharparkar cattle. The NSC was highest at the fourth lactation for F_1 crosses with Brown Swiss. Kumar and Bhat (1979) noted that Haryana heifers needed more services per conception than cows.

Researchers using 3 local Ethiopian breeds, the Barca, Horro and Boran, found that NSC was lower for animals from wet areas than for those from drier areas (1.74 ±0.6 vs 1.98 ±0.07). Crossbred cows required 0.12 and 0.14 fewer services per conception than local zebu cows in wet and dry areas, respectively. Researchers also concluded that NSC did not differ significantly between Red Butana and Red Butana crosses (average 2.6) but was influenced by month of calving. NSC increased over the study period, probably due to changes in management. This is partly supported by an analysis by Busch and Furstenberg (1984) of 483 600 inseminations performed by 379 technicians on 623 farms in the USA, which showed that the 90-and 120-day non-return rate differed significantly among inseminators and the inseminator effect was greater than the farm effect. However, non-return rate did not differ among bulls.

CALVING INTERVAL

Calving interval can be divided into three periods: gestation, postpartum anoestrus (from calving to first oestrus) and the service period (first postpartum oestrus to conception). Factors affecting gestation length. The factors that influence the length of the postpartum anoestrous and service periods. This is sometimes also called the 'days open', period and is the part of the calving interval that can be shortened by improved herd management.

The 'days open' period should not exceed 80-85 days if a calving interval of 12 months is to be achieved. This requires re-establishment of ovarian activity soon after calving and high conception rates. The duration of this period is influenced by nutrition, season, milk yield, parity, suckling and uterine involution. At any time, the effects of one or more of these factors may be confounded. Calving interval has been extensively analysed and reported. It is probably the best index of a cattle herd's reproductive efficiency. Resumption of ovarian activity in the postpartum period does not necessarily lead to conception and methods of stimulating oestrus must be considered in relation to their effect on conception and, indirectly, calving intervals. The estimates of the duration of the various phases of the calving interval are based on averages in the literature for cows raised under traditional management.

Genetic Effects

Researchers observed that genotype had a significant effect on the calving interval of Brahman cows in Venezuela. In Mexico, found calving intervals of 18.1 months for Gir and InduBrazil cattle, 18.8 months for Brown Swiss × zebu crosses and 20.3 months for pure Brown Swiss cattle. The long calving interval of the Brown Swiss probably reflects lack of adaptation to the humid environment. Researchers also reported that calving interval was affected by maternal grand sire. However, researchers found no significant effect of genetic grouping (proportion of zebu blood) among cows in Brazil.

Estimates of the repeatability of calving interval range from near zero to 0.37. Heritability estimates range from 0.003 to 0.33. The heritability values of 0.68 ±0.14 obtained by researchers in Tharparkar cows in India, and 0.81 to 0.86 found by Weitze (1984) among Nellore cows in Brazil, appear to be exceptionally high.

Researchers working with Nellore cattle, observed that animals calving in the dry season had an average subsequent calving interval of 13.9 months, compared with 14.5 months for those that calved in the wet season. Researchers working with White Fulani heifers, found calving intervals of 15.3 and 18 months for the dry and wet seasons, respectively. The authors suggested that the difference was due to the fact that cows calving in the dry season could take advantage of improved nutritional conditions during the subsequent rainy season to meet their total requirements for maintenance, growth and lactation. In addition, a larger proportion of dry-season calves die due to inadequate nutrition. Both factors lead to earlier re-establishment of oestrus in cows that calve in the dry season. These suggestions were supported by the scientists who found that cows calving in October in Côte d'Ivoire usually conceived again in the following January while those calving in January were unlikely to conceive during the subsequent mating period. Early death of calves also reduced calving interval by more than 2 months and abortion shortened it by several days. The calving interval for cows whose calves died prior to fertile mating was estimated by the formula: CI = 328.3 + (0.992 x age of the calf at the time of death) days. A similar estimate by Wilson (1985) among Sudanese Fulani cattle in Mali yielded a prediction equation of CI = 499.5 + (0.318 x age at calf death) days.

Table 6.8 : Some Estimates of Repeatability of Calving Interval

Breed type	*Estimate*
Zebu	0.022
Brahman	0.05-0.50
Butana	0.111 ±0.039
Deoni	0.20
Deshi	0.21
Kenana	0.23 ±0.03
Haryana	0.24
Haryana	0.27

Malvi	0.29 ±0.02
Brahman	0.32
Gir	0.37

Although these observations involved cows that aborted or lost their calves, they indicate that calf rearing strategies, such as early weaning, bucket feeding or partial suckling, can influence subsequent dam reproduction. For example, researchers found that partial suckling in Africander cows significantly (P<0.01) reduced the number of cows that were anovulatory for 100 days postpartum and increased conception rates (P< 0.001). Partial suckling reduced the interval from parturition to first ovulation by 20 days and the mean interval to conception by 21 days averaged over all cows. In a study of 6-to 10-year-old Bunaji cows, the interval from calving to conception averaged 232.5 and 72.6 days for suckled and non-suckled animals, respectively. The associated calving intervals were 512.5 and 352.6 days with 60-90 day pregnancy rates of 21.1 per cent and 72.7 per cent, respectively. Serum progesterone levels showed that suckling interfered with ovarian activity and thus conception during the postpartum period, resulting in a prolonged calving interval.

Table 6.9 : Some Estimates of Heritability of Calving Interval

Breed type	*Estimate*
Haryana	0.003-0.33
Nellore	0.022
Deshi	0.09
InduBrazil	0.10 ±0.08
Gir	0.22 ±0.11
Guzerat	0.24

Effect of Nutrition

Underfeeding delays puberty in taurine heifers Joubert, 1954a) and stops oestrus and ovarian activity in heifers that are already cycling. The cows were fed a high-or a low-energy ration before calving; half of the animals in each group were then fed a high-or low-energy ration after calving. The resulting pregnancy rates were 95, 77, 95 and 20 per cent on the high-high, high-low, low-high and low-low ration, respectively. These results, indicate that level of feeding after calving has a greater effect on subsequent pregnancy than level of feeding before calving. The high level of feeding after calving shortened the interval from first breeding to conception and thus reduced calving interval. In zebu cattle, Researchers found a calving interval of 780 days (26 months) in traditionally raised Ethiopian highland zebus. Lactation length was 239 days (8 months). Cows thus failed to conceive for more than 8 months after lactation had ceased. This may be the average period required to gain sufficient bodyweight and condition to start cycling and conceive again, given the limited nutritional resources of the traditional system.

Calving intervals also tend to be shorter in animals that are more productive in other respects. This may be a reflection of the effect of nutrition, since more productive animals are usually fed better than unproductive animals.

Effect of Age

In zebu cattle, calving interval is longest in first-calf heifers and older cows, and shortest in cows of intermediate age (6-9 years old). Researchers reported a maximum calving interval of 496 days in 12 to 16-year-old cows, with similar values for young cows 3-6 years old. Calving interval was shortest (424 days) in cows of intermediate age (6-9 years old). Earlier, researchers had also observed a tendency for calving intervals to shorten with increasing age in Brahman cows, as did researchers in a commercial zebu herd in Mexico.

In an analysis of data collected over 20 years on zebu cattle in Venezuela, Researchers found that calving interval was longest between the first and second calving, and shortest between the fifth and sixth calving.Researchers working with Brahman cattle in Costa Rica, also found the longest calving interval between the first and second calving, and the shortest between the fourth and fifth calving. These observations were consistent with those of researchers working with Nellore cattle in Brazil, researchers, who studied Guzerat cows, and researchers working on Haryana cows in India. The last authors found that calving interval continued to shorten until after the sixth parity.

Other Factors

Calving interval can be influenced by the sex of the calf. In a study of zebu cows in Kenya, scientists observed that cows with male calves had a longer calving interval than those with female calves (430 vs 383 days). Subsequently, researchers found that dams stopped suckling, and therefore weaned, female calves earlier than males (8.8 vs 11.3 months). The cows with male calves had a calving interval 19.1 days longer than that of cows with female calves.

Calving interval may be influenced by placenta expulsion time and uterine pathology. Hinojosa *et al.*, (1980) found a favourable mean calving interval of 383 ±3.7 days (12.8 months) in a well-managed herd in Mexico. They attributed the shortness of the calving interval to the absence of brucellosis, which reduced abortion rate, and stringent culling of infertile cows.

THE RELATIONSHIP BETWEEN BODY CONDITION AND COW REPRODUCTION

Ward (1968) suggested that every cow has an optimum bodyweight for conception, the so-called 'target' or 'critical' bodyweight. Animals weighing less than this are less able to reproduce. Wiltbank *et al.*, (1964) added that breeding cows must be improving in 'condition' during the mating period. This is emphasised in the work of Wiltbank (1977) and Haresign (1984).

Table 6.10: Effect of Cow Body Condition at Calving on the Cumulative Percentage Return to Oestrus

Body condition	*Cumulative percentage return to oestrus*					
	Days after calving					
	40	*50*	*60*	*70*	*80*	*90*
Thin	19	34	46	55	62	66
Moderate	21	45	61	79	88	92
Good	31	42	91	96	98	100

Source: Wiltbank (1977).

Condition scoring was started in Australia for assessing sheep fatness: it was introduced into the United Kingdom for the same purpose, and has since been extended to cattle. Condition scoring is a subjective visual assessment of animals, but with practice a high level of repeatability, both between measurements and between scorers, can be obtained. A condition score is based on the amount of fat and muscle tissue covering the skeletal frame and is indicative of the animal's nutritional status.

The relationship between condition score and body fatness has been established from data on cows slaughtered at different body condition scores. Although the condition score gives a good indication of fatness, breeds differ in the way they deposit fat reserves. This is especially true of cows with more than 15 per cent body fat. Dairy cattle generally deposit more fat internally than do beef cattle. Condition scoring tends to assess subcutaneous fat reserves, and therefore at a given condition score value dairy cows tend to have more fat reserves than beef cows.

Changes in bodyweight or condition score of cows indicate likely levels of subsequent reproductive performance. The fertility of cows in poor condition is low.

Researchers compared the conception rates of cows of similar weight that differed in condition score and found that condition at mating was more important than weight. This agrees with the findings of van Niekerk (1982), who observed a calving rate of 78 per cent for cows in optimum condition compared with just 8 per cent for animals in the poorest condition. The feed costs of maintaining the animals in this better condition are more than covered by increased reproductive performance.

Thus animals should be fed well to promote good reproductive performance. It is more efficient to feed animals to maintain good body condition than to allow them to lose weight in the hope that it can be regained before the mating season. Researchers estimated that the loss of one unit in condition score would supply 3200 MJ of metabolisable energy: restoring the animal's condition score would require about

6500 MJ of dietary metabolisable energy. This agrees with van Niekerk (1982) who concluded that the feed cost of maintaining a cow at a condition score of 3.0 was half that required to raise a cow's condition from 1.5 to 3.0. The benefits of feeding animals well in terms of better reproductive performance are often easily appreciated by peasant farmers.

However, smallholders usually have only small supplies of supplementary feed and will need advice on which animals to feed it to, how much to feed and when.

HORMONAL CHANGES ASSOCIATED WITH UNDERNUTRITION

Few studies have been made on the relationship between bodyweight, condition and hormone synthesis or secretion in zebu cattle, and their results are inconsistent. However, in general the results suggest that poor feeding postpartum reduces luteal function and responsiveness of the ovaries to luteinising hormone.

REPRODUCTIVE HERD HEALTH PROGRAMMES

Reproductive herd health programmes are necessary to achieve and maintain the reproductive efficiency of cattle and hence boost the income from them. Such programmes consist of visits every 2 weeks or a month by a veterinarian to farms or cows. Where the number of cows owned by individual farmers or herders is small, groups of farmers can assemble their animals in one place to make fullest use of the veterinarian's visits. During his or her visits, the veterinarian should examine:

- Cows that calved in the last 15 to 45 days (postpartum examination) for normal recovery;
- Cows bred within the last 35 to 60 days (pregnancy diagnosis);
- Cows that have not shown oestrus at the expected time or those that have been served but failed to settle;
- Cows and heifers known to have reproductive abnormalities, infections and other causes of infertility; and

- Bulls used for natural service to determine their breeding soundness. Each visit should have four 'phases': identification and history, clinical examination, rectal examination and treatment.

Identification and History

Animal records should include the cow number or other means of identification, and its origin, breed, age, weight, body condition score, parity, date and ease of last calving, pueperium, lactation, nutrition management, housing, dates of heat and last service, and type of service (artificial insemination or natural), with details of the bull or semen used. Comments about sexual behaviour may be added if available. All records should be organised on a well planned, individual animal record card.

Clinical Examination

After identifying the animal it should be clinically examined. In particular, the external genital system should be examined; observations should include the size, position and shape of the vulva, and the presence and type of any discharges and crusts. Ideally the vagina should be examined using a speculum and a light for discharges (their amount and origins), degree of closure (pneumo-vagina), mucosal lacerations and cervicitis. All equipment used should be properly cleaned between animals.

Bibliography

Ainsworth, G.C., P.K.C. Austwick: *Fungal Diseases of Animals*, Farnham Royal, Slough, United Kingdom: Commonwealth Agricultural Bureau; 1973.

Asdell, S.A. : *Cattle Fertility and Sterility*, Greenworld, Delhi, 2002.

Bennett, J.E. : *Principles and Practice of Infectious Diseases*, New York: Churchill Livingstone Inc.; 1990.

Bhatia, S.K. ; Shiv Kumar and D.C. Sangwan: *Advances in Buffalo-Cattle Nutrition and Rumen Ecosystem*, International Book Distributing Co, Delhi, 2004.

Carter, G.R.: *Diagnostic Procedures in Veterinary Microbiology*, Springfield: Thomas; 1973.

Dale, Edward Everett: *The Range Cattle Industry. Norman,* Oklahoma: University of Oklahoma Press, 1969.

Fincher, M.G. ; W.J. Gibbons, Karl Mayer and S.E. Park: *Diseases of Cattle : A Text and Reference Work*, Greenworld, Delhi, 1998.

Hill, J.L.: *The End of the Cattle Trail. Austin,* Texas: The Pemberton Press, 1969.

Jennings, Robert P. : *Handbook of Common Cattle Diseases and Breeding Management*, Dominant Pub., Delhi, 2010.

Mandal, A.B. ; S.S. Paul and N.N. Pathak: *Nutrient Requirements and Feeding of Buffaloes and Cattle*, International Book Dist, Delhi, 2003.

Morgan, P.B.: *Complement and Infectious Siseases*, Harcourt Brace Jovanovich, London, 1990.

Satya, Laxman D : *Ecology, Colonialism, and Cattle : Central India in the Nineteenth Century*, Oxford University Press, Delhi, 2004.

Soltys, M.A.: *Bacteria and Fungi Pathogenic to Man and Animals*. London: BaillièreTindall; 1963.

Soni, Lok Nath : *The Cattle and The Stick : An Ethnographic Profile of the Raut of Chhattisgarh*, Anthropological Survey of India, Delhi, 2000.

Vohra, Vikas and A.K. Chakravarty: *Sustainable Breeding in Cattle and Buffalo*, Satish Serial Pub, Delhi, 2011.

Wannemuehler, M.J.: *Role of Cytokines in Intestinal Health and Disease*, Marcel Dekker, New York, 1995.

Yapp, William Wodin and William Barbour Nevens: *Dairy Cattle Selection : Feeding and Management*, Biotech Books, Delhi, 2011.

Index

B

C

D